The art of
TYPOGRAPHY
An introduction to Typo.icon.ography

The art of
TYPOGRAPHY
An introduction to Typo.icon.ography

MARTIN SOLOMON

Watson-Guptill Publications / New York

Copyright © 1986 Watson-Guptill Publications

First published in 1986 in New York by
Watson-Guptill Publications,
a division of Billboard Publications, Inc.,
1515 Broadway, New York, N.Y. 10036

Library of Congress Cataloging-in-Publication Data

Solomon, Martin.
  The art of typography.

  Includes index.
  1. Printing, Practical—Layout.   2. Type and type-
founding.   3. Graphic arts.   I. Title.
Z246.S655   1986   686.2′2   86-230
ISBN 0-8230-0285-3

Distributed in the United Kingdom by
Phaidon Press Ltd., Littlegate House,
St. Ebbe's St., Oxford

Manufactured in U.S.A.

First printing, 1986
1   2   3   4   5   6   7   8   9   10/91   90   89   88   87   86

Typefaces on pages 182–236 from Visual Graphics Corporation.
Reproduced by permission.

Contents

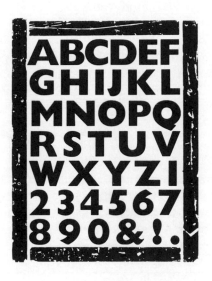

Introduction

I had been an admirer of the art of the letterform long before I was aware of the term *typography*. The mystical shapes called letters that make up words, lines, and pages of symbols truly have to be among the greatest creations of the civilized world. Writing preserves knowledge, for it transcends time and space.

To me, typography is the art of mechanically producing letters, numbers, symbols, and shapes through an understanding of the basic elements, principles, and attributes of design. I define the art of typography as *typoiconography*—a word I developed to combine my perception of symbolism and art as they relate to typography.

Ancient civilizations created symbols or pictorial representations of sacred figures and events. These icons were venerated and became companions to those who possessed them. Because early writings communicated sacred events, their symbols were inscribed with respect and retained a mysticism associated with symbolic art. Medieval manuscripts maintained the iconic feeling through illuminated letters and beautiful pages of calligraphic words and flourishes. This art is still held in high esteem, and even the smallest remnants have been carefully preserved. Typography must be treated with the same respect today so that we do not lose this noble legacy.

As an art, typography can be compared to painting, sculpture, music, and dance. All these arts seem to follow a natural source of power, one influenced and directed by nature. The similarities in their structure often reinforce specific points about typographic design.

In this book, I make numerous references to the various schools of experimental art that emerged in the early twentieth century. The impact of these movements was felt not only in the immediate realm of the fine arts, but also in the commercial, industrial, and domestic arts. One art that underwent accelerated changes was typography. The design of the letters themselves was revolutionized, as was their application to the page. As Futurist Filippo Tommaso Marinetti wrote: "Our revolution is directed against the so-called typographic harmony of the page, which is opposed to the flux and reflux, the jerks and bursts of style that are represented in it. We shall use, therefore, on the same page three or four different colors of ink and, if necessary, even twenty different forms of type." I consider myself an experimentalist, striving to find new methods of communication. I therefore feel an affinity to the art of these pioneer designers.

My education and subsequent professional endeavors are in both the fine and the communication arts. I perceive no division between the two and approach each project with the same sensitivity and logic. When typography is used in my work, it becomes more than just a means of communication. I view letters as shapes, tones, and placements of abstract forms. My designs take on personalities, the medium and the message becoming one. I project this theory to my students at every level in their education in typographic design. Museums become an extension of my classroom and a sketch pad an extension of the hand. Since typography is a personal art, revealed through individual statements of design, I encourage personal development through experimentation.

Designers should bear in mind that typography can wear two hats. It can be treated as an art form or as an undiscerning method of communication. Yet even at its most basic, typography should not be visually offensive. My own approach to typography is a classical one, taking into consideration the refinements that elevate typesetting to the art of typography.

In some ways, letters may be considered chameleons that blend into their surroundings. Determining their intent is the responsibility of the designer or type director. The nature of their subject must be analyzed; it cannot be taken for granted. While typographic letterforms offer a variety of styles, sizes, weights, and personalities, it is mainly through the designer's direction that the technical craft becomes an art.

Over the past twenty-five years, I have worked directly with people involved in all phases of the production of typography. I have expected from these people the same high standard of professionalism that I demand of myself. This standard of excellence is the common bond that unites the designer, type director, and production manager with the typographer. When letters were composed in metal type, it was not uncommon for writers and designers to spend hours with the compositor altering words to create a better-looking line formation without changing the copy's meaning. All creative forces worked in concert, and the result was excellent typography.

For the designer to communicate a concept effectively, the specific typographic vocabulary must be understood. It is this terminology that verbally expresses the designer's abstract intuition. Terminology is also essential in directing the technical manufacturing of an art. It is through this language that refinements in the reproduction of typography are manifested. To enable you to understand and apply the aesthetic and technical aspects of typography, I have developed a series of exercises to stimulate creativity and build your skills.

Overall, typographic design is a special art, which requires considerable training—training that encompasses not only letters themselves, but also study of the dimensional arts. On one level, typography performs the task of conveying ideas. Yet by themselves, unincorporated into words, letters are beautiful abstract shapes.

For those who wish to broaden their artistic abilities, I feel that drawing letters is synonomous with studying the fine arts. It is a disciplined art because of its exactness, yet within its rigorous requirements, it reveals the free flow of mystical lines. It can stand alone as a thing of beauty, or it can support the aesthetics of other elements. The art of typography contains an energy that few art forms possess. It is as personal as one's signature. It is truly typoiconography.

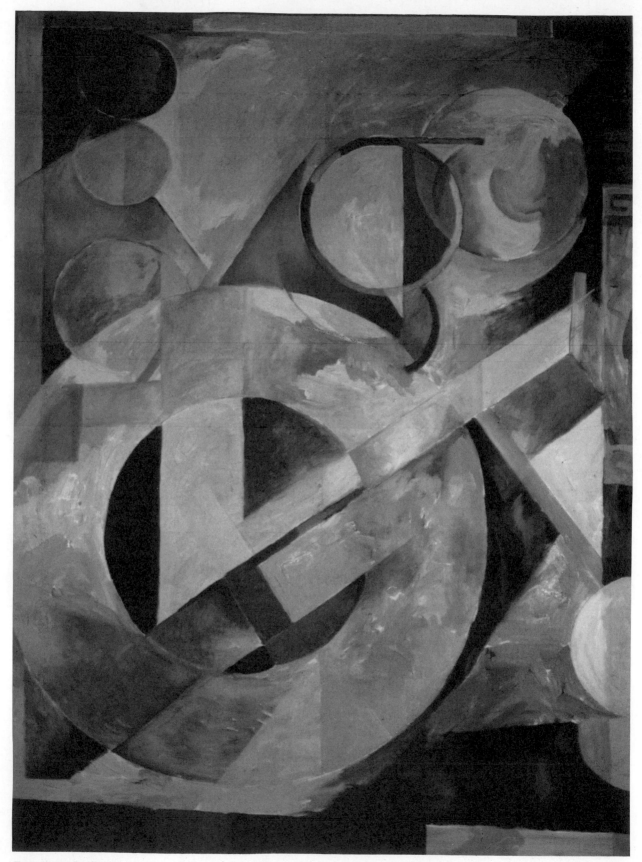

Experimental painting of letter G by Martin Solomon.

Part One
Typography as an Art Form

Nature and its physical forces follow their own laws, sculpting and shaping the earth's surface. By studying these natural laws, we can adapt them into rules that become the guidelines for art. I define these basic rules as elements, principles, and attributes of design. At times these rules may appear to control the development of a creative theme, but there may be times that they can be interpreted according to the artist's intent. In the arts, as in nature, the forces can range from calm to intense.

Typography conforms to the same rules as the other arts. These rules form the foundation for the aesthetic formulas creating typoiconography. They are the designer's tools for transforming the mechanically manufactured composition of letterforms into a visual art.

The elements, the basic parts making up the whole, are the structural foundations of design. Space and line are the purest of these, with solids and masses, tonal values, textures, and planes completing the typographic palette. It is not enough to know of these elements; their usage must be practiced. Observing and understanding them in all forms of nature and art will increase the sensitivity essential to the design's development.

The principles of design direct the elements. Relationship is the most basic principle, with repetition the most common. In nature, repetition is reflected in such multiples as clouds, leaves, waves, or hills. Opposition, transition, position, and priority are the other principles of design. Although some of these are more dominant than others, all must be considered, for each affects the details that make up the whole.

The attributes, or qualities, of design are directed by the principles. These attributes include balance, contrast or emphasis, and rhythm. Much as in painting, poetry, music, or dance, they are used in typography to create definition.

The primary factor that ultimately governs all these components is composition. It is the summation, the bringing together of all the parts. In working with the elements, principles, and attributes of design, you must constantly keep in mind the effect you wish to achieve.

Although good composition is directed by rules, the designer must not be content with mere repetition of proven techniques. An exciting part of designing is discovering, through experimentation, the various possibilities that go beyond convention. To experiment logically, however, you must understand the traditions on which the rules are based. By altering what generally has been considered fundamental usage of the elements, principles, and attributes, you can achieve an exciting energy, one that defies convention and enters the arena of creativity.

1. Elements of Design

The elements of design—space, line, solid and mass, tonal value, texture, and plane—are the major forces of a composition. These constituents perform in whatever manner you direct. They are the purest palette of design. Each contains its own individuality, and it is this independence of energy that gives rise to your design. Because these elements are totally unrelated to each other in form, they must be brought together through the principles and attributes of design.

The designer must understand the characteristics of each element, not only in typography, but in relation to the other arts as well. I urge you to observe classical painting, architecture, industrial design, and dance as well as to listen to music. It is through these observations that you will gain greater understanding of the elements of design.

Space

Space is the area in which the other elements act. It is like the air around us. It begins as a void and becomes a design element, taking on form and acquiring dimension as other elements are added to it. It functions as a blank canvas or empty stage—the background to and against which everything is applied. The success of a composition is determined by the selection and juxtaposition of the other elements within a designated space.

Designers must learn to perceive space. Think, for example, of how space works in relation to a building. Surrounding forms can change a building's lines. An architect must consider how the environment will influence the completed structure; it cannot be planned as a solitary entity, standing alone in a void. New York's skyline demonstrates how adjacent forms affect each other's silhouettes, how space and line work together.

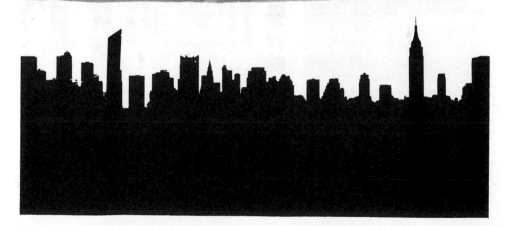

In a sense, space is an ambiguous element: it can be as definite as a planographic surface or as limitless as infinity. The specifications for a project, however, place physical limitations on this potentially infinite element. Among the first factors designers must consider are the size requirements of a project and the environment into which the project will be placed. Both considerations relate to space. The first deals with an internal space—the area the design itself occupies and the elements contained within it. The second relates to an external space—the area surrounding the design and the elements within that environment. Both internal and external elements will influence each other, whether these involve a cityscape or facing pages of a magazine.

The Seagram Building on Park Avenue in New York City illustrates how space relates to the internal and external environments. Designed by Mies van der Rohe and completed in 1959, the Seagram Building is a vertical, flat-topped, metal and glass structure, which encompasses a full block in width. The building adheres to the basic Bauhaus philosophy of minimalism, and form follows function. The design of the internal structure supports the simplicity of the overall concept. Within the space the building itself occupies, the exterior and interior façades merge to form a unified design that makes a decisive statement.

Surrounding the building on three sides is a plaza. Although designed as part of the building's space, it serves as a transition from the structure to its environment. It enables the building to maintain its own identity while relating it to neighboring structures. By introducing the principle of relationship to space, Mies van der Rohe created a complete design solution. Space without relationship is total isolation, completely unconnected to its surroundings.

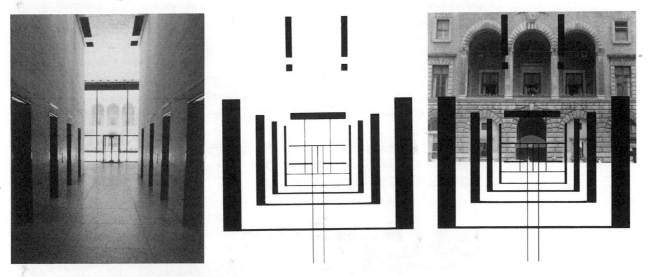

Both the building and the plaza are above street level. The elements in the plaza are unobtrusive and encourage interaction between internal and external space. The design of the building also allows interaction of elements in related spaces. The large glass windows of the lobby, for example, permit contact between inside and out, since the transparent glass does not establish a solid dividing line between environments.

Left to right: lobby of Seagram Building; graphic interpretation of lobby; relationship of lobby to building across street, which is in the Italian Renaissance style.

Mies van der Rohe positioned the Seagram Building to align with the existing structure facing it across the street. The plaza was designed as a continuing form, joining together the two otherwise unrelated periods of art to create a bisymmetry with geometric shapes. By uniting his design with the external environment, Mies van der Rohe used space to the fullest extent to support his design.

Relating this example to typography, the designer must realize that the elements within the internal space of a design have to support the central theme and work well within the given space. Designers must also be aware that external space will influence the design and, whenever possible, use that space to support it, creating a harmonious flow between inside and out.

Think of space in relation to individual letters and of the letterforms in words and lines as creating a neighborhood. When designing with type, a designer directs the three most important types of space: letter space, word space, and line space. It is obvious that, without all three kinds of space, there would be a confusing mass of overlapping shapes. There are also supporting spaces, such as paragraph indents and column and margin spacing. A designer must know how to direct space optically as well as mechanically.

One consideration is the space that defines the areas within some letters (called counters) and between the letters themselves (called letter space). Again, there is a comparison to architecture, where spacing articulates the design of a structure's two-dimensional façade and also emphasizes the structure in relation to surrounding buildings.

Word space is necessary to distinguish words. This kind of space gives words their own identity so that they are immediately recognizable. Word space is as essential to legibility in typography as pauses are to timing in music. It becomes as difficult to read

wordsruntogetherwithoutspace

as it is to listen to music without pauses between notes. You can't hear a melody or set up a tempo without spacing. In fact it is the rests and the tempo that help bring a musical score to life.

The third kind of priority space is line space, also known as leading because of the material used to create it in metal composition. Line space is the horizontal space between lines; it can be used to support readability.

When combined with other typographic elements, space can be considered an energy force. Letters rely on space to emphasize their weight and shape. The weight of type is determined by the amount of space it absorbs or displaces. In addition, the amount of positive mass within an area will affect how space is perceived. If mass is increased until it visually outweighs the space, the space becomes the shape and the mass is perceived as the negative area.

A continuous metamorphosis—with the space becoming the shape and vice versa—can be seen in some two-dimensional art. The painters M. C. Escher, Robert Motherwell, Clyfford Still, and Franz Kline have all taken advantage of the relationship of space and shape in their work.

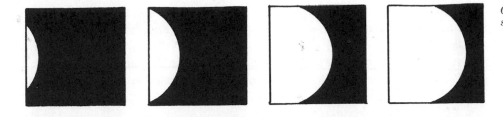

Think of space as a chromatic "mixing agent." In oil painting, white pigment functions as a tinting agent when mixed with black. You need it to make different values of gray. In typography there is no actual gray, but an illusion of gray is created by the placement and spacing of black type on a white background. The white of the paper acts as the tinting factor that determines, along with the type's style, the illusion of gray. The type will appear to be darker, for example, if spacing is reduced.

Although space implies nothingness, its hidden strength is monumental. To understand its true power, it must be studied in relation to the other components. Observe the shapes between the forms as well as the forms themselves, and you will begin to understand the power of space.

Line

Line is an energy force that can divide, penetrate, enclose, or otherwise define a space. It can convey not only shape, but also stability, movement, action, and direction. Lines fall into several categories, with each performing a particular function in relation to the space around it. The dominant lines are those that direct motion, force, opposition, or shape. It is these physical lines that are considered elements, whether they are created with a single mark or by grouping units together. There are also guidelines, which support the dominant lines or shapes of letters. They maintain the natural flow of individual letters so that they relate to one another. Then there are predetermined grid lines, which direct the placement of elements on a page. Guidelines and grid lines can be real or imaginary. Yet imaginary lines, such as those the eye projects to connect isolated points or shapes, can be just as forceful as physical lines.

A line that encloses a space becomes a powerful structure. The energy of the confined space creates strong outward tension on the line, while

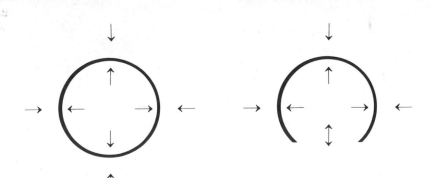

the external space exerts a weaker, but opposing tension. A partially closed line, although less powerful than a fully enclosed one, is still very protective of its internal space. The ends of the line create a visual connection, separating internal from external space. When, however, a line does not have an opposing internal energy force, the converging external energy forces tend to be equal.

Each letter relies for support on the energy forces created by its design. Fully exposed letters rely on external space for support, while letters with fully or partially enclosed counters are supported by space both inside and outside the letterform. Counters thus belong to the letterform and not to its adjacent spaces. Study the energy forces in each individual letter. These become particularly important when letters are isolated as initial capitals and increase in emphasis with larger sizes.

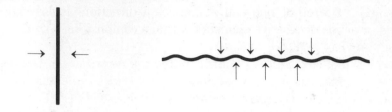

Line, then, is the basic element that gives form to a letter; it is the design of the line that determines the style of type. A letterform with an additional structure that helps you associate one letter to the next is called a serif letter. Block letters or sans serif letters—from the French meaning "without serif"—function more independently of each other. In both cases, proper spacing between letters, words, and lines makes the styles readable.

Left to right:
serif and sans serif letters.

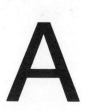

Line also describes the direction in which type flows. Our eyes follow lines of type, seeking the next word, until they reach the end of the line and then go on to the next. If adjacent lines are too close, however, the continuity becomes confused—the areas merge to become a mass.

Lines are the simplest of typographic devices: by definition they connect two points. Typographic lines called rules come in various thicknesses and perform different functions. Used as an underscore, a rule can emphasize words. Tapered at one end, it implies a direction. Rules can create borders or act as decorative elements within a composition. All these ways of using line can enhance a design.

In addition to the physical lines within the composition, the designer can suggest imaginary lines that direct and support the actual elements. Often designers use imaginary lines to establish a grid or graphic formula to which the other elements conform. These lines set up reference points from item to item, establishing a format to which adjacent elements should relate. This permits visual continuity to flow from page to page.

Before beginning a design project, you should define the area within which you will be working. This space is contained by the four imaginary lines that define the borders of the picture plane. They do not become energy forces until you set your art close to the edge of the picture plane. In a rectangular or square space, these four lines are connected at right angles to form corners. These corner angles can become escape areas. Think of them as the corner pockets of a pool table. Once the ball hits that point, it is gone. Although these corners appear to be a void, an improperly placed line, shape, or form can lead your eye out of the space entirely.

These are great similarities to line in art and music. Line, as it relates to both the visual and auditory senses, can be perceived as a continuous element. A finely drawn graphic line is comparable to the high tonal quality of a violin, while a heavier line is comparable to the lower-pitched tone of a cello. The intensity with which an instrument is played also relates to the intensity of a drawn line.

Some musical instruments are not linear in tonal character but relate to individual beats. The beat of a drum or the striking of a piano key resembles a dot, rather than a line. The combination of individual notes can be related to a line of dots, similar to individual letters making up lines of type. If the spaces between the typographic elements are close enough to relate to each other, they create a unity that we perceive as a line. If, however, letter and word space are excessive, the illusion of a line is lost and another element will take over.

Solid and Mass

By definition, a solid is an unbroken area having definite shape and volume. In typography, the term *solid* describes the visual weight of a typographic element. A mass is an assemblage of individual parts, which collectively form a unit. The term *mass* denotes either a unit weight or the collective weight of a grouping of elements.

Solids and masses are usually strong statements of shape with a decisive intent. They establish and sustain priority within a composition.

To intensify a typographic mass, for instance, you can increase the weight and size of the letterforms and tighten the letter, word, and line space.

The degree of power generated by a letter relates directly to the intensity and thickness of its line. In general, medium-bold and extra-bold letters emit a greater energy force than thinner structures because they have a greater weight in proportion to the space they occupy. If, for example, you compare a bold and a thin letter E, they take up almost the same space on the outside, but on the inside the bold E's counters have far less space. The weight then takes priority over the space and advances forward visually. Conversely, the thinner letter, with its more open counters, has a greater feeling of space around it, so that its line appears less intense.

BB EE GG

A typographic line becomes a solid when the mass of the letterform outweighs the volume of space it replaces or absorbs within a contained area. To visualize this, notice how a solid increases in intensity in proportion to the area it consumes within a given space.

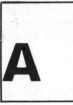 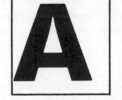 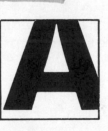

Compare three different weights of the same typeface: Futura Light next to Futura Bold and Futura Extra Bold in the same point size. Although theoretically all these weights of type consist of lines, the extremely bold letters appear as a visual mass when compared with the lighter styles.

Top to bottom:
Futura Light, Futura Bold,
Futura Extra Bold.

EOYeoy

EOYeoy

EOYeoy

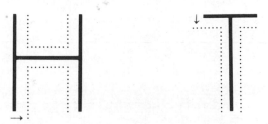

Solid letters usually retain the outer shape of their lighter counterparts. In general a letter is made solid by "heavying" the letter from within, reducing the counter space. After a certain weight has been achieved, however, the counters cannot be reduced any further without affecting the legibility of the letter. At this point, weight also has to be added to the exterior. Such reproportioning is done to create extra-bold typefaces.

A different kind of visual metamorphosis takes place when you thicken an outline letter. As the lines become heavier, the letter is transformed into an inline letter (where the line defines the interior shape of the letter). Eventually, it becomes a solid letter.

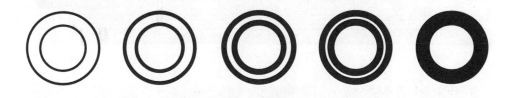

It is the designer's responsibility to find effective and aesthetic ways to use spacing in relation to solid and mass. Consider, for example, that when bold letters are set with very tight letter spacing, they tend to generate an optical magnetism. Each letter "attracts" adjacent letters so that legibility is decreased.

Dada gives itself or nothing, for Dada is priceless.

Dada gives itself or nothing, for Dada is priceless.

In typography the position of each solid or mass within a space must be carefully thought out. If there is more than one element on a page, the objective is to make each element harmonious with the others. Many factors influence the visual weight of a mass, and it is the combination of these factors that determines an object's placement within a composition. Some of these considerations include intensity, priority, and contrast. Moreover, you can select from a variety of typographic symbols to support mass. Such devices as heavy rules and ornaments should be part of your typographic palette.

Artists such as Jean Arp and Henry Moore have mastered combining solids and space in both two- and three-dimensional forms. Observation and experimentation will help you understand how these elements relate in design. No set formula applies to every design project. What is important is what you want to communicate. Ultimately, the designer's eye determines the most comfortable and appealing juxtaposition of letters, just as the artist plans a painting or sculpture.

The work of the De Stijl school of art illustrates the graphic effectiveness of line and solid. This influential Dutch movement, which lasted from 1917 to 1931, emphasized functional minimalism in line, mass, and color in painting, architecture, furniture and graphic design, as well as typography. The essential aim of De Stijl work was harmony achieved by abstract means, disassociated from objects in nature. Its concern was to establish a new link between life and art by creating a new visual style for living. In this style all solids and masses were related to basic geometric shapes. The paintings of Piet Mondrian and the furniture and architecture of Gerrit Rietveld used the basic concept of organizing line, solid, and mass into a two-dimensional or three-dimensional space.

The typographic style of De Stijl was revolutionary compared with other typography of that period. Mainly block letters with square-box and angle shapes were used. These abstract shapes served as solids and masses creating the representative shapes of letters. Other typographic forms were developed from quarter, half, and full circles. Triangular shapes also related perfectly to the typographic style of the De Stijl art form.

Lettering by
Theo Van Doesburg, 1917.

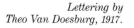

Tonal Value

Typography, when prepared for reproduction, is produced in black and white. Yet the letters, when placed next to each other, lose their individual blackness and collectively appear as a shade of gray. The intensity of the gray depends on the type style, its weight, and the density of the letters in relation to one another. Text-size type is more sympathetic to creating gray values, since larger letters tend to maintain a more identifiable character structure.

I analyze the optical gray masses to determine the tonal value. Although the tonal value of text-size type can be any percentage of gray, it is convenient to visualize it in intervals of 10%. The tonal value scale thus ranges from 0% for white to 100% for black, with values of gray increasing in intensity at 10% intervals. Tonal values are your palette for choosing the correct style, size, and weight of type for any project.

Tonal value is a gauge that helps you determine levels of contrast, thereby enabling you to be more decisive when creating emphasis within copy. Although tonal value is apparent in all sizes of type, it is most predominant in 6 to 14 point, which are considered the type sizes for text. To see the different tonal values of gray produced by type, compare a 9-point medium-weight Spartan set solid with the same face set solid in 12-point type. The 9-point type appears much lighter in value and also has less mass. Remember, however, that contrast reacts in both directions—it is not always the darker image that is the most dominant.

The main purpose of letters is the practical one of making t houghts visible. Ruskin says that "all letters are frightful thi ngs and to be endured only upon occasion, that is to say, in places where the sense of the inscription is of more importa nce than external ornament." This is a sweeping statement, from which we need not suffer unduly; yet it is doubtful wh

The main purpose of letters is the practical o ne of making thoughts visible. Ruskin says th at "all letters are frightful things and to be e ndured only upon occasion, that is to say, in

Top to bottom:
9-point Spartan Medium,
12-point Spartan Medium.

Note that paper also has a tonal value, which will influence the intensity of the type. Newsprint, for example, is considered a white stock, but when placed next to the coated white stock used for a magazine, the newsprint appears to be grayer. The gray of the paper reduces the contrast with the black of the type. If type with an 80% tonal intensity is printed on newspaper stock with an inherent 20% tint, the tonal value of the type will be reduced to 60%. The same type printed on a pure white stock will retain its full value. Designers must be aware of this relationship in choosing the point size and weight of the type.

Another relationship to consider concerns mass and tonal value. Mass refers to the area of type, and tonal value refers to its weight as measured in degrees of gray. The tonal value is created by the amount of text-size type on a page, or the ratio of black type to white space. The heavier the typeface, the more surface it covers and the more intense the tonal value. In other words, letters with small counters, very tight letter and word spacing, and no leading will appear to be darker. Conversely, the thinner the typeface, the more white space remains and the lighter the tonal value. Letters with large counters, open letter and word spacing, and extensive leading appear lighter. Obviously, an invaluable visual mixing agent here is the spacing within and around each form. Just as white or lighter areas are needed to achieve contrast in a drawing, so in typography spacing helps create different tonal values. Notice, for example, how much lighter the same style and size of type appear when leading is added between the lines. Similarly, the same body copy with the same leading and the same word and letter spacing will have a slightly different tonal value if you change the measure it is set on.

Top to bottom: 9-point Spartan Medium with 1-point, 2-point, and 3-point leading.

The main purpose of letters is the practical one of making t houghts visible. Ruskin says that "all letters are frightful thi ngs and to be endured only upon occasion, that is to say, in places where the sense of the inscription is of more importa nce than external ornament." This is a sweeping statement, from which we need not suffer unduly; yet it is doubtful wh

The main purpose of letters is the practical one of making t houghts visible. Ruskin says that "all letters are frightful thi ngs and to be endured only upon occasion, that is to say, in places where the sense of the inscription is of more importa nce than external ornament." This is a sweeping statement,

The main purpose of letters is the practical one of making t houghts visible. Ruskin says that "all letters are frightful thi ngs and to be endured only upon occasion, that is to say, in places where the sense of the inscription is of more importa

Refer to the tonal value scale when selecting your type for contrast. At least a 20% variation between tones is necessary for contrast to be effective. Anything less can be mistaken for a poor printing impression or insertion of the wrong font.

Contrast in Futura family.

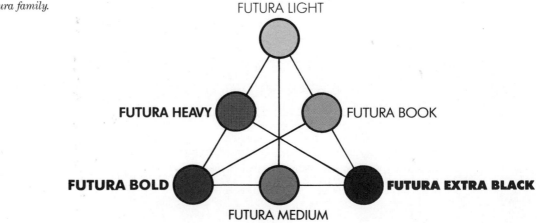

FUTURA LIGHT

FUTURA HEAVY   FUTURA BOOK

FUTURA BOLD   FUTURA EXTRA BLACK

FUTURA MEDIUM

Texture

Texture is the interwoven pattern of light and dark tones created by the precise repetition of letterforms or shapes in relation to the space around them. It is present whenever letters or symbols are printed together in blocks of type. The weaving of this texture may be loose, random, or tight. Consider how you might describe the texture of a musical composition by the prolonged repetition of the same notes or the texture of a building façade by its arrangement of windows. The relation between texture and the arrangement of type is similar.

The history of the modern alphabet is one of the most convincing testimonials to the slow but inevitable progress of the human race. Of all the evidences which have remained to us of the ancient civilizations, none is so complete, so unaffected by the passage of time and so near to its original relationship to humanity, as the little group of phonetic symbols which form the basis of expression for the intellectual world.

The history of the modern alphabet is one of the most convincing testimonials to the slow but inevitable progress of the human race. Of all the evidences which have remained to us of the ancient civilizations, none is so complete, so unaffected by the passage of time and so near to its original relationship to humanity, as the little group of phonetic symbols which form the basis of expression for the intellectual world.

Top to bottom: different textures of 10/10 Helvetica Regular and 10/10 Futura Light.

Textures can be created by repeating the same or similar shapes, or they can vary in surface structure. When, for example, you use letters in the same type style that are isolated from each other, they create a two-dimensional texture, on the surface of the page. On the other hand, the repetition of a decorative border with strong light and dark contrasts may establish a three-dimensional texture, much like a coarse fabric.

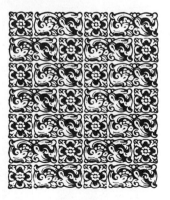

Left to right: excerpt from forty-two-line Mazarin Bible with two-dimensional texture; repetition of decorative border with three-dimensional texture.

Texture, however, differs from repetition in the sense that texture is not a separate grouping of shapes, whereas repetition is. When repetition of the same shape is closely regimented in a design, it may become a texture.

Obviously the strength of texture relates directly to the type's spacing as well as to repetition. Generally, the spaces between letters separate them enough so that they are independent of each other, and their texture does not interfere with readability. Any additional space between letters, regardless of the letters' size, tends to isolate each character, thereby lightening the texture. If set too tight, however, they may become abstract and overly textural, decreasing readability.

S P A C I N G

S   P   A   C   I   N   G

S   P   A   C   I   N   G

Another important consideration in texture is the type's weight. Bolder type, with its more intense tonal value, has a stronger texture. The reverse is true for light or thin faces. Compare the differences in texture, for instance, between Helvetica Regular and Futura Light (see page 23). The designers must control texture so that it does not interfere with other elements in the design. A line of type can lose its legibility, for instance, when it is printed over a texture of similar or greater intensity. Even the most minute texture will disturb the legibility of text type. Conflicting interactions of tonal intensity set up an optical disturbance, reducing clarity and diminishing the overall effectiveness of the composition. Since nontypographic textures are energetic elements that contain a series of intensities of light and dark tones, they usually work best when they are not overprinted with type.

Type loses its legibility when overprinted on a texture of similar or greater intensity.

Type loses its legibility when overprinted on a texture of similar or greater intensity.

Type loses its legibility when overprinted on a texture of similar or greater intensity.

Type loses its legibility when overprinted on a texture of similar or greater intensity.

Plane

Typography is essentially a two-dimensional art form because all the elements lie on the same plane—the flat surface of the paper. In this way typography is similar to painting, where the flat surface of the canvas defines the picture plane. Yet the designer, like the painter, can create the illusion of different planes and three dimensions by setting up a perspective, a visual depth of field. There is a transformation so that, instead of perceiving everything on the same plane, we see some components as close and others as further away.

With type, depth is suggested by varying the size and weight of letters and shapes. Smaller and lighter letters, for instance, appear to recede, while larger and bolder letters advance. Although, in fact, these design elements rest on a single flat plane, their placement in various sizes throughout the composition generates the feeling of a third dimension, with closeup and more distant planes.

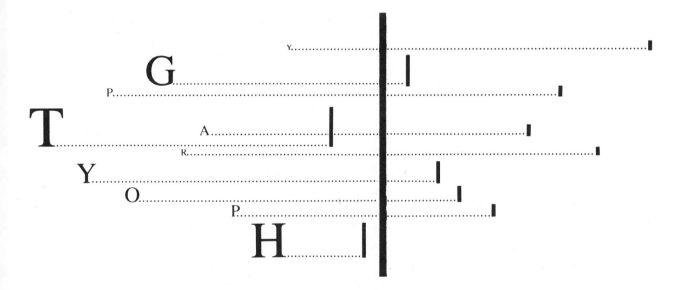

Instead of focusing on a readable word, try to visualize the individual letters floating above the surface of the plane. Think of them as sound that moves through the air. If you accept letters as lying on a piece of paper, you will lose the depth of field inherent in sound. Light musical tones recede while strong sounds project off the same imaginary plane. Visual intensities react in much the same way.

Architectural structures offer good examples of planes for the designer to study. Both the interior and the exterior of a building have surfaces that relate to each other through depth and elevation. Translating the interplay of light and shadow in these three-dimensional forms into a two-dimensional medium poses a problem for the designer working with type. To create the illusion of depth or multileveled planes in typography, you must understand the principles of perspective and how they affect what we see.

The long vertical represents the side view of the plane, while the smaller bars indicate the visual distance in front of or behind the plane.

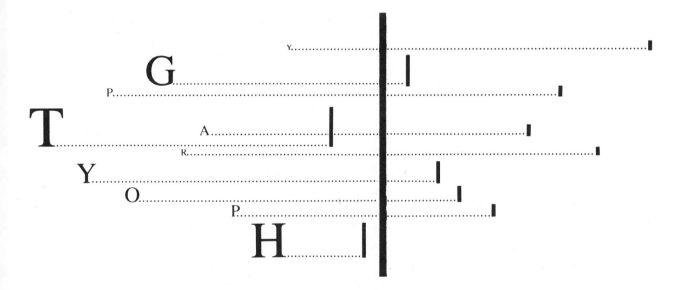

25

Although three dimensions can be suggested by flat letters and forms alone, you should be familiar with type styles that contain an illustrative dimension. These letters usually reveal a crisp interplay of line and solid. The contrasting black and white surfaces create what is called a drop shadow. Our visual imagination then perceives the form as having a third dimension.

HARK! AWAKEN,

HARK! AWAKEN,

Hark! Awaken,

Hark! Awaken,

Review the examples of drop-shadow and dimensional letters. Notice that the letter's focal point never changes in relation to an imaginary vanishing point. Most drop shadows are typographically uniform in the dimensional effect they create. Although they place the viewer at a hypothetical location and specific eye level from the page, they do not fully follow the rules of perspective. To understand this, think of a page as a landscape with a horizon. Once the first drop-shadow letter is placed within the space, a perspective, or depth of field, has been established. The lines of each subsequent letter should then recede to the same vanishing point. Note the change in the perspective lines for each of the letters as you scan the line of type below. Also observe how these letters seem to dictate the distance from which they should be viewed.

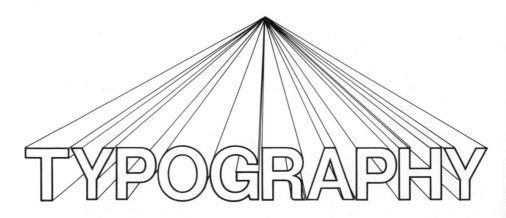

Visually dimensional letters tend to be more pictorial than typographic. They are best used when you feel display heads require decorative or ornamental designs. Keep in mind that dimensional letters establish a definitive point of view. They are illustrative and therefore do not mix easily with other styles. Notice how the letter A below and the Flat Iron Building both demand a frontal view. In addition, their impact depends on their isolation, with ample space around them.

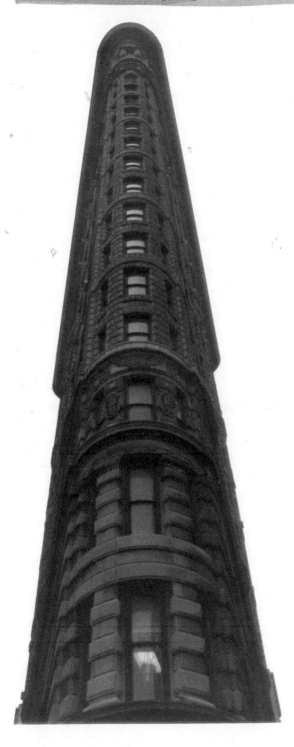

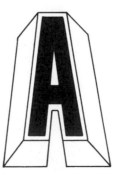

2. Principles of Design

Each work of art establishes a theme, to which all the elements within that composition must relate. The principles of design are the basic theories on how to build and work with these elements. The six principles are relationship, transition, repetition, opposition, priority, and position. All these principles are interrelated and depend on or overlap each other to some degree. Such unifying concepts as harmony and proportion, while not principles in themselves, are also important.

Relationship

Although a particular composition may not use all the principles, relationship must always be present, for it is the connecting force. In every art form, the elements must be related to each other in some fashion. In a musical composition, for example, all the notes produced by the instruments must relate at any given time, or the piece lacks harmony and coherence.

Setting up relationships is the designer's task. There are infinite variations of elements from which to choose. Not only do you have to select elements that will work together, but you must also understand how to control them in the design process. All compositions, no matter how abstract, rely on an underlying order to establish and maintain a theme. Harmony and proportion also contribute to the compatibility of elements within a design.

One of the major principles in establishing harmony and proportion is the golden section, also known as the divine proportion. This principle was used in the pyramids of ancient Egypt and it underlies classical architec-

To construct the golden rectangle, bisect side AB of the square ABCD at point E. With center E and radius EC, draw the arc of a circle intersecting line AB at point F. Then draw a line perpendicular to AF which meets line DC at point G. The rectangle AFGD is the golden rectangle.

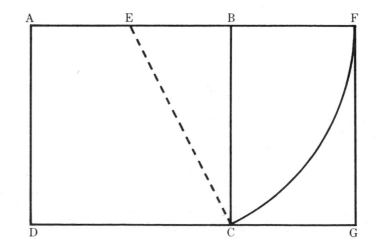

ture, painting, and graphic design. The golden section is based on a mathematical proportion in which the smaller part is to the greater as the greater is to the whole. Related to this concept is the golden rectangle, in which the width is to the length as the length is to the sum of the width and the length. Anything designed within these invisible confines contains a harmonious relationship to its own parts.

In addition to the overall proportions, you must consider how the individual letters relate. One of the most common techniques for establishing a relationship in typography is to use what is known as a "family" of type. A complete family includes all the variations of weights, sizes, and styles that relate to each other in one type grouping.

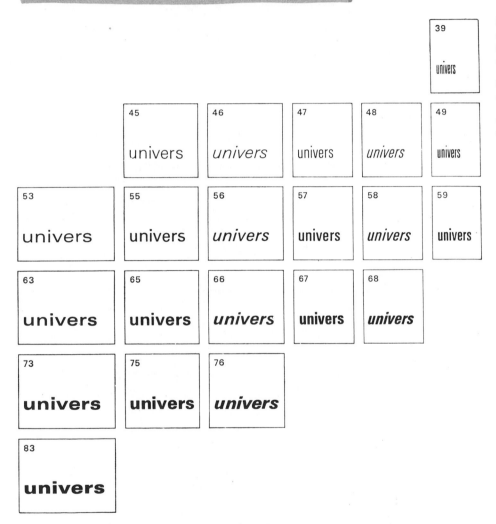

Compatible styles and weights of the Univers family are arranged vertically and horizontally on this chart. Univers 45, for example, is the lighter version but same style as 55, 65, and 75. Univers 53 is the same weight but more extended than 55, 56, 57, 58, and 59.

By selecting combinations of type in contrasting weights and sizes within one family, you can create comfortable relationships. Such relationships, however, tend to be less dramatic than those developed through experimentation. Being overly conservative can limit your creativity. Experimenting to develop new relationships is an exciting challenge. By studying the varied combinations of type encountered every day, whether on television or in periodicals or newspapers, you will become aware of what is currently in use and gain ideas for experimentation. Note, for example, how combining Franklin Gothic with Century Expanded Italic creates a more unusual relationship than using a single typeface with an underscore. The other type style combinations shown below also have strong, harmonious relationships.

Quotation from "Paul Rand" by L. Moholy-Nagy, 1940.

The Constructivist movement in Europe originated in countries with undeveloped industry... in Russia, Hungary and Holland. **The marvels of technical civilization as they were described in reports about the U.S.A. were a great incentive for the young painters, sculptors and architects of those countries.** *The message about American organization, production processes, life standards, created a Utopian picture in the mind of these young European artists. Their imaginative picture of America governed their thinking and their work.*

The Constructivist movement in Europe originated in countries with undeveloped industry... in Russia, Hungary and Holland. The marvels of technical civilization as they were described in reports about the U.S.A. were a great incentive for the young painters, sculptors and architects of those countries. **The message about American organization, production processes, life standards, created a Utopian picture in the mind of these young European artists. Their imaginative picture of America governed their thinking and their work.**

The Constructivist movement in Europe originated in countries with undeveloped industry... in Russia, Hungary and Holland. **The marvels of technical civilization as they were described in reports about the U.S.A. were a great incentive for the young painters, sculptors and architects of those countries. The message about American organization, production processes, life standards, created a Utopian picture in the mind of these young European artists. Their imaginative picture of America governed their thinking and their work. They admired exactness and precision, smooth functioning, the skyscraper, the highways, the immense span of bridges, the power plants of Niagara Falls, the autos and airplanes of America. They tried to be as contemporary and efficient in their own work as the Americans and without sentimentality for the old and traditional. They tried to be the children of a new age as they believed the Americans to be.**

The past holds many valuable lessons in relationships. One example is the magnificent marriage between the initial capital letter and text in medieval manuscripts.

Sequitur Commune sanctorum. Et primo In vigilia vnius apli. Intro.

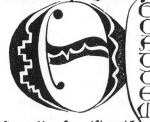

sicut oliua fructificaui i domo dñi. speraui in miscdia dei mei. et expectabo nomé tuũ. qm bonũ est ante cospectũ sctorũ tuorũ. ps Quid gliaris in malicia q potens es iniqtate. Kirie. feriale Cõcede nob' Colla qñs ops deus vẽ turá beati M. apli tui solénitate cõgruo puenire honore. et veniente digna celebrare deuotõe. p dñm. sola. Jté alie colle q videbũtur expedire. Lcõli. sapie Ecci xliiij Benedictio dñi sup caput iusti: ideo dedit illi hereditaté. z diuisit ei pté in tribub' duodecim. et inuenit gratiã in gspectu omnis carnis.

Magnificauit eum in timore inimicoʒ: z in verbis suis monstra placauit. Glorificauit eum in cospectu regũ: z ostédit illi gloriã suã. Jn fide et lenitate ipius sanctũ fecit illũ: et elegit eum ex omni carne. Dedit illi pcepta et legé vite et discipline: z excelsũ fecit illũ. Statuit illi testamentũ sempiternũ: circũcinxit eũ ʒona iusticie. z induit eũ dñs corona gle. Hʒ Justus ut palma florebit. sicut cedrus libani multiplicabit' in domo dñi. ʒ Ad annũciandũ mane miscdiã tuã et veritaté tuã p nocte. Alleluia non cantatur. Scõm iohãnem xv. Jn illo tépe: D. i. d. s. Ego sũ vitis vera: et vos palmites. Qui manet in me z ego in eo hic fert fructũ multũ: qʒ sine me nichil potestis facere. Si quis in me non mãserit: mittetur foras sicut palmes z arescet. et colligent eum. et in igné

From Missael Herbipoiense, *Wurzburg, 1481.*

In designing any project, whether a bottle cap or an editorial spread in a magazine, you must first consider what use or function the item has and how your design will relate to that. Then you must establish a coherent relationship among the individual elements. This unit, in turn, must relate to its environment. An ad that looks good in a magazine, for instance, may not be visually effective if enlarged to billboard size. You must consider not only the internal relationships of elements within a composition, but also the external relationships of your subject to its environment.

Consider a book with these relationships in mind. A book is an individual item, designed with its own identity even when it is part of a series. Its design must comfortably accommodate the user. A compatible relationship between such factors as the size, feel, and weight of a book, as well as the legibility of the typeface, must be established in order for the reader to enjoy using it.

Another consideration involving relationships is posed by a product's package. To create sales, each package design must stimulate consumer attention. Not only must the package identify its particular product and define its own interest, it must promote its purchase by establishing a unique identity in relation to similar, competitive products. Its appeal on a store shelf is largely determined by the overall effectiveness of the relationships created by its design.

Of course, the positioning of an item, whether it be a product on a shelf or the order of advertisements in a magazine or newspaper, cannot always be controlled. It is therefore essential that the design be strong enough to maintain its own identity.

Transition

The principle of transition is used to create an orderly progression, so that the passage from one element to another remains related to a given subject. The concept of direction, movement, or flow through time and space is thus essential to understanding this principle. In classical music, for example, the theme flows rhythmically, even if the tempo changes. Certainly there can be abrupt variations, or opposition, but for the most part the elements must flow smoothly for a composition to be harmonious.

Transition is usually so taken for granted that it appears to be the natural order of things. It is like the seemingly effortless way in which an outfielder catches a fly ball. Compare that to what happens when the ball hits the wall and bounces off, sending several players into a frenzy as they try to anticipate where the ball will go next. A similar disruption occurs in a finely tuned string quartet when one string breaks and the delicate and precise flow of notes is abruptly disturbed.

Transitions in typography are essential for ease in reading and comprehension. A certain uniformity and predictability are needed. An area or page composed of words in incompatible typefaces or widely differing sizes is visually disturbing. When incompatible elements are arbitrarily introduced, they disrupt the flow of relationships. It is difficult to read a passage where the leading is inconsistently increased or decreased for no apparent reason or where the right-hand margin is staggered randomly between 20 to 40 picas. Legibility in text-size type requires a more controlled stagger, creating a more comfortable transition from line to line.

Assume that you are preparing a design that includes a main headline, subheads, and text. The text and subheads could be set in the same type style as the main headline, varying only in point size, or you could select different type styles that complement the headline.

The variations are as vast as the designer's creative talents and levels of experience and skill. Keep in mind, however, that the success of your design depends on a harmonious transition between the elements. Just as sharps and flats serve as shifting devices in music, bold and light typefaces, expanded and condensed styles, italics and obliques can provide transitions in typography. You can experiment with typography, detouring from the norms and varying your applications, as long as you maintain proper control of relationships and establish transitions.

THE FROG THAT BECAME THE PRINCE.

(OR, HOW TO IMPROVE YOUR GAME BY LEAPS AND BOUNDS)

ONCE *upon a time all racquets were pretty much the same. The same aluminum, the same wood, but more importantly, the same size.*

So when Prince introduced the very first over-sized racquet in 1976 the court jesters laughed.

"Ho. Ho. Ho. Look how big it is!" one said. "It looks like a frog," said another. You'll never serve an ace with that," they cried. And they all made merry.

THE UPSTART

But a few brave players ventured forth and tried this upstart. They were astounded with the results.

And when they won more games than they were supposed to be winning, their opponents took notice.

Realizing that playing against a Prince® racquet placed them at a great disadvantage, they too, soon switched.

THE LEGEND GROWS

And so the legend grew till it became a ground swell.

By 1983 Prince had become the number one racquet at the U.S. Open.

More top ranked juniors and fully 45% of the finalists at the NCAA® championships used a Prince.

More amazingly, 94% of the players who switched to Prince said it

improved their game an average of 35%.

The court jesters panicked. They examined The Prince more closely. "It does have a bigger sweet spot," they said.

"Look, it's wide enough so that it doesn't twist! Everybody knows that gives you more control!

"Oh my. What should we do?" they cried.

THE HEAD MAN SPEAKS

"We'll make a racquet just like it, that's what we'll do," roared the head man.

But alas, it was not to be.

What they had failed to observe was that Prince had been awarded an exclusive patent by the U.S. Government.

The Prince racquet could not be copied without the approval of, you guessed it, Prince.

And so, today mid-size racquets are made as ovals, oblongs, tear drops and pear shapes.

And it has been whispered that some have even taken to kissing their racquets hoping to create a Prince. All to no avail.

Which is why, today, more people buy Prince than all

mid-size racquets combined.

MORAL

There is no other racquet out there that can do more for your game than a Prince. So why play anything less.

Advertisement for Prince tennis rackets prepared by Waring and LaRosa Inc. Reproduced by permission.

Repetition

The recurring use of the same element or theme establishes a harmonious relationship through repetition. This principle is common to every art form. A theme in a musical score, while not identically duplicated, can create a harmonious flow, with variations in pitch, intensity, tempo, and instruments preventing the repeated sounds from becoming montonous. Beethoven's Fifth Symphony is a powerful example of such use of repetition. The first four notes appear throughout the symphony, with changes in pitch and tempo creating exciting recurring patterns.

Painters often use variations of the same colors and shapes to create a binding force. These repetitions may be subtle, but they work subliminally to strengthen relationships and transitions within a composition. In architecture the repetition of windows, for example, may be more obvious, although the cellular effect may be broken by introducing different angles, varying shapes, or changes in material.

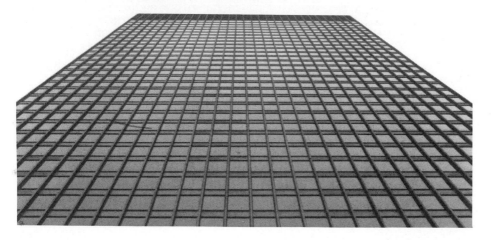

Seagram Building, New York City.

In typography, repetition is a device that is often taken for granted. You do not consciously think about repeating letters to form words, lines, paragraphs, and pages of a book. Yet repetition is present when the relationships among type styles, sizes, and weights are harmonious. If, for instance, you use a Helvetica Light followed by Helvetica Medium and then Helvetica Bold, you will have a visual transition of weight. But if you introduce a Helvetica Bold immediately after a Helvetica Light, the repetition will be disrupted by a contrast.

The Constructivist movement in Europe originated in countries with undeveloped industry…in Russia, Hungary and Holland. The marvels of technical civilization as they were described in reports about the U.S.A. were a great incentive for the young painters, sculptors and architects of those countries. **The message about American organization, production processes, life standards, created a Utopian picture in the mind of these young European artists. Their imaginative picture of America governed their thinking and their work. They admired exactness and precision, smooth functioning, the skyscraper, the highways, the immense span of bridges, the power plants of Niagara Falls, the autos and airplanes of America. They tried to be as contemporary and efficient in their own work as the Americans and without sentimentality for the old and traditional. They tried to be the children of a new age as they believed the Americans to be.**

The Constructivist movement in Europe originated in countries with undeveloped industry…in Russia, Hungary and Holland. The marvels of technical civilization as they were described in reports about the U.S.A. were a great incentive for the young painters, sculptors and architects of those countries. **The message about American organization, production processes, life standards, created a Utopian picture in the mind of these young European artists. Their imaginative picture of America governed their thinking and their work. They admired exactness and precision, smooth functioning, the skyscraper, the highways, the immense span of bridges, the power plants of Niagara Falls, the autos and airplanes of America. They tried to be as contemporary and efficient in their own work as the Americans and without sentimentality for the old and traditional. They tried to be the children of a new age as they believed the Americans to be.**

Only when repetition is interrupted by other, more powerful design components, such as opposition or contrast, are our visual senses detoured by the more dominant design force. It is important to determine the priority of repetition in your design. You must know what you want to design in order to control it. Note that the differences in weight within some type families may be more intense than those within the Helvetica family. Changes in letter, word, or line spacing will also affect repetition.

Certain decorative typographic elements are created through repetition. A scotch rule, for example, is composed of repeated lines of varying thickness. Similarly, a border is formed by combining ornaments in some repetitive pattern.

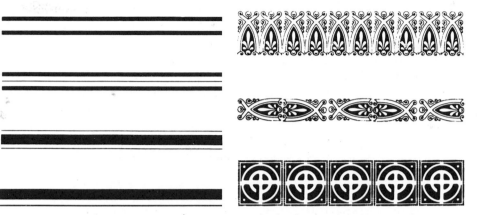

The theories of repetition have remained the same through the centuries, but the devices have changed. The decorative ornamentation popular in the eighteenth and nineteenth centuries, for instance, gave way to the simplified rules and bars of Russian Constructivist design.

Below, left to right: border and title initial design in style made popular by William Morris in late nineteenth century; page from Mayakovsky's book of poems, entitled For Reading Out Loud, *designed by El Lissitzky in 1923.*

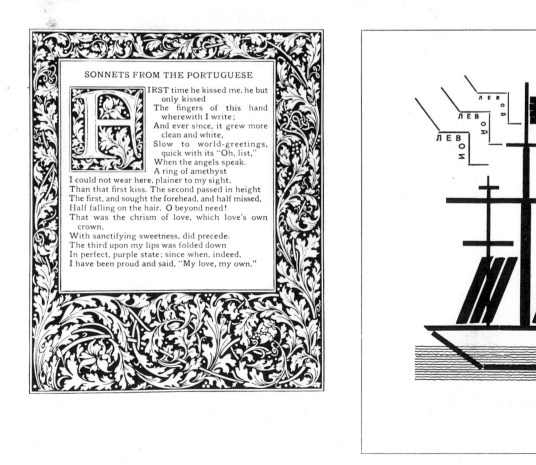

SONNETS FROM THE PORTUGUESE

FIRST time he kissed me, he but only kissed
The fingers of this hand wherewith I write;
And ever since, it grew more clean and white,
Slow to world-greetings, quick with its "Oh, list,"
When the angels speak. A ring of amethyst
I could not wear here, plainer to my sight,
Than that first kiss. The second passed in height
The first, and sought the forehead, and half missed,
Half falling on the hair. O beyond need!
That was the chrism of love, which love's own crown,
With sanctifying sweetness, did precede.
The third upon my lips was folded down
In perfect, purple state; since when, indeed,
I have been proud and said, "My love, my own."

If a new factor such as a different type style or weight is introduced within your design, it may seem awkward and disassociated if it is not repeated elsewhere. This certainly holds true if the project you are designing is several pages long. Repeated discreetly throughout the pages, the "different" element can become a delightful highlight or accent. Remember that the repeated similarity of lines, shapes, and color throughout a composition promotes unity within a design.

Opposition

Opposition takes advantage of the attraction of extremes. When used effectively, the strength of opposing forces can stimulate excitement and tension. In music, opposition can be created by changing the tempo and intensity of sound or by introducing additional instruments with opposing themes. Imagine the powerful impact when the smooth sounds of violins, rising and falling like waves, are suddenly confronted by blaring brasses. The intensity of this opposition can act as a crescendo, bringing a statement to a climax, as if the waves were breaking upon hitting a formation of rocks. Or the effect may be of an undercurrent, so that the waves continue to flow but in a different direction. Too much opposition, however, may become disruptive. It is important that you determine the right amount in order to maintain a cohesive composition.

Opposition can be as graceful as the beautiful lines formed by the opposing weight of two dancers. Or it may be as simple as the interplay between abstract shapes moving in different directions. The lines may complement or dominate each other, setting up priority.

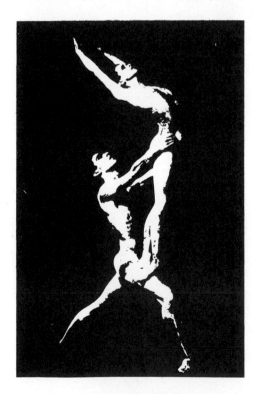
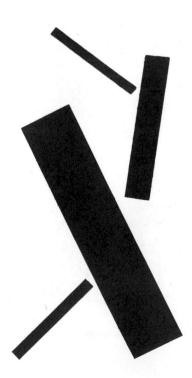

In typography, several techniques can be used to create opposition. The shape, size, and weight of letters; the relationship of type to the picture plane; the use of space, tonal value, and texture—all these elements should be considered. Note, for example, how a greater emphasis can be created by opposing an 18-point solid black rule with a 2-point rule rather than a 12-point rule.

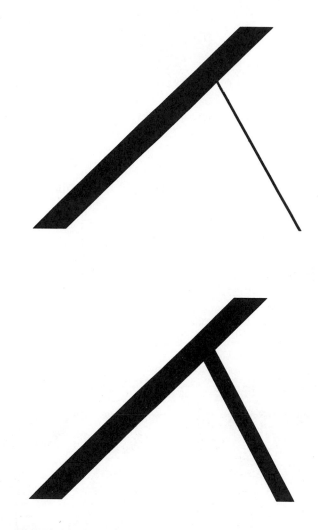

Letters have various levels of energy that generate opposition within the structure of the characters themselves. The degree of opposition varies, depending on the typeface.

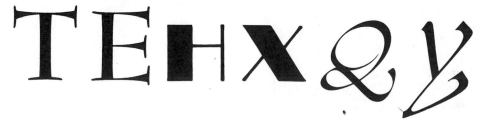

Left to right: letter pairs are set in Bernhard Modern Bold, Broadway, and Legend.

Pi symbols can be used alone or in combination to produce opposition. Note that the energy in letters and pi symbols is often used to form memorable logotypes, trademarks, and corporate images.

Top to bottom: logos for Planned Parenthood of New York City, Qiana for Du Pont, Raytex Textiles, and Eagle Transfer Corporation–all designed by Martin Solomon.

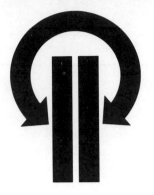

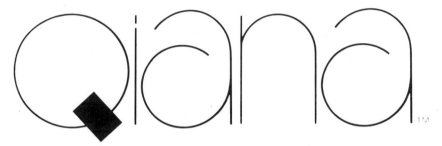

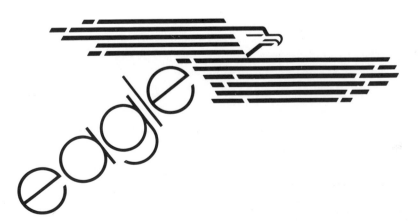

Opposition can also be created within a column of type. With Bodoni Book Italic, for example, you can generate an oppositional force by introducing a condensed face. The radicalness of the change determines the strength as well as the effectiveness of the opposition.

It may be made beautiful by the beauty of each of its prints—its literary content, its material or materials, its writing or printing, its illumination or illustration, its binding and decoration—of each of its parts in subordination to the whole which collectively they constitute: or it may be made beautiful by the supreme beauty of one or more of its parts, all the other parts subordinating or even effacing themselves for the sake of this one or more, and each in turn being capable of playing this supreme part, and each in its own peculiar and characteristic way. **On the other hand, each contributory craft may usurp the functions of the rest and of the whole, and growing beautiful beyond all bounds, ruin for its own the common cause.** *The whole duty of typography is to communicate to the imagination, without loss by the way, the thought or image intended to be communicated by the author.* **And the whole duty of beautiful typography is not to substitute for the beauty or interest of the thing thought not intended to be conveyed by the symbol, a beauty or its interest of its own.**

It may be made beautiful by the beauty of each of its prints—its literary content, its material or materials, its writing or printing, its illumination or illustration, its binding and decoration—of each of its parts in subordination to the whole which collectively they constitute: or it may be made beautiful by the supreme beauty of one or more of its parts, all the other parts subordinating or even effacing themselves for the sake of this one or more, and each in turn being capable of playing this supreme part, and each in its own peculiar and characteristic way. **On the other hand, each contributory craft may usurp the functions of the rest and of the whole, and growing beautiful beyond all bounds, ruin for its own the common cause.** The whole duty of typography is to communicate to the imagination, without loss by the way, the thought or image intended to be communicated by the author. **And the whole duty of beautiful typography is not to substitute for the beauty or interest of the thing thought not intended to be conveyed by the symbol, a beauty or its interest of its own.**

Opposition, however, is only one aspect of a composition. It must be used with discretion and control so that it supports but does not dominate the overall design statement you choose to make.

Priority

Priority determines the order of dominance among the various elements within a composition. It organizes them according to levels of importance, which are necessary to create a logical flow within a design.

In typography, as well as other two-dimensional arts, the surface usually isolates priorities by confining the elements within the picture plane. If, however, more than one element within a design strives for visual dominance, too great an opposition may occur. Unless visual supremacy is established, there will be confusion of priority.

In typographic design, priorities can be established through size, weight, spacing, tonal intensities, and position. If all the typographic elements are equally spaced on a white page, the type style, point size, and type weight become the devices for setting up priority among the elements. It is the dominant factor that determines the priority. By experimenting with different combinations and variations of the same typographic character, you can explore some of the many ways to create priorities in a design.

Page of typographic poetry by Martin Solomon.

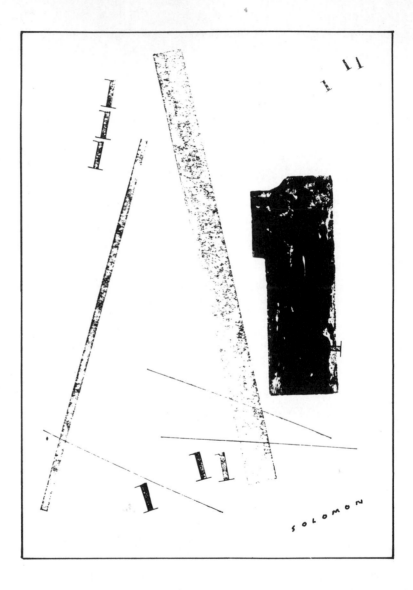

Introducing a tone or a bright color stimulates the eye and rearranges the order of priority among the elements. Two tones of the same intensity, however, create an optical halation—an illusion of vibrating tone at the point of contact—and thus prevent any priority from being established. One tone must vary enough in contrast or chromatic value to yield to the other for a compatible relationship to be created between the two and priority established. Subtle variations in tone can produce exciting results.

Establishing priority does not mean that the primary element should overpower the rest of the composition. Rather, it should be a starting point for the eye on its trip through the page. The other elements then move the eye through the rest of the design, bringing continuity to the composition.

Position

Position involves the placement of elements in a specific area. Painters, architects and designers have always considered position one of the main principles of design. Once an element is placed within a space, a definite relationship is established between that element and its space. Once the element takes possession of that position, it owns it and stands firmly committed to that area. Since position influences the forces within a picture plane, a designer must carefully plan the placement of elements within the space.

It is difficult to understand position without being aware of the effect it has on balance. Certain spaces, for example, are more protective of their elements than others. A dot placed in the center of a square will appear secure in its position because the energy forces of the surrounding space contain it within the area. If that same dot is placed off center, the composition may appear more interesting, but it will not appear as secure. A dot too close to the edge can lead the eye off the page, since the corner of the picture plane acts as an outward directional force.

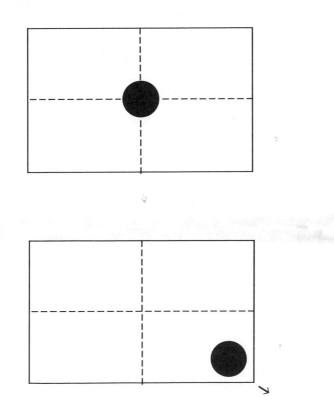

The masters of the Renaissance were aware of the importance of position and carefully determined the placement of shapes in their paintings to create what I call "dynamic symmetry." The power of their work derived from an underlying grid, which is still used by designers today. This guide for planning the space within a design combines dynamic lines of motion with a balanced, symmetrical division of the picture plane. To use this method, take a sheet of paper and draw a grid that divides the picture plane into equal vertical, horizontal, and diagonal parts. The example below illustrates only one of several possible ways in which you can do this.

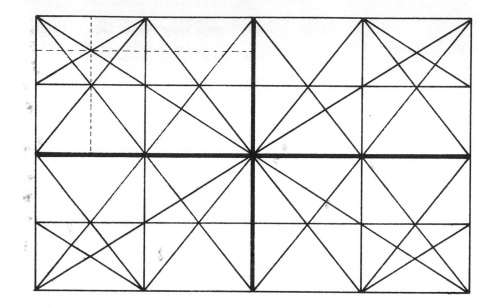

Although intuition may guide the placement of elements on a surface, by using these guidelines to break down your space mathematically, you become more aware of the energy forces within each segment and how the size and shape of each element relates to the whole. There is no formula for positioning elements within a space, but you can use this grid to arrive at a logical solution. Once you are satisfied with the position of your elements, remove your tracing-paper guide and begin making typographic refinements to finalize the composition. As you develop your skills as a designer, you should begin to perceive your elements within an imaginary grid, without having to use the tracing.

Position demands an understanding of space as an organized totality to which elements are applied according to the various principles of design. In our culture, tradition dictates that letterforms are read horizontally and vertically, and typesetting machinery is geared to follow this format. In most cases, typographic elements are positioned along horizontal and vertical lines, parallel to the edges of the picture plane. Newspapers, periodicals, annual reports, and books are usually designed according to this traditional system. No interpretation of a tradition, however, is absolute. After type is produced, designers can position it in any way they choose. The work of the Russian Constructivists is a good example of the possibilities for revolutionary changes in position.

CZas° pismo

revue

1927
1928
1929
1930

praesens

nr 2

warszawa a sovie

ce na 15 zł

Henry Stazewski, cover for second and last issue of the Polish Constructivist journal Praesens.

3. Attributes of Design

The attributes of design are qualities or characteristics inherent in any art form, such as balance, emphasis or contrast, and rhythm. These attributes are used to support the feeling of a design and project the personality of a piece. To convey a fast-paced, rhythmic flow, for example, the designer must establish attributes that support this intent by combining elements in accordance with the appropriate principles. If the pace is to be slowed, the attributes will change. Careful control of the attributes of design is necessary to successfully project an intended image.

Balance

An arrangement of one or more elements so that visually they equal each other creates a balance. This principle is a basic phenomenon in nature and a universally accepted concept in art. Nature has designed a balanced world, with north opposing south, east facing west, and the whole rotating on an axis. Every object in nature has its own structural balance, from the symmetry of a flower petal to the chambers of a snail's shell.

Our bodies are designed with bisymmetrical unity. The balance needed every time we perform a movement is automatically maintained by a built-in equilibrium that we take for granted. Man-made structures, even if they are not formally equal on all sides, must maintain a balance in relation to a perpendicular surface. No doubt the Leaning Tower of Pisa will someday fall when a greater portion of its weight shifts off balance.

Sound must also be balanced, both in its production and in its reproduction. Every instrument in an orchestra is directed to ensure that one does not unintentionally overpower another. This balance is further monitored during a recording session by highly sophisticated equalizing equipment. When you adjust the dials on your audio system at home, you are also striving to control fidelity and balance.

Achieving a physical balance is simple: the weight of one object must be counterbalanced by the weight of another on the opposite end of a fulcrum. If, however, the objects are of different materials, the masses may not appear to be balanced. Because steel is heavier than wood, for example, a large piece of wood is needed to balance a small piece of steel.

Physical balance can be measured; there is no scientific method, however, for determining the weight of shapes in the arts. Instead, balance is determined by weighing the objects visually. Optically, a large mass of gray can be balanced by a small mass of black. But the visual weights of elements are not constant; they change depending on the other elements in the composition. Every time an element is added to or removed from a composition, the balance shifts. Moreover, an object that is the dominant weight in one composition may be subordinate in another.

As the eye moves through a composition, it seeks compensating balancing factors. The position of elements thus affects the feeling of balance. When elements are placed near the center of the picture plane, they will appear to be supported by the space around them. As the elements move closer to the edge, however, the weight and energy forces shift and some sort of compensation is required.

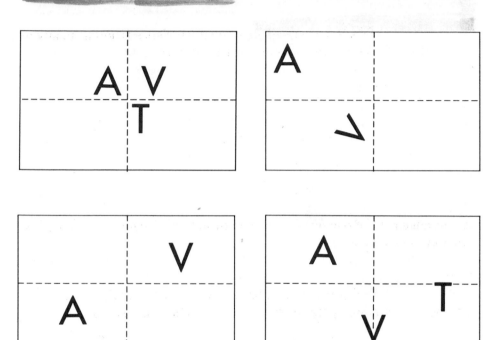

Balance may be symmetrical or asymmetrical. Symmetrical balance is visually equal on both sides in weight and tone, while asymmetrical balance may be unequal in position and intensity. In the example below, the two circles at equal distance from the centerpoint are symmetrically balanced. As one moves toward the center, the weight shifts. To create an asymmetrical balance, there must be an increase in intensity to compensate for the change in position. Intensity can be increased by changing size, shape, or tone.

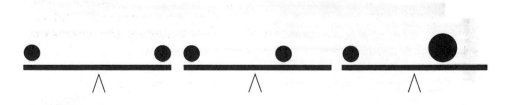

Symmetrical balance is static, with a specific gravity that creates a formal relationship between the elements and the picture plane. The equality of the elements holds the eye in a fixed focus within the picture plane. If the eye moves from one object to another, it is not because of a directional force created by the objects or their placement within the composition, but because of the attracting power of the object itself.

A directional force can be introduced to set up movement among the elements of a composition. In typography, letter shapes, arrows, leaders, triangles, and bullets can all serve as directional forces, actively leading the eye through the picture plane. The directional forces, however, must be balanced in some way or the eye will wander off the page. A dynamic element, for instance, can be balanced or partially balanced by a static element toward which it is directed.

Typographic composition by Martin Solomon.

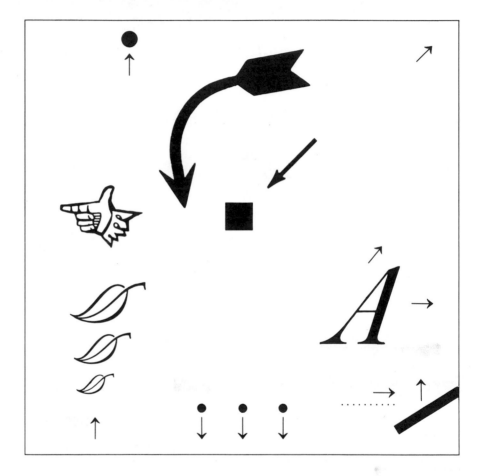

There are many different ways of achieving an asymmetrical balance. For a particular project, a designer might choose to position the elements on one side of the picture plane. The opposing white space must then act as a counterbalancing force. The deliberate "off-balance" becomes aesthetically pleasing if the relationship of mass to space is proportionally correct.

In manipulating the visual qualities of weight and position, the designer must consider the composition as a whole. Although not all letter shapes are symmetrical in design, they can create a formal symmetry when they take on overall shape as units of words, lines, columns, or pages. One way to determine the balance of elements on a page is to compare one area with another. Again, it is helpful to analyze the space with an imaginary grid (see page 42). In this way you can optically weigh the masses and determine their intensity and direction.

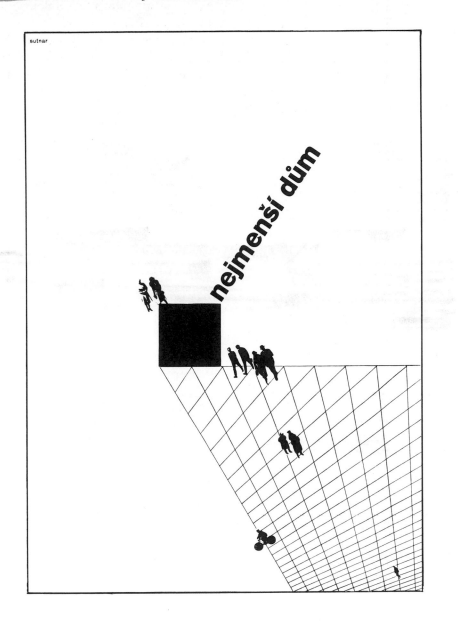

see page 42

Title page designed by Ladislav Sutnar for Nejmenšsi Dům *("Minimum House"), 1931.*

Emphasis and Contrast

Of all the attributes, emphasis and contrast are probably the most important. Although the terms are often used interchangeably, I perceive emphasis as providing a sense of transition, whereas contrast entails a more abrupt shift.

Emphasis and contrast are very specific and do not lend themselves to interpretation. In music, a sharp or flat outside the primary tonality is a modest but definite emphasis. Similarly, in typography an italic of the same point size as its roman counterpart provides a modest but definite change.

Statement by Jan Tschichold.

All abstract pictures, particularly the quite simple ones, show elements of painting or graphic art which are at once clearly defined in form and in plain relation to one another. From this to typography is no great step. *The works of abstract painters are symbols of the subtle arrangement of simple yet strongly contrasting elements.* Since the new typography sets itself no other task than the creation of just arrangements, it is possible for many works of abstract painters and sculptors to act as inspirational models.

The proportions of elements within a composition are also important factors in determining contrast. While the lack of contrast can be boring, too much contrast can be irritating. The correct level of contrast is arrived at by analyzing the different potentials and choosing those that proportionately complement the subject.

In typography there are various ways to achieve contrast. A frequently used device is tonal value, since most type styles offer a full family of weights, ranging from thin to extra-bold. Some also include a variety of widths from extra-condensed to extra-wide or expanded. Contrast can also be created by combining type styles, spacing, and ornamentation in various ways. The typographic palette holds innumerable possibilities. It is up to you and your imagination to find the devices that best indicate emphasis.

Using an underscore.

All abstract pictures, particularly the quite simple ones, show elements of painting or graphic art which are at once clearly defined in form and in plain relation to one another. From this to typography is no great step. <u>The works of abstract painters are symbols of the subtle arrangement of simple yet strongly contrasting elements.</u> Since the new typography sets itself no other task than the creation of just arrangements, it is possible for many works of abstract painters and sculptors to act as inspirational models.

Specifying condensed letters with a regular style.

All abstract pictures, particularly the quite simple ones, show elements of painting or graphic art which are at once clearly defined in form and in plain relation to one another. From this to typography is no great step. The works of abstract painters are symbols of the subtle arrangement of simple yet strongly contrasting elements. Since the new typography sets itself no other task than the creation of just arrangements, it is possible for many works of abstract painters and sculptors to act as inspirational models.

All abstract pictures, particularly the quite simple ones, show elements of painting or graphic art which are at once clearly defined in form and in plain relation to one another. From this to typography is no great step. ▌The works of abstract painters are symbols of the subtle arrangement of simple yet strongly contrasting elements. ▌ Since the new typography sets itself no other task than the creation of just arrangements, it is possible for many works of abstract painters and sculptors to act as inspirational models.

Bracketing a section with vertical rules.

All abstract pictures, particularly the quite simple ones, show elements of painting or graphic art which are at once clearly defined in form and in plain relation to one another. From this to typography is no great step. The works of abstract painters are symbols of the subtle arrangement of simple yet STRONGLY CONTRASTING ELEMENTS. Since the new typography sets itself no other task than the creation of just arrangements, it is possible for many works of abstract painters and sculptors to act as inspirational models.

Using small capitals (if available) or capital letters one or more point sizes smaller than the rest of the text.

All abstract pictures, particularly the quite simple ones, show elements of painting or graphic art which are at once clearly defined in form and in plain relation to one another. **From this to typography is no great step. The works of abstract painters are symbols of the subtle arrangement of simple yet strongly contrasting elements.** Since the new typography sets itself no other task than the creation of just arrangements, it is possible for many works of abstract painters and sculptors to act as inspirational models.

Introducing a boldface into light-face copy (or vice versa).

All abstract pictures, particularly the quite simple ones, show elements of painting or graphic art which are at once clearly defined in form and in plain relation to one another. From this to typography is no great step. The works of abstract painters are symbols of the subtle arrangement of simple yet s t r o n g l y c o n t r a s t i n g e l e m e n t s . Since the new typography sets itself no other task than the creation of just arrangements, it is possible for many works of abstract painters and sculptors to act as inspirational models.

Inserting letter space.

You can also indicate a second color for emphasis. Remember, however, that the degree of contrast will be affected by the surface the color is printed on. The brilliance of white paper varies, depending on the stock you use, and this must be considered in planning your composition. With a multipage format, you can also add contrast, both visually and tactilely, by introducing different paper stocks.

Obviously, in the design of multipage formats such as magazine editorials and text pages, the considerations about emphasis are different from those for a single page. The design theme must follow through with consistency, but there is greater latitude for contrast. You can, for instance, introduce more variations of tone than would be possible in a more confined space. This does not, however, imply that you should use every device available in a single piece. Good design requires a deliberate choice of the levels of emphasis most applicable to the subject.

When first designed, some typefaces did not have a full family of weights and widths, so other typefaces were used for contrast. News Gothic provides an interesting case study of typeface design and use. In 1909 Morris F. Benton designed News Gothic in a regular weight, along with News Gothic Condensed and Extra Condensed (which had approximately the same weight as the regular). These were the contrasting alternatives in the family. When a bolder face was needed to create contrast for the regular News Gothic, Franklin Gothic, designed by Benton in 1904, was used. Alternate Gothic No. 2 was the bold companion of News Gothic Condensed, and Alternate Gothic No. 1 became the companion face of News Gothic Extra Condensed. When companion faces were not readily available, an underscore was usually used to supply contrast.

News Gothic **Franklin Gothic**

News Gothic Condensed **Alternate Gothic No. 2**

News Gothic Extra Condensed **Alternate Gothic No.1**

It wasn't until 1958 that a more complete family for News Gothic, with a bold and an italic, became available. Many designers, however, continue to use Franklin Gothic as the companion face, contending that the bold version of News Gothic does not provide a sufficiently strong contrast. They value the additional weight and classic style of Franklin Gothic, which they feel creates a more compatible and exciting contrast. Many other typefaces have a similar history.

News Gothic Bold

News Gothic Bold Italic

Rhythm

Derived from the Greek word for "flow," rhythm is an essential attribute of all art forms. It is the moving force connecting the elements within a composition. While the principle of transition is based on maintaining flow, providing for gradual change, rhythm is the heartbeat of flow. At the same time rhythm is a subtle, poetic trait.

In music, rhythm refers to a definite, orderly movement that can create various moods from excitement to sadness, depending on the tempo. Although different instruments may play different notes of varying duration and intensity, the composer weaves the individual rhythms into a whole. The designer can also employ several rhythms simultaneously, using different lines, shapes, colors, and textures, each compatible with the others.

Rhythm is a state of movement that is generated from within the composition. It need not be formal, but it must convey the designer's intent. All rhythm is supported by secondary forces—undercurrents that often go unnoticed, but nonetheless energize the overall dramatic intent. In typography these secondary forces are the eddies found within the shapes of letters. The beautiful grass-style writing of Chinese calligraphy, developed by Wang Hsi-Chih in the Han Dynasty, suggests the simple, pure rhythm inherent in the speed of line.

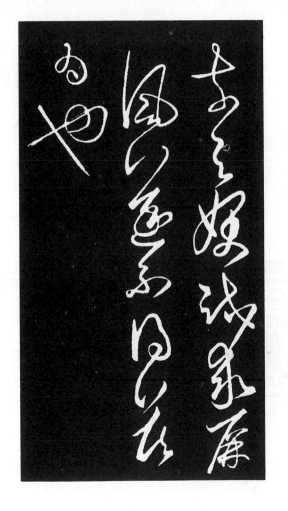

Rubbing of grass-style writing taken from stone engraving.

A different kind of rhythm is found in the Dada artists' combination of letters and words into abstract groupings. Although this Dada poetry is nonobjective as language, it has a visual and acoustic rhythm. In the example here, you can see the typographic rhythm set up through the use of space, position, and size.

Raoul Hausmann, "Sound-Rel," 1919.

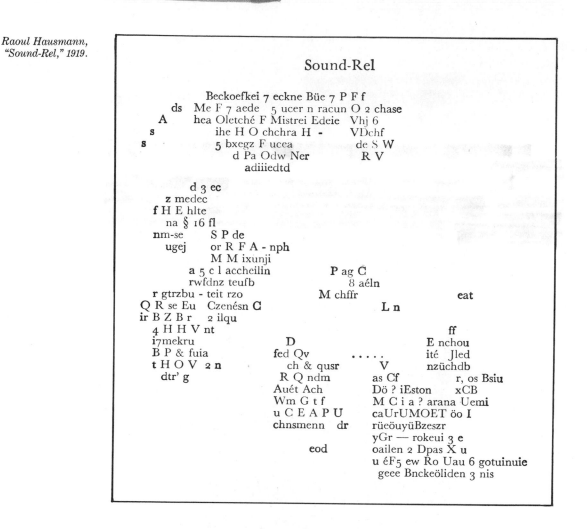

The simplest form of rhythm in typography involves the continuous flow of lines of type on a page. Here the supporting elements of the design must be close enough to relate visually, maintaining the continuity of movement. The type is united into a solid mass, with letter, word, and line spacing directing its flow. Just as you can change the rhythm in music by altering the tempo, you can add space between lines to slow reading or tighten letter or word space to increase speed. You can also extend the lines of type, but if they extend too far, it becomes difficult for the eye to pick up the next line and the continuity is disrupted. Obviously, the designer must visualize the type's next movement to maintain rhythmic flow.

Although rhythm appears to be a continuous flow, it must in fact end. The point of conclusion must not be abrupt, but rather fade, as if the rhythm were passing rather than ending.

Poster designed by Martin Solomon.

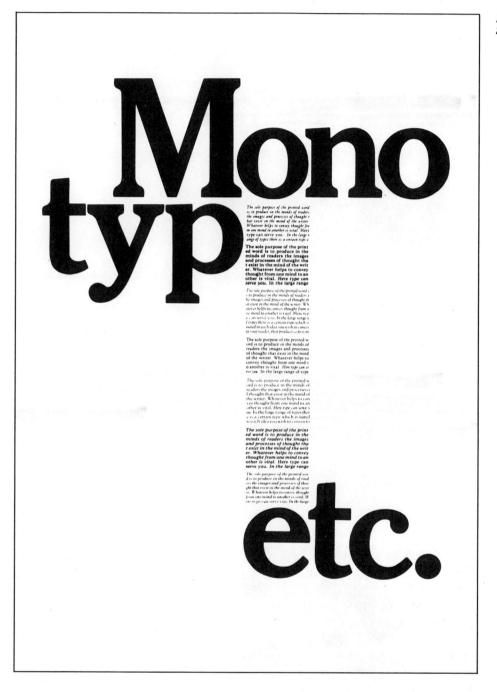

4. Composition and Experimentation

Composition brings together all the elements, principles, and attributes of design in a pleasing, logical display of unity. Although good composition defies definition, no one can deny that you can acquire the ability to recognize it. When I watch a musical performance, the movements of the conductor's baton seem to create a musical design, while the notes and tempo resemble the visual abstractions of letterforms. Much as a conductor unites the instruments, an art director orchestrates and directs all the elements, using the principles and attributes of design. If one aspect of the design does not comply with the specifications, it is like a discordant note in a concert—the whole composition is jeopardized.

There is no formal explanation for what makes a composition good. Each subject establishes its own criteria for a successful composition. For a composition to be effective, however, the order of things must conform to the subject's priorities. The design must fulfill its intended purpose within the framework of sound aesthetic judgment. A Dada poem, for example, demands different aesthetic treatment from a romantic sonnet.

A composition must rely on all its parts in order to be effective. Even the smallest detail is critical to the success of the composition. Yet you must never lose sight of the overall surface area. The intensity and mass of the parts must be compatible with the surface plane.

The importance of these considerations can be seen in Chinese calligraphy, an art form requiring great discipline. The master calligraphers were highly skilled in controlling the substance of each line. Even a dot became decisive statement. Moreover, each calligraphic shape and its placement within the composition were predetermined to ensure a proper relationship within the whole.

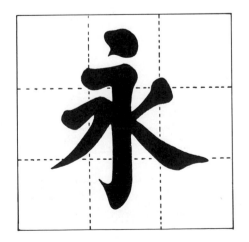

Typography is also a finely tuned art form. At first, in developing a concept, explore alternative compositions. Prepare many rough layouts, pulling apart and reassembling the components of the design. Keep adjusting the positioning, spacing, and other aspects until the whole coalesces. Subtleties, in the form of typographic refinements, can be used to enhance the composition. As you can see in the following examples, there are many different ways to design an effective composition.

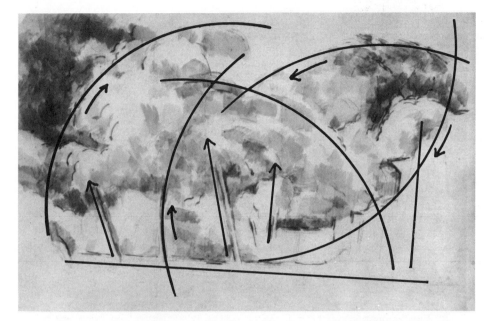

Diagram of directional lines in watercolor by Paul Cézanne.

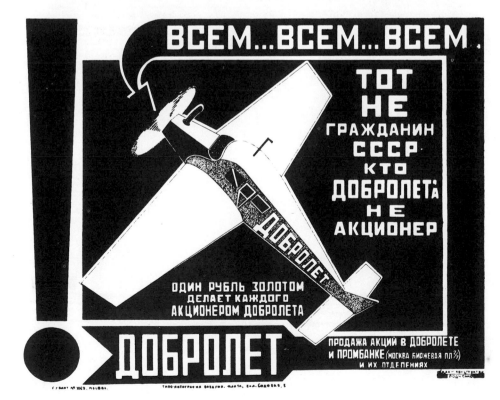

Alexander Rodchenko, poster for New Economic Policy, 1923.

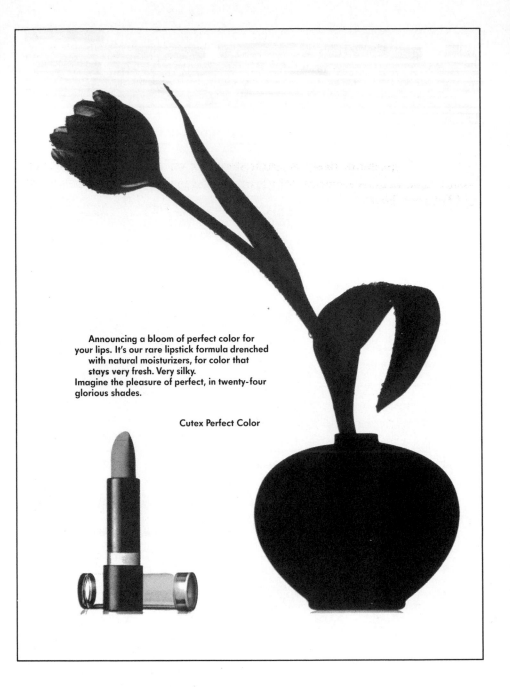

Announcing a bloom of perfect color for
your lips. It's our rare lipstick formula drenched
with natural moisturizers, for color that
stays very fresh. Very silky.
Imagine the pleasure of perfect, in twenty-four
glorious shades.

Cutex Perfect Color

Experimentation

A designer's sensitivity to the arts and personal growth should be developed through experimentation. First, however, you must understand design traditions, for they provide a foundation on which to build. Experimentation requires ideology, research, application, and perception, all of which stimulate your imagination and increase the scope of your design.

By looking at the development of letterforms in Chinese calligraphy, one can gain insights into how change occurs. The evolution of the symbol shapes from the original pictograms to classical Chinese writing is attributed to a change in writing mediums, specifically the invention of paper and the replacement of the bamboo stylus with the brush. New shapes emerged from the old: round areas became square, angles were thickened, horizontal lines became thinner, and vertical lines broader.

A more contemporary example of experimentation is the work of Giorgio Morandi, a twentieth-century painter who never spent much time outside his native town of Bologna in Italy. In his still lifes Morandi used the same objects continuously, but each time he created a different composition, with a new arrangement of shape, color, and form. The effectiveness of Morandi's designs often depends on the interplay between positive and negative shapes, which can be compared to the shapes within and between letters.

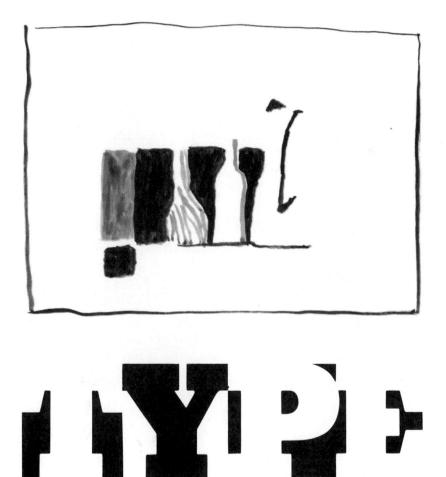

Study of positive and negative shapes in still life after Giorgio Morandi.

As abstract forms, typographic letters lend themselves to innumerable possibilities for experimentation. Indeed, artists have long held typography in high esteem and have used its symbols in practically every medium. In the early twentieth century, the mysticism of random letters was incorporated into the paintings and collages of Pablo Picasso, Georges Braque, and Juan Gris. Later, Ben Shahn created marvelous artworks with hand lettering on newspaper. More recently, Jasper Johns has used newspaper to create a foundational texture for his encaustic paintings; he has also made stenciled letters and numbers central elements in some of his artwork.

Ben Shahn, seriograph on newsprint, 1958.

Within the twentieth century, various revolutionary art movements have been dedicated to innovative changes in art and its philosophy. The ideas of the Dada, Constructivist, De Stijl, and Bauhaus artists are particularly important for the typographic designer. These movements opposed traditional restrictions on artists and developed a new ideology, in which artists and designers were encouraged to explore unorthodox approaches. For all these movements, experimentation was a major force in the development of their philosophies.

Typography was greatly influenced by these progressive changes. Type was no longer just flush left and right in vertical columns; it found new directions in space not seen before. The Constructivists, for example, introduced the idea of assembling abstract shapes into a nonobjective composition. When letters were taken out of the normal reading pattern and type was no longer parallel to the page, the letterforms could be seen more as shapes than as phonetic symbols. Changing the position or angle of type on a page offered a different insight into design.

Typographers and designers also made extensive use of block letter faces. Experimental typefaces developed by Herbert Bayer of the Bauhaus and Wladyslaw Strzemínski, a Polish Constructivist, reflected the prevailing aesthetic of minimalism. The simple geometry of these letterforms exemplified the belief that form should follow function. Several typefaces that we today accept as classical, such as Futura and Kabel, were inspired by the Bauhaus and similar movements.

Top to bottom: alphabets designed by Wladyslaw Strzemínski in 1931 and by Herbert Bayer in 1925.

Although the Dada, Constructivist, De Stijl, and Bauhaus movements all began in Russia and Europe, their influence spread. With the increasingly uncertain political climate in Europe, some of the more prominent artists and designers emigrated to America. In particular, several of the Bauhaus's most influential designers—Walter Gropius, Mies van der Rohe, Herbert Bayer, and Josef Albers, for example—accepted teaching positions at top American universities. In their own way, the artists in these movements were responsible for the design concepts that so many architects, graphic designers, and industrial designers practice today. They made an indelible mark on all phases of the arts as well as on everyday items and living conditions.

Marcel Janco, poster for Dada exhibition and Tzara lectures, 1917.

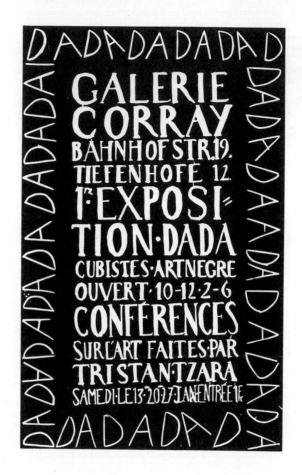

An innovation developed through experimentation is often looked upon as an oddity—a statement that shocks the viewer through unconventionalism. Most oddities are rejected. If, however, an oddity is exciting enough and makes a sufficiently powerful statement, it will gain momentum and be developed and perfected. If an oddity withstands the test of time, it is embraced as an innovative part of history. Periodically, philosophies of design emerge in modifed forms under different names. Although surface changes are made, the traditional design concepts remain consistent. The High Tech and New Wave movements of the late 1970s and early 1980s, for example, were based on the Constructivist art of the early 1920s.

The philosophy and tradition of a movement are the foundation and substance of its art. Without an understanding of motivations, an elaboration of an original work is only a modified reproduction. It is therefore essential to understand the impetus behind a movement in order to expand upon the past intelligently. Experimentation is the bridge connecting past traditions to those of the future.

When I think of experimenting with type, the material used to execute the project becomes as important as the design itself. New possibilities and priorities for dealing with space, mass, weight, and dimension as well as the other elements of design release new energies, stirring visual excitement. Even if the initial experiment is not a graphic success, an intellectual statement has been made, encouraging further experimentation.

Often the impetus for experimentation comes from one of the other arts. Architects, for example, require typography for street numbers, elevator panels, building directories, and directional signs. Here typography is not restricted to a two-dimensional surface. Materials such as plastics, metal, wood, and glass may be used to present typographic forms in innovative ways. The same is true in industrial design. An example is the typography on automobiles, which is often enameled on the front hood, door panels, or other sections of the car. This type is an extension of the car's design—it not only identifies the vehicle, but also puts forward the image with which the car and owner will be associated.

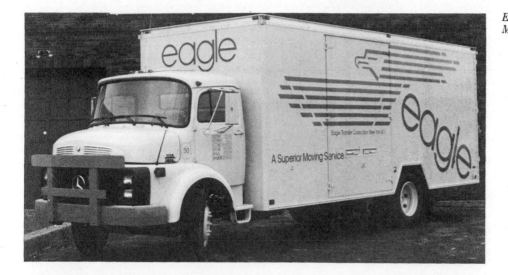

Eagle Transfer design by Martin Solomon.

Experimentation is a very personal reflection of your ability to think and create. To begin, you must become thoroughly familiar with your subject. Research your subject and its relation to the past, for the past can be inspirational as well as informative. Reviewing the movements and the artists who were instrumental in establishing a concept provides the background necessary to intelligently correlate your own ideas.

Document every step of your experimental process. Explore new mediums. If applicable, think beyond a purely graphic representation to a collaboration with sound and movement. Remember, however, that expanded technological capabilities are no substitute for creativity.

Do not be timid in executing new concepts. If tradition is to be broken, break it boldly and with conviction, always guided by sound aesthetic judgment. Do not, however, break tradition for the sake of change itself. If you deviate from tradition, it should be because you believe it is the only way to achieve the effect you want. A knowledge of the past coupled with observations from the present will create the future.

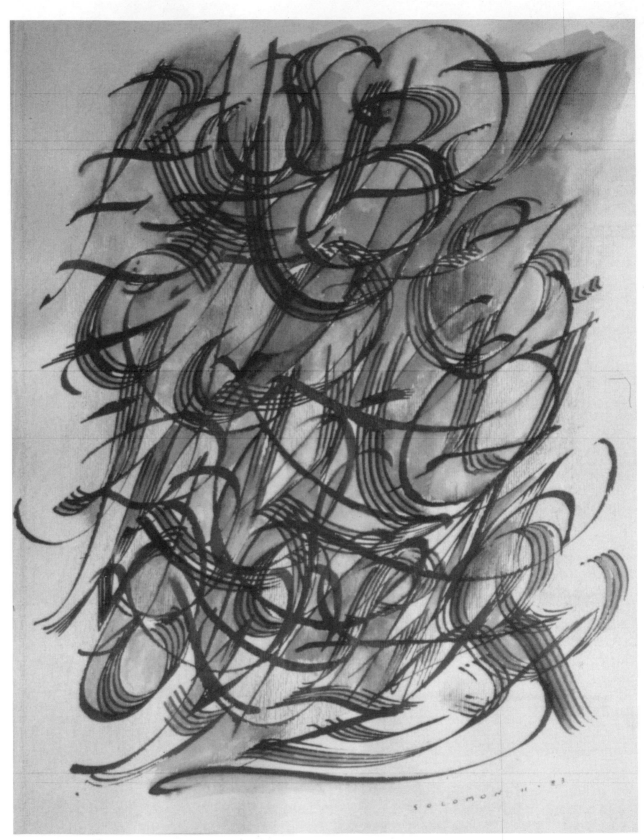

Composition of calligraphic letterforms by Martin Solomon.

Part Two
Type and Its Refinements

All the arts have their own technical languages, which permit you to communicate with the proper terminology. Learning the specific language of an art is essential, for it enables you to use and interpret the elements, principles, and attributes of design. It is difficult to play a musical instrument and communicate with sound in an intelligent manner without knowing what musical symbols and notations represent. Yet once this vocabulary has been learned, the creative musician can develop any number of interpretations.

Typography is an exceptional art because mechanical technology is required to direct its aesthetics. Many of the typefaces and most of the basic terminology in use today originated in metal type composition. By familiarizing yourself with the history and mechanics of metal type, as well as new phototypesetting methods, you will increase your command over the typographic vocabulary.

Although typographic terminology is standardized, it can be interpreted in different ways. Once you are familiar with the basic terminology, it is important to learn how to read the basic information on a type specimen sheet and how to translate this information into specifications that will ensure the typographic impact you want. It is important to understand the possible variations—for instance, in word and letter spacing—as it may not be enough to let the typographer interpret general specifications. Elaborations through refinements add the finishing touches to a design and distinguish typography from typesetting. Adding refinements is like polishing a marble sculpture to bring out its inner illumination.

For most projects, there is still another consideration—the reproduction of the design through printing. Here the designer needs to be aware of printing methods, as well as available paper and color choices. Selecting paper and color requires the same care as selecting type and its refinements. Typography is an exacting art, necessitating clear specifications at every point in its creation.

5. Basic Styles of Type

Johann Gutenberg of Mainz, Germany, is generally cited as the inventor of movable type, although a more accurate assessment would credit him with perfecting printing and casting processes and not their invention. The forty-two-line Mazarin Bible, printed around 1455, has become known as the first book produced with movable type. Both the type style and its composition were produced by Gutenberg. Attempting to simulate the formal manuscript style popular during that period, Gutenberg modeled his typeface after the gothic-style black letter. The letters in this style had a solid, pointed look, stressing the perpendicular, and tended to be heavy and ornamented, like Teutonic architecture of the time.

Beginning of Proverbs from forty-two-line Mazarin Bible, with illuminated initial representing King Solomon.

64

Generally, the design of the printed letterform followed the development of handwriting styles, along with improvements in materials and machinery. Type comes in a variety of styles, and each has its own history of development. Nearly all typefaces, however, can be grouped in categories, according to certain shared characteristics. The most broadly defined categories are roman, script, gothic, ornamental, and period.

Different typefaces have different personalities. Some styles emphasize a full-face view; others stress the profile. The larger the type size is, the more animated and pictorial the appearance of the type will be. A character or mood is created beyond the words or message. It is as if the letters were wearing a uniform or costume, ready to perform within a designated stage area or space.

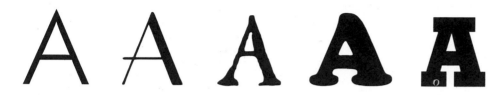

Left to right: Futura Light, Parisian, Caslon Antique, Copper Black, Stymie Extra Bold.

Roman

As the early German printers emigrated to other European countries to escape political turmoil, they found that the black letter was not only unpopular in other countries, but was rejected as barbaric. In Italy, the Renaissance had revived an interest in the classics. Renaissance scribes modified and beautified the Caroline minuscule, an eighth-century script, which was believed to represent traditional Roman writing, unlike the "barbaric" black letter. This modified script—the Neo-Caroline minuscule—became the model for the earliest roman typefaces.

Actually, it was the carvings on the Trajan Column (built in Rome in A.D. 114) that established the format for the classical roman letter style. The letters were chiseled into the stone, creating an intaglio or V shape, with sunlight reflecting on one side of the letter while a contrasting shadow was cast on the other. To prevent the stone from chipping or cracking around the letterforms, score lines called serifs were cut at the ends of

Inscription cut in stone at base of Trajan Column in Rome.

SENATVSPOPVLVSQVEROMANVS
IMP·CAESARI·DIVI·NERVAE·F·NERVAE
TRAIANO·AVG·GERM·DACICOPONTIF
MAXIMOTRIBPOT·XVII·IMP·VI·COS·VI·P·P
ADDECLARANDVMQVANTAEALTITVDINIS
MONSETLOCVSTAN̄   IBVSSITEGESTVS

the letters. The serifs also helped compensate for the optical distortion in the center of the verticals, making them appear to bulge outward. Eventually serifs were designed to blend into the letter's structure.

Roman letters are by definition structures with thick-and-thin weights. They may or may not have serifs, although most do. Within this classical style, several variations developed, due to influences of geography, popular cultural and intellectual philosophies, politics, and technology. These variations of the roman letter include old style, transitional, modern, and primer (or book). In addition, there are some faces that appear to follow the roman format for thick-and-thin letters, but introduce modifications by exaggerating weights or displacing emphasis; they thus begin to indicate a change in personality. Included in this category are fat face and Egyptian (Antique).

Optima

Old Style

In 1470 Nicolas Jenson, a Frenchman who established himself as a printer in Venice, cut one of the earliest roman typefaces, based on the handwriting used in the finest humanist manuscripts of the day. But it was not until the end of that century, in 1495, that Aldus Manutius, another Venetian printer, introduced the first old style roman type. Aldus's letter design served as the model for the classical font cut by Claude Garamond in 1530. Garamond's old style roman had thick-and-thin variations within the parts of letters, including serifs. The letters were crisp, beautiful, and more informal than the carvings on the Trajan Column.

Garamond No.3

In 1734 William Caslon I, the first in a long line of type designers, cut an old style type, which was influenced by Garamond's design and which, like Garamond's font, has since become recognized as a classic. Caslon's font was styled after the effect created by a flat brush, as lettered by the Romans—unlike Garamond's font, which was fashioned after the effect of the more flexible quill pen. The Caslon font followed a more formal, structured letterform design with fewer variations in line weight.

Caslon Old Face No. 2

Although Caslon's typeface gained increasing popularity in England, the popularity of old style faces declined in general in Continental Europe. In France Philippe Grandjean in 1702 and Pierre Simon Fournier (le Jeune) in 1737 designed and developed new letterforms, which eventually led to what we now call transitional or intermediate roman letters.

During this period a new handwriting style, the roundhand, was developed. The Renaissance scribes had written with broad-nib pens, held approximately at a 30-degree angle. This gave the curved letters of the humanist hand a more informal appearance, since they were drawn asymmetrically to the baseline. The heaviest parts of the letters were drawn from a 12 o'clock position to a 3 o'clock position, with the curve continuing from 6 o'clock to 9 o'clock. The eighteenth-century scribes used the same pen but changed the writing angle, keeping the flat edge of the pen parallel to the baseline. This made the down-stroke main line the heaviest line and the horizontal lines the lightest.

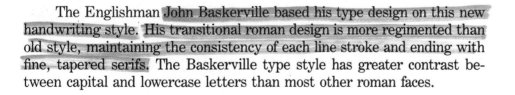

The Englishman John Baskerville based his type design on this new handwriting style. His transitional roman design is more regimented than old style, maintaining the consistency of each line stroke and ending with fine, tapered serifs. The Baskerville type style has greater contrast between capital and lowercase letters than most other roman faces.

Baskerville

The modern roman letterform was introduced by the Didot type foundry in France in 1784. Improvements in press and paper enabled printers to obtain clearer impressions, and the Didot face was reworked until it acquired the ridged, untapered, fine-line serif structures we recognize today as characteristic of modern roman letterforms.

Firmin Didot

Giambattista Bodoni, a printer from Parma, Italy, copied the Didot style and in 1787 introduced his version of modern roman. Bodoni's face is also mechanically precise and projects a feeling of sophistication. The exaggerated contrast between the thick-and-thin strokes is characteristic of modern roman.

Bodoni

The Bodoni face was used more extensively and became the more popular of the two faces, if only for practical reasons (the serifs of the Didot face were finer and often cracked or broke during printing). Since the introduction of photocomposition, which eliminates concern over damaged serifs, the Didot face has gained in popularity.

Primer (or Book)

There is also a group of typefaces specifically designed to facilitate readability—called primer or book faces. Their characters are usually full-bodied, with serifs, open counters, and soft contrasts between the different parts of the letters, so that the character structures are easy to identify. Primer faces are set with ample letter, word, and line space, which creates a comfortable reading pace. These qualities are beneficial to someone who is learning to read, and textbooks, especially those written for younger children, are often set in these faces. Indeed, primer faces were probably your first introduction to the letterform. The full potential of a primer face is apparent in display sizes. Here the subtleties in the character structure are more prominent and expressive so you see the full beauty of the letterform design.

Century Schoolbook

Bookman

Fat Face

Families of type usually range in weight from light to extra-bold. Any roman letter that extends beyond that range falls into the category called fat face. These letters are either the most exaggerated, weighted version of a family or individual designs, unrelated to any other style. What generally distinguishes a fat face is that there is less counter space in relation to the mass of the letter structure itself.

Fat faces were the earliest typefaces used in advertising. The originator of this letter style is not known with certainty: some attribute its development to Thomas Cotterell in 1765; others, to his pupil Robert Thorne, in about 1803. Fat face was used extensively during the early part of the nineteenth century; however, by the end of that century, it had declined in popularity. During the 1920s there was a renewed interest in these faces, and they regained popularity in the United States and Germany. Two examples are Poster Bodoni and Figgin's Fat Face.

Poster Bodoni

Egyptian (Antique)

During the nineteenth century, basic roman letterforms with bold, squared-off serifs were introduced. These typefaces became known as Egyptian or Antique because their "slab-like" serifs reflected the rigidness of ancient, Egyptian hieroglyphics. Egyptian letters are either considered part of the roman category or placed in a category by themselves.

The Egyptian style of type was first shown in a type specimen book by Vincent Figgins in England in 1815, although it may have been originally designed and named by Robert Thorne. Some present-day Egyptian faces are Consort, Clarendon, and Antique.

Antique No.3

Italic

The term *roman* has two meanings. The first, as discussed above, defines a thick-and-thin letterform. The second refers to the vertical stance of a letterform. Any straight, vertical letter in any type style is considered a roman letter.

Upright characters that slant to the right without changes in the letters' design are known as oblique letters. These letters are either drawn or constructed through camera or lens modification, which alters them to an oblique angle, generally varying from 11 to 30 degrees. Often oblique letters are mistakenly referred to as italics. Italic letters also slant to the right at an angle of 11 to 30 degrees, but they have been redesigned in structure.

Italic letters were introduced by Aldus Manutius in 1501. At this time there was an increasing demand for small, pocket-sized books, and it was

Aldus's intent to design a condensed typeface that would fit a greater amount of text on each page. He based his design on the chancery hand, a cursive script developed from the Neo-Caroline script. The chancery hand was written quickly, so the letter shapes became condensed.

Times Roman
Times Roman Oblique
Times Roman Italic

Aldus's original design was quite complicated and contained many imperfections. Around 1542, Ludovico Arrighi, a Roman printer, designed several faces (also modeled after the chancery hand), which were superior to Aldine italic. This style became known as Vicento italic.

Italic faces were very popular during the sixteenth century. The initial Aldine and Vicento italics were designed as independent faces, not as companions to roman fonts. Although italics remained separate from the roman fonts throughout the seventeenth century, corresponding italic faces were being developed by the end of the sixteenth century, which indicated the changing status of italic type. The first attempt to associate an italic with a roman was made by Grandjean in France. Fournier, Bodoni, the Didots, and Baskerville followed by cutting italic faces to be used with their respective roman fonts.

Italic faces have strong contrast between the thick-and-thin strokes. The weight of the letter's structure is designed to complement its roman counterpart. The slope of the italic letter is mechanically regulated and angled anywhere from 11 to 30 degrees. Since italic faces reflect a handwriting influence, at times there may be a tail at the end of a lowercase letter, eliminating the serifs that are usually part of the roman versions.

Script

Italic handwriting was eventually modified and cut into a type style called script. Scripts fall into two main categories: gothic and Latin.

Gothic Scripts

The earliest gothic script typefaces, developed in Germany around the middle of the sixteenth century, were based on the formal cursive handwriting used in the chanceries (*Kanzleischriften*). These typefaces were intended to be used for printing texts, but few books were actually set in script type. In England a typeface styled after the Elizabethan hand, called Secretary, was cut in 1576. Again, it was used for miscellaneous printing and not texts.

In France, the type designer Robert Granjon developed a script type style named Civilité in the late 1550s, which was styled after the French gothic hand. Script writing, however, was not popular in France. As a nation, France was more concerned with producing letters that would depict definite French characteristics. The first half of the sixteenth century proved to be a golden age of French letter design.

Gothic bâtarde type.

Latin Scripts

The Latin script, which was based on the Italian hand, was developed in the sixteenth century, but was not widely used until the eighteenth century. The French styles of this script had the most influence on other areas. They were divided into three categories: the *ronde*, actually a gothic-style script similar to Civilité, frequently used in books as a decorative type; the *bâtarde coulée*, a less formal hand, also referred to as *financière* because of its use by the Ministry of Finance; and the *bâtarde ordinaire* or *italienne*, which remained the purest form of Latin script, most closely related to the Italian hand. These styles of Latin script spread to England, where in 1700 the British developed their own distinctive style called Cursoriols, which followed the flow of the Italian hand.

Pierre Moreau's bâtarele italienne.

Another popular style was the Spencerian system. "Professor" Spencer, who laid claim to developing an efficient handwriting script, taught his style to business colleges in as many as forty-four English cities during the eighteenth century. His style was also widely used throughout the United States, though it was not adopted on the Continent. The semi-angular script typeface, designed in about 1857 to resemble Spencer's handwriting system, became the basis for such formal type styles as Commercial Script, Bank Script, and Typo Script Extended.

Commercial Script

In the eighteenth century, the Romantic period inspired the further development of the script style of writing. Earlier, with the increasing use of the flexible quill pen, scribes had begun to create a continuous line, thick-and-thin in style, and flowing from letter to letter. As early as 1712 John Snell developed a script upon which the type style known as Snell Roundhand was based. Then, in 1733, George Bickham's Universal typeface was designed, with uniform, flowing letters that were connected.

Snell Roundhand

Script writing became extremely decorative and very popular. Many people pursued it as a hobby, and most educated people began writing in the controlled penman manner, a formal style of handwriting. Typographic cartouches and decoration were developed in keeping with the penman hand. The cartouche, a decorative extension with elaborate curves of the script line, was an important part of everyday, or genre, writing, and many contemporary type specimen books featured cartouches in their showings of decorative styles. Because, however, the elaborate swirls were difficult to reproduce with the printing methods of the time, an engraver had to hand-etch the very delicate cartouche into a copper plate, which could then be printed along with the type. These engravings could be positioned only as close to the shoulder of the corresponding type as was mechanically feasible.

From Compendium of Usuall Hands, *written and invented by Richard Daniel and engraved by Edward Cocker, London, 1664.*

Scripts are still frequently used for announcements, invitations, and inscriptions for ceremonial occasions. In addition to traditional flowing scripts, there are nonflowing scripts, which are similar in character, except the letters do not touch. Each letter is an independent form and does not have a tail connecting it to the next letter. One kind of nonflowing script is the brush script, which was originally drawn with a brush and which is considered a modified or contemporary script. Brush scripts were popular in the 1950s, with several different faces designed to simulate the brush quality—for example, Mistral, Brush Script, Dom Casual, and Balloon. Technically, however, such a face is not a script; the only related characteristic is that it appears to have been written quickly, as if it were drawn by hand.

Brush Script

Mistral

Gothic

Although initially the term *gothic* related to the black letter used by early German printers, in contemporary usage it designates a monoweight letter structure—one without the thick-and-thin line variations of the traditional roman letterform and without ornamentation. These gothic letters were introduced in the early nineteenth century, with the first such typeface appearing in 1816 in a type specimen book by William Caslon IV, who called this face Egyptian. It was followed in 1832 by a face designed by Vincent Figgins and given the name *sans serif*, as well as one by William Thorowgood, which he termed Grotesque. The reason for associating the word *gothic* with these letters was because the tonal value of these extremely bold sans serif letters resembled the intensity of the German black letter. Although these letters are now designed in a full range of weights, the name *gothic* still remains.

Top to bottom: old gothic, contemporary gothic.

Gothic

Gothic

Unlike traditional roman letterforms, most gothic letterforms are sans serif. If they do have serifs, these are generally little hairlines that protrude slightly from the letter structure, thereby creating a more formal-looking letter, as in Copperplate Gothic.

COPPERPLATE GOTHIC

Some gothic typefaces do not strictly adhere to a pure monoweight structure. With the Futura typeface, for instance, there is a slight tapering of the curved sections where they meet the straight stems. This modification, however, maintains the optical feeling of the monoweight form. If the letter structure were not modified, the connecting areas would appear visually to be heavier. Compare Futura with Avant Garde, which is a mechanically drawn monoweight.

Futura Medium

Avant Garde Medium

Gothic letters were originally used as novelty display faces for advertising, and the early gothic fonts contained only capital letters. Gothic faces did not gain prominence until the 1920s, when the Constructivist experimentalists introduced them into their posters, books, and other typographic media.

Ornamental

The great manuscripts written during the twelfth century contain early examples of ornamental letters, which were used to introduce chapters in a book. These letters were laboriously drawn and painted by master artists, who worked closely with the scribes writing the manuscripts. We refer to them as illuminated letters because their intense colors (derived from such quality materials as ground gemstones and pure gold) illuminated the entire page, making all the letters look alive. Although illuminated letters are seldom used today, they were the forerunners of the contemporary title initial, which is used to indicate beginning paragraphs in both book and advertising copy.

Eventually complete alphabets of decorative letters were designed. Examples of decorative capitals first appeared in France around 1680 and in England around 1690. It was Fournier's ornamental letters, introduced between 1764 and 1766, however, that set the standard for typographic ornamental letters.

Numerous ornamental type styles were designed during the Victorian period. Often these letters were elaborately decorative and too intricate to be cut as foundry type, so an engraving was made in copper from an original drawing. These engraving plates were trimmed to size and mounted on a box of wood, which was cut to type-high specifications (see page 92). This method permitted virtually any letter design or ornamentation to be printed along with type.

Lilith

Today, these decorative letters are photographically reproduced from the originals or facsimiles. Keep in mind, however, that because of their decorative design, ornamental letterforms are not practical for text or display copy of more than a few lines.

Period

The intended function, physical appearance, or emotional appeal of any creation is influenced by the environment in which it is produced. Moreover, most major periods of history have had artistic styles uniquely their own. Period art is a conscious application of popular styles created to visually express the times. It is difficult, however, to determine when a period emerges, and why some have longevity, while others become passé. In transitional stages there is a tendency to return to the obvious.

Often the style of architecture prevalent during a period is represented in the shapes of letterforms, which are then referred to as period typography. Two examples are the faces designed for the Bauhaus and Art Deco periods. The Bauhaus (1919–1933), through its philosophy of form follows function, simplified architecture and the plastic arts. Although typography deals mostly with two-dimensional design, a similar energy flows between an architectural mass in a space and abstract shapes in a space. Futura and Kabel, with their basic, anonymous geometric structure, are two typefaces representative of the simple yet functional concepts of the Bauhaus.

Art Deco was another powerful art style during the 1920s and '30s. Its pleasant geometric shapes seemed somewhat solidified, compared with the flowing, curved lines of the preceding Art Nouveau period. Adaptable to all materials, but especially glass, plastic, and marble, this style introduced exciting new shapes and colors. Many of the buildings constructed in New York City during this period exemplified the Art Deco style. The Empire State Building, the Chrysler Building, as well as the Rockefeller Center complex, are a tribute to this era. Although quite decorative in its adaption of shapes, Art Deco design was basically simple and honest, with balance as a major theme.

The typography of the time reflected a similar attitude. Geometric shapes were the main force behind the design of letterforms, including such faces as Broadway, Bernhard, and Parisian. Moreover, Art Deco was a period in which architecture and typography collaborated. The letters and words on building directories, elevator banks, and store signs all had a unity of design following the Art Deco theme.

Top to bottom: Oscar's restaurant, Waldorf Astoria Hotel, New York City; General Electric Building, New York City.

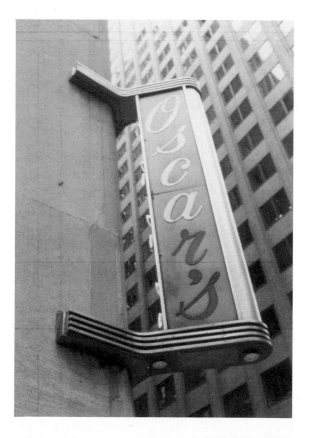

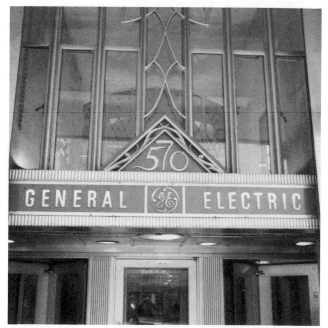

Although both Bauhaus and Art Deco typefaces are based on geometric forms, there are differences. The Bauhaus style consists predominantly of monoweight block letters, following the true simplicity of the geometric shape. The Art Deco letterform has more contrast, with extreme thick-and-thin forms giving character to the letters.

Broadway

Parisian

6. Typographic Terminology

Typography has its own language and scales of measurement, which do not relate to any other industry outside its allied art—printing. An explanation of typographic terms, both traditional and contemporary, will give you an understanding of how type is composed. Although most typesetting today is done by photocomposition, the traditions of typography were established in metal type. When you understand the function of certain terms in metal type composition, their meanings will become evident. Moreover, with this knowledge, you'll be able to communicate clearly with those responsible for setting your type. Clear communication is essential to directing typography as an art form.

Methods of Setting Type

One of the first things to understand is how type is physically produced. In learning about the development of typesetting machinery, as well as the advantages and limitations of different kinds of equipment, you will become more aware of all the elements that contribute to excellent typography.

Foundry Type

The name of this method of setting type derives from its manufacturing process. Each individual letter is cast into a body of type using a mixture of lead, tin, and antimony. The letters must then be composed by hand to form lines of type. Because of this procedure, foundry type is often referred to as hand-set.

The desire for precision and quality directed the use of materials and methods in the early casting of type. The letterforms were designed from manuscript writing, and type founders depended on the scribe's artistic efforts in developing a style to be cut into type. Throughout the centuries, the typefaces produced have combined the designer's art with the technical skill of the craftsman and engineer.

After the letterforms were designed, they were given to a punch cutter, who fashioned the master punch for the matrix (or mold) from which the type was manufactured. The traditional procedure for cutting the punch involved preparing the steel blank (a block of metal), inscribing guidelines on the face of the blank, and drawing the letter character within those lines. The letter was finished with files and gravers (engraving tools) until the desired letter was produced. Gauges were used to control the proper depth of the letter's impression. Once the punch was approved, it was tempered to a proper hardness so it could be struck on a matrix. Today, modern routing tools are used to make the master punch.

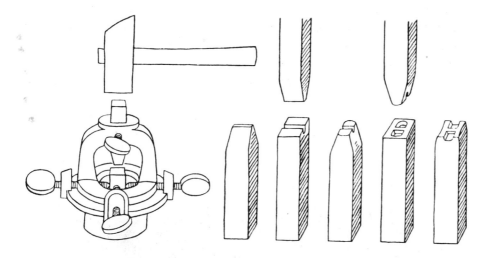

Hand type required a skilled compositor, who had to fit every line of type with extreme accuracy. A composing stick was used to hold the letters in the line of type before it was put into a form (also called a chase or lockup), which held an entire galley of type. Spaces between letters, words, and lines often depended on optical judgment rather than mechanical setting. Spacing materials were either precast to sizes corresponding to the type or cast to special specifications to accommodate an unusual combination of letters or words, such as notching in underscores below letters without descenders.

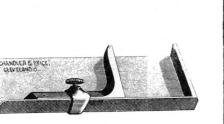

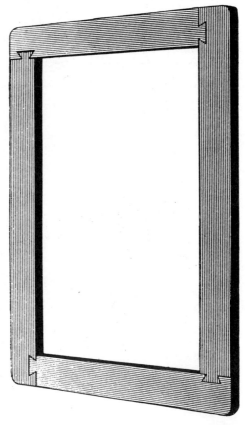

Left to right: common screw composing stick; chase ready for use.

Foundry type was stored in a drawer, called a case, according to point size and type style. The case drawers were specially designed with compartments to separate the letters. The upper case of a specific type size usually contained the capitals, while the lower case housed the small (minuscule) letters. It is from this organization of foundry type that the terms *uppercase* and *lowercase* derive. Once a proof of the set type was pulled and approved, the type was removed from the chase, washed, and redistributed to its proper job case, ready for the next use.

Cabinet with California job cases.

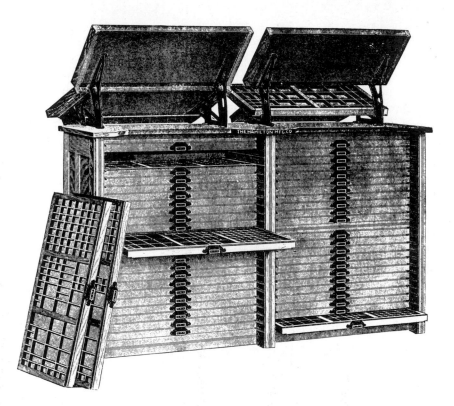

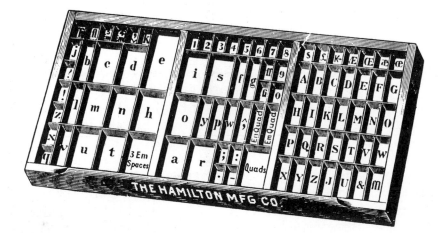

Linotype

Attempts to invent a machine to replace the laborious process of hand-setting type date as far back as 1822. A major obstacle to overcome was to design a machine that would distribute the letters for reuse automatically rather than by hand. The breakthrough came with the linotype method of setting type, which revolutionized the printing industry by automatically producing a line of type. Its invention in 1876 has been attributed to Ottmar Mergenthaler, a clockmaker by trade, who spent ten years perfecting his machine. The first commercial test of his blower linotype was in the office of the *New York Tribune* on July 3, 1886. By the close of that year about a dozen of these machines were in use in the *Tribune* composing room, as well as in other newspaper plants.

The linotype method worked on a system of cams, belts, and gravity. The type was composed from individual matrices, usually made from brass, held in a container called a magazine. Each magazine held a complete font of type in one size and one type style, although each matrix usually contained a companion of the same or contrasting face. Times Roman, for example, might have either Times Roman Bold or Times Roman Italic cut into the same matrix. The chosen style was positioned for casting by raising the assembling elevator rail, which acted similarly to the shift key on a typewriter. Each matrix had a code key, which allowed the individual matrix to be redistributed into its proper channel in the magazine housing after it had been used for casting.

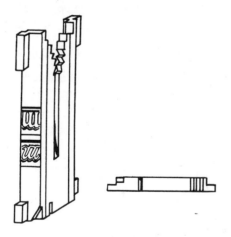

Linotype double-letter matrix, face, side, and bottom views.

The linotype machine was controlled by a keyboard operator, who typed out individual letters on a three-part keyboard. Every time a key was struck, a lever released an individual matrix. It was then transported to the head casting section, where the line of type was cast. It was at this point in the operation that refinements could be made in an individual line.

The length of a linotype bar was either 30 or 42 picas, depending on the capacity of the machine. If a narrower type width was required, the excess metal was trimmed off the 30- or 42-pica bar. Word space was inserted by depressing space bands, fed by the operator as the line was being composed. These space bands were designed to force the set line to the predetermined pica width—they adjusted the widths to whatever space was remaining on a given line. It was left to the discretion of the linotype operator to determine the consistency in word spacing.

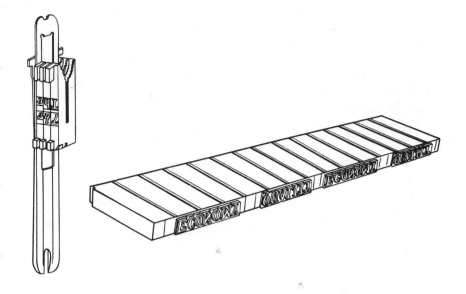

Spacing could also be controlled by hand, with individual matrices inserted into the line. The matrices, called pi sorts, were not returned to the magazine via the pickup arm, but instead were redistributed through a separate channel, to be put in a sort case.

After a line of type was composed, the operator tapped a release bar, which transported the matrices to one of four channels gauged to relate to the size of the type. At this point the gauging was adjusted to add leading. Once the matrix was in position, a plunger forced molten lead into the matrix channel. The lead solidified immediately and was trimmed off, automatically forming a line of type.

This procedure was continuous: as one line was being molded, the next was being set. All these separate bars of type were then assembled by a compositor and prepared for proofing.

Mergenthaler's initial machine did not have all the capacities described. It was really his last machine—the Square Base Model I, introduced in 1890—that marked the advent of modern linotype. This was the first machine to have a 90-character keyboard and to use matrices similar to the ones now in use. For convenience, the matrices were stored in an inclined magazine at the top of the front. This magazine could accommodate matrices up to and including 11 points.

Additional improvements were made to fit the needs of typography. In 1897 the wide-measure, 42-em linotype was developed, eliminating the need to set two separate slugs and butt them together for measures wider than 30 picas. Then, in 1898, the two-letter matrix was created. Before this, matrices had had only one character punched in them. This two-letter matrix doubled the variety of typefaces that could be set on a given ma-

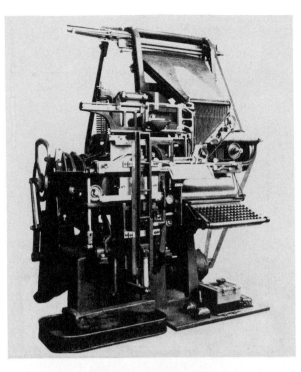

*Mergenthaler's Square Base
Model I linotype machine.*

chine at any one time. In 1906 the Quick-Change Linotype was introduced, in which the magazine could be removed from the front, allowing for "quick changes." Later in 1909, display-size matrices were developed, increasing the range of type the machine could set.

For many years, linotype was regarded as the workhorse of typesetting. It was used for newspapers, books, catalogs, and general typesetting of all kinds. Until the 1960s and the introduction of photocomposition, it was one of the most efficient methods of typesetting.

Monotype

The monotype typesetting machine was invented in 1885 by Tolbert Lanston, an inventor who knew very little about printing. It was the first machine that both molded type and assembled it in justified lines in a single operation. Many other machines, either single-type assembly or slug-line (linotype) machines, were already in use when monotype was fully introduced in the late 1890s. Typographers selected the system that they felt would be most productive for them. Sometimes both monotype and linotype equipment were employed in the same shop.

The monotype machine could set type in 4 to 18 points. Unlike the linotype machine, it cast each character separately and then assembled the characters into a line, much as in hand composition. Indeed, the appearance of type produced from a monotype matrix resembled foundry type, and monotype characters in display sizes were often cast and used in place of foundry type.

The set of the letter (the given width of the type body) was controlled by the casting matrix so that letter space could be tightened or widened and the shoulder could be cast to a predetermined width. The em established for each set (see page 94) was divided into 18 equal parts, or units, and each character in the font was designed to be cast on a body that was a certain number of units wide. (In a few faces the capital W, for instance, was wider than 18 units.) This method of assigning a definite body width to each character was known as the monotype unit system. (A similar system is used for establishing the widths of characters and spaces in photo-composition.)

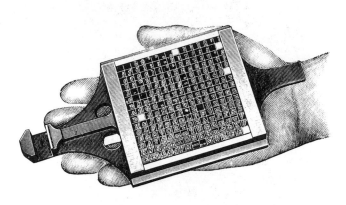

Monotype matrix case, which holds 225 cellular matrices.

The monotype was a two-machine operation. The first machine involved the keyboard, on which the operator typed in the copy to be set. The operator—aware of the point size and set size of the type to be cast, as well as the pica width of the lines—set the em scale (the line width) on the keyboard and then proceeded to strike the keys corresponding to the characters and spaces desired. As the operator struck the keys, punches rose and perforated holes in a roll of paper (known as controller paper) and then receded. These holes represented the selection of characters as well as the width of the type body on which each character would be cast.

Monotype keyboards.

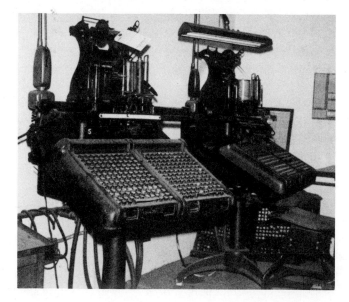

During the keyboarding procedure, a mechanism added up the widths of the characters being set. A bell rang to notify the operator when the line was almost full. After glancing at the justifying scale, the operator decided whether to finish the final word or hyphenate it. By touching special keys indicated on the justifying scale, the operator also directed the machine to automatically control the width of the spaces between the words to completely fill (justify) the line. This procedure was repeated for each line.

Once the job was keyboarded, the tape was put on a type caster, which glided over the matrices. Compressed air was forced through the holes in the controller paper, pushing the letter matrix directly into position over the opening of the mold. This process established the width of the body of the character or space to be cast. Hot metal was then forced into the mold, forming each character individually. The operation was continued automatically until the full line was composed. The line was then pushed into a galley and another line was started. This procedure was repeated at an average rate of 150 casts per minute, varying according to the point size of the type being set.

After the job was completed, the type was not redistributed, but was remelted, replenished with antimony for hardness, and molded into new ingots for reuse. Larger-size monotype letters, rules, and ornaments, however, were redistributed in the same manner as foundry type.

Several features increased the flexibility of monotype. Although most monotype typefaces were made with close-fitting widths to assure good design and proper typesetting, the width could be "opened up" by increasing the set width, thereby extending the body width and increasing the letter space. Usually the roman and italic styles of the same size and face were designed to have the same set and were combined in the same keyboard arrangement for machine setting. It was possible, however, to produce combinations of roman, italic, and boldface to meet the individual requirements indicated in a type specification. Two different type styles of different set widths (for instance, light- and boldfaces of the same point size) could be combined in the same matrix case by increasing the set width for the narrower face and vice versa. It was also possible to combine two faces of different point sizes but the same set width in the same keyboard arrangement.

Although refinements and improvements of the monotype process were made, the structure of the keyboard and the typesetting mechanism remained the same. One improvement increased the line width from 60 to 90 ems and provided automatic spacing for close or wide casting. An attachment for automatic leading was also perfected.

Ludlow

Ludlow composition was an economical method of setting large-size type without an extensive inventory of foundry type, because after each line was cast, the matrices could be reused for the next line. This method was first used commercially in the composing room of the *Chicago Evening Post* in 1913. The Ludlow company believed that whatever was normally set by hand in a well-operated composing room could be produced more efficiently and economically with the Ludlow.

With this system, individual matrices were assembled from the matrix case by hand in a special composing stick, which was then inserted in the casting machine, where the line of type was produced in slug-line form. The Ludlow was specially designed to cast slugs or lines in any type larger than 12 points. It is worth noting that Ludlow italics have a characteristic spirit due to the machine's unique, angular italic matrix, which makes full kerning possible (see page 99).

Ludlow composing stick.

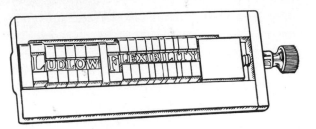

Photocomposition

The need for increased speed in production has been a major priority for typographers ever since letters have been produced mechanically. For more than one hundred years, metal type production, referred to as hot type, was the state of the art in typography. Then, in the early 1960s, huge innovative strides were made with the introduction of phototypesetting, or cold type, which considerably reduced composing time for both display and text. It also eliminated the concern about having enough display type to complete a job. (Often in hand composition, if there was not enough type to complete a job, individual letters were lifted from the part of the form already proofed—a procedure called "jumping the type.")

Photocomposition is essentially a multistep process. The first step is to input on a computer all the copy to be set. The operator uses a keyboard similar to that of a typewriter, except that there are additional keys for special formatting instructions. A video display of the copy appears on a CRT screen (cathode ray tube), usually located just above the keyboard. In this way the copy and all the control information can be viewed and checked during composition. One of the limitations, however, is that the copy displayed is running copy, and does not show the line breaks for justified or ragged lines. Moreover, since the computer itself is incapable of determining an aesthetic rag, this must be programmed according to specifications supplied by the designer. If these specifications are not included, some alteration of computerized line breaks is usually necessary.

With the equipment commonly in use today, the input copy is stored on a floppy disc, which is a magnetic tape resembling a small record. This disc retains all the instructions needed to set the type and is later fed into a printout machine to produce the type. With these discs, a complete photocomposition job can be stored in a simple, flat envelope weighing only a few ounces. Compared with the much heavier metal forms of type, floppy discs obviously provide a considerable savings in storage space.

If the type font is in the form of a film negative, high-intensity light is flashed through the characters, projecting them—through a series of lenses and prisms—onto film or photosensitive paper. The exposed film or paper is then developed and becomes the master setting.

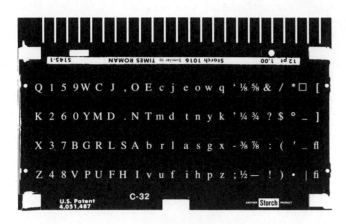

Font on film for Mergenthaler VIP photocomposition.

Some computers use a digitized system rather than actual letter fonts. The digitized system produces letterforms through a series of fine dots or lines that create the shapes of the letters. The resolution of dots or lines for text size is 900 dots per linear inch; the resolution for display type is nearly 2,000. Point sizes range from 4-1/2 to 96 points, with a maximum pica width of 80 picas. The result of this composition is a master film in positive form. Printouts can be produced on film or paper.

Preparation of type specifications for photocomposition is essentially the same as it is for metal composition. With the exception of a few computer words, the terminology is basically the same. Even the type styles in photocomposition are generally called by the same name as their metal counterparts, although, for legal reasons, some metal faces have been altered by different equipment manufacturers and given other names. In specimen books, these changes are usually qualified with a reference to the original name. Because of slight differences in style, however, the designer should take care to specify the chosen type style from a specimen sheet representing the system composing the type (see Chapter 7).

A major difference between metal and photographic composition is in the letter's proportions. In photocomposition a single master drawing is used for all sizes, rather than the multiple drawings used to manufacture the various sizes of metal type. When photocomposition was first introduced, this difference was obvious because metal type was still readily available. Today, except for a few typophiles, most designers and type directors are unaware of this proportional difference since metal composition is less visible. Discriminating designers and type directors should compare a manufacturer's translations of type styles with the original for accurate size, weight, x-height, and letter style (see page 114).

The industrialization of an art does not always improve its well-being. Most of the typefaces designed today, for instance, do not go beyond the capital and lowercase letters, numbers 0 through 9, monetary signs, and necessary punctuation marks. Rarely are any "sorts," such as arrows, fractions, old style numbers, or small capitals, included. Much of the sensitivity and variety of the typographic palette has been sacrificed for speed and convenience; the designer is deprived of the full range of characters available in metal type. In the illustration below, for example, the original foundry showing of (Bauer) Futura Light includes old style numbers, which are not included in the version available for photocomposition.

ABCDEFGHIJKLMNOPQRS
TUVWXYZ&   .,-:;'!?
abcdefghijklmnopqrstuvwxy
1234567890$ 1234567890$

One of the main advantages of computer typesetting, however, is that it can take all the variables or refinements of typography and store them in a memory bank. The storage capabilities are innumerable and include such modification formats as notching, undercutting letters, minus leading, inserting underscores between baseline and descender, as well as joining or overlapping vertical and horizontal rules. Additional modifications such as expanding, condensing, obliquing, or backslanting can be done through programming. Variations in typefaces and point sizes are automatically base-aligned.

In metal typesetting, although new equipment was constantly introduced, most of it increased the speed of composition or the pica measure, but did not change the set or fit the type. With photocomposition, however, there is much more versatility in the machine's capabilities. With these increased capabilities, there is a greater responsibility for controlling type production on the part of the designer and type director. It is up to them to indicate any needed refinements in their specifications.

The Anatomy of Type
As I have already indicated, although most typography produced today is composed by photographic and computer technology, the terminology is still based on metal type composition. Actually, many of the terms used to describe the structure of metal type are derived from human anatomy.

The position of each letter on a type body is not arbitrary. All letters share common areas defined by four imaginary guidelines: the baseline, x-height, ascender, and descender. These guidelines designate specific areas to which parts of the letter are confined. Together, they establish a continuity for reading letters into words and words into lines.

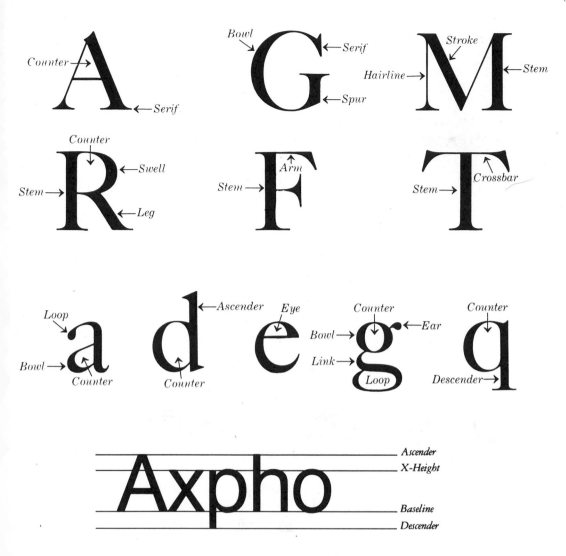

The *baseline* is the foundation and the main point of reference from one letter to the next. In a given typeface and point size, it is the common line on which all x-heights, ascenders, capital letters, and lining numbers rest, as well as the starting point for descenders. The *x-height* is the vertical space occupied by lowercase letters (excluding ascenders and descenders). The letter x was chosen to describe this height because all four ends of its lines touch a point of measurement. An *ascender* is that portion of a lowercase letter that protrudes above the x-height, while a *descender* is that portion of a lowercase letter that goes below the baseline. In some typefaces, however, the capital letters or numbers do not share the common ascending guideline. There are also faces with letters deliberately designed to extend below the descending guideline. These characters require an additional guideline.

Because different type styles favor different design proportions, it is unlikely that the same point size in different styles will share common guidelines. In the four different styles of the same point size shown on page 90, note the differences in x-height, as well as in the ascenders and descenders.

AHMS ahxp

AHMS ahxp

AHMS ahxp

AHMS ahxp

Type Measurement

In the United States, typography is based on a system of measurement known as the American point system. In this system, a point equals 1/72 or 0.0138 of an inch. (Although technically a 72-point unit is 0.9961 of an inch, or slightly under 1 inch, the difference is insignificant.)

Traditionally, points are used to designate the vertical height of letters. They indicate the physical height of the metal type body, however, not the size of the printed letter. Points are also used to indicate the spacing between letters, words, and lines. To adjust space, points may be broken down into smaller divisions such as half-points, quarter-points, or smaller fractions. In photocomposition systems, these detailed increments are called units or tracks. The computer measures the amount of unit space each letter occupies within the line. The tracking or unit spacing designation is usually included on a type specimen sheet supplied by the typographer (see Chapter 7). Along with the style and size of type, the designer must specify which unit of spacing is to be used in setting the type. Letter and word spacing usually work together harmoniously, but the designer may choose to alter the spacing.

The pica is the other basic unit of typographic measurement, with 12 points equaling 1 pica and 6 picas approximating 1 inch. Picas are used mainly in the horizontal direction. The width of a line, for instance, is specified in picas. All contemporary typesetting equipment is geared to measure line widths in picas.

Picas are rarely used to measure the size of type. You would not refer to a 12-point typeface as a 1-pica typeface. On the other hand, you would specify a line of type to be set 18 picas wide, not 216 points wide. You might, however, specify a line to be set 18 picas and 7 points wide, with the 7 points serving as a subdivision of a pica.

Points and picas only became standard measures in the last century. The point system was first devised in France by Pierre Simon Fournier in the 1730s and later revised by François Ambroise Didot. It was not until 1878, however, that Marder, Luse & Co. of the Chicago Type Foundry began to use the point system in the United States. At the time each

American foundry used its own system of measurement, and thus type was not produced in uniform, interchangeable sizes. In 1886 the United States Typefounders Association formed a committee to consider instituting the point system. They decided to base the common measurement for all type bodies on the metric system, with 83 picas equaling 35 centimeters.

There are now three basic measurement systems used for typesetting throughout the world: the American-British, the Didot (accepted throughout most of Continental Europe), and the Mediaan (adopted by the French). The following guide should prove useful.

Points	American-British	Didot	Mediaan
1	.01383	.01483	.01374
2	.0277	.0296	.0275
3	.0415	.0445	.0412
4	.0553	.0593	.0550
4¾	.0657	.0704	.0653
5	.0692	.0742	.0687
5½	.0761	.0816	.0756
6	.0830	.0890	.0824
6½	.0899	.0964	.0893
6¾	.0934	.1001	.0927
7	.0968	.1038	.0962
7½	.1037	.1112	.1031
7¾	.1072	.1149	.1065
8	.1107	.1186	.1099
8½	.1176	.1261	.1168
9	.1245	.1335	.1237
10	.1383	.1483	.1374
10½	.1452	.1557	.1443
11	.1522	.1631	.1511
11½	.1591	.1705	.1580
12	.1660	.1780	.1649
14	.1936	.2076	.1924
16	.2213	.2373	.2198
18	.2490	.2669	.2473
20	.2767	.2966	.2748
21	.2906	.3114	.2885
24	.3320	.3559	.3298
27	.3736	.4004	.3710
28	.3874	.4152	.3847
30	.4150	.4449	.4122
34	.4704	.5042	.4672
36	.4980	.5339	.4946
42	.5810	.6229	.5771
48	.6640	.7118	.6595
54	.7471	.8008	.7420
60	.8301	.8898	.8244
72	.9961	1.0678	.9893

The three principal measurement systems, with points in decimals of an inch.

Type-High Measurement

There is another kind of measurement that affects typography, although it is not included in design specification. To ensure accurate reproduction of the type style and tonal value, all elements to be printed must conform to the requirements of the printing process. In metal type, 0.918 of an inch is the standard height from the face to the feet of the metal body. This measurement conforms exactly to the height from the press bed to the paper in letterpress printing; in other words, in order to print properly, the type body must be this high (called type-high).

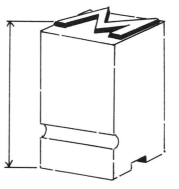

Type-high 0.918 inch

The type-high requirement reveals the tradition of typography and printing as exacting arts. To check that impressions were type-high, a sheet of paper was first run through the press over the uninked plate to create a blind embossed impression of the image to be printed. Holding the reverse side of the proof horizontally up to a light source, the press operator could determine high and low areas by studying the slight shadows cast onto the paper. If any of the type was over or under type-high, adjustments in the tissue-paper packing of the cylinder were made, adding or removing layers of tissue to coincide with the problem areas. This procedure, known as make-ready, was time-consuming, often requiring adjustments in thousandths of an inch. Without such careful preparation, however, impressions that were less than type-high would appear light or broken. Those higher than type-high would push through the paper or spread the ink, distorting counters and tonal value. Once these adjustments were made, the plate was inked and a final set of reproduction proofs was pulled.

In photocomposition there is no physical type-high measurement since the typographic images are photographically produced on film or paper, without the use of ink. There is, however, a photographic equivalent of the type-high requirement—maintaining a consistent intensity of reproductive black. Several factors affect the blackness of photographically reproduced characters. Variations in the exposure time, the temperature of the chemicals used to develop the film, the developing time, or the speed with which the reproduction proofs pass through the light source and developing baths—all create corresponding variations in the degree of blackness. Excesses, which intensify the blackness, are equivalent to more than type-high; while insufficiencies, which produce light blacks, are comparable to less than type-high.

It is absolutely necessary for the typographer to exert quality control with regard to the consistency of reproduction. A densitometer can be used to measure the intensity of the black areas. This machine accurately indicates on an intensity scale or in digitized numbers the physical density of black by measuring the amount of light penetrating through an area of black type of a reproduction proof or transparent film. The type specimen sheet then serves as a guide to determine the correct intensity of black for a given type style.

Alignment

In metal type a single unit of lead usually houses only one character. Each piece of metal type thus has to relate physically to others of the same face and point size to ensure unified base alignment. Different type styles and point sizes cannot be set on the same line with a common base alignment because of the physical structure of the metal form and the position of the letterform on its body. A 12-point Helvetica, for example, cannot be aligned with a 10-point Helvetica or a different typeface in 12-point without mechanical adjustments.

In comparison, photocomposition has a built-in alignment feature whereby the same baseline is common to all typefaces in all point sizes. Nevertheless, if you choose to mix typefaces, point sizes, or modifications, you must provide enough space between lines to avoid overlap.

ALIGNMENT

ALIGNMENT

Top to bottom: metal composition, photocomposition.

Leading

In setting foundry type, pieces of lead (or sometimes paper or copper) of a specified point size and width were inserted by hand between the lines to separate them. Because these pieces of lead—called leading—were not as high as the type, they did not print, thus creating visual space between the lines. Leading could be increased or removed, depending on the given specifications.

In monotype, leading could be molded onto the top of each individual type body. With linotype machines, which cast a whole line of type in one bar rather than assembling individual letters as the monotype machine did, leading could also be molded onto the lower body of type when the line was cast. As in monotype, this meant space could be added, but not removed. If the leading specifications were decreased, each line had to be recast.

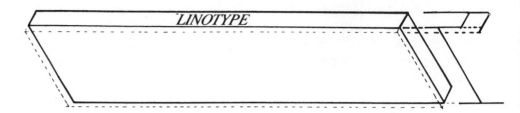

Although lead is not employed in photocomposition, the term *leading* is still used to specify line spacing. Because photocomposition does not have the physical restrictions imposed by actual pieces of metal type, it is possible to specify minus leading. Points are removed from the hypothetical type body to bring the lines closer together. Before making this specification, however, you should study the character of your type to ensure that the descenders of one line will not overlap the ascenders of the next line.

Leading must always be specified. One way to indicate 12-point type set with 2 points of leading is 12/14. With metal type, this meant that 2 points of lead were cast onto the original 12-point body, yielding 14 points. If 1-point minus leading is indicated, it is specified as 12/11, since it is hypothetically a 12-point typeface on an 11-point body.

Em and En Spacing

An em is a unit of measurement that represents the square of any point size of type. It is also called a quad, which is short for "quadrilateral," meaning four equal sides. In early letterform design, when only capital letters were used, the capital M filled the entire piece of metal, forming a perfect square within the type body. Based on this M, the em became the accepted designation for the square of a given point size. With 12-point type, for example, an em would be a 12-point square. A unit of space half the width of an em is called an en, since the capital N was originally drawn to half the M's width. A 12-point en space is therefore 12 points high and 6 points wide.

Because the em relates in size to the point size of the type being set, a division of the em is used to designate word spacing. Only the width of an em is divided, however; the vertical height remains the same. The average amount of word space is 3- or 4-to-the-em, which represents one-third or one-fourth of the total em. The size of type then determines the em spacing. If, for example, you use a 24-point typeface and specify 4-to-the-em word space, 6 points of space will be placed between words. The division of the em space does not have to be a whole number; it can be a fraction. You can, for example, specify 5-to-the-em word spacing for a 24-point typeface, so that 4.8 points of space will be inserted between each word. When you specify word spacing with photocomposition, you don't have to calculate it; the machinery will do it automatically.

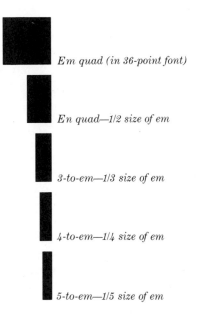

Em quad (in 36-point font)

En quad—1/2 size of em

3-to-em—1/3 size of em

4-to-em—1/4 size of em

5-to-em—1/5 size of em

In addition to word spacing, typographers have traditionally used ems and ens for paragraph indentions. Ems have also served as a convenient piece of typographic furniture to absorb large empty spaces within the type makeup. When the type did not fill the entire width of a line, ems, ens, and points were inserted to make up the space. Since these pieces of "dead metal" were less than type-high, they did not print. In a similar way, ems were used to center or position lines in hand-set composition.

Type Fonts

A complete range of characters of a single type style is called a font. Usually a font consists of capital and lowercase letters, numbers, some fractions, ligatures, punctuation marks, and signs. Some fonts contain small capitals and old style numbers as well (see the illustration on page 96). The number of individual characters in a particular font, not including additional sorts, ranges from 90 to 130, depending on whether it is for domestic or international usage. Because European languages include such alternative characters as accents, cedillas, umlauts, and various currency marks, they require more characters per font than English.

Type Families

Most fonts are members of a family of type. Families, which are identified through similarities in character structure, usually range in size from 6 to 72 points. Most type styles have companion faces that act as members of a real family. These include bold, italic, extended, and condensed faces.

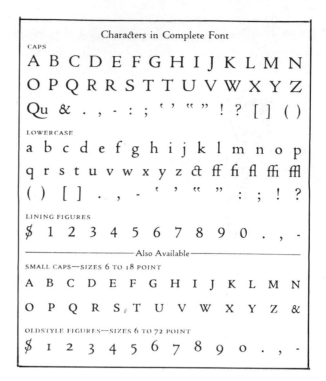

Characters in Complete Font

CAPS

A B C D E F G H I J K L M N
O P Q R R S T T U V W X Y Z
Qu & . , - : ; ' ' " " ! ? [ ] ( )

LOWERCASE

a b c d e f g h i j k l m n o p
q r s t u v w x y z ct ff fi fl ffi ffl
( ) [ ] . , - ' ' " " : ; ! ?

LINING FIGURES

$ 1 2 3 4 5 6 7 8 9 0 . , -

———————————— Also Available ————————————

SMALL CAPS—SIZES 6 TO 18 POINT

A B C D E F G H I J K L M N
O P Q R S T U V W X Y Z &

OLDSTYLE FIGURES—SIZES 6 TO 72 POINT

$ 1 2 3 4 5 6 7 8 9 0 . , -

Small Capitals

Some fonts include small capitals (or small caps), which are capital-shaped letters that are the same size as the x-height of the typeface. They are usually roman rather than italic and normally have the same tonal value as the lowercase letters. Since they do not have ascenders or descenders, they can be set with minus leading. Small caps are used primarily for creating contrast and variation. Often they are used at the beginning of a chapter, immediately following a single full-capital letter.

ONCE UPON A TIME there was...

ONCE UPON A TIME there was...

ONCE UPON A TIME there was...

ONCE UPON A TIME there was...

Biform or Commoncase Letters

Biform, or commoncase, letters are lowercase in appearance, but match the height and weight of that style's capital letter. The concept of the biform letter dates back to medieval times when the half uncial—which combined large, rounded letters with cursive forms—was introduced into manuscript writing. Biform letters have a tendency to bring more attention to words or phrases than do words with all capitals, lowercase, or both. Biform or commoncase letters are not included in most fonts as alternative letters, but do appear in some popular typefaces such as Folio Medium Extended (shown below).

Aa Ee
Mm Nn Rr
abcdefghijklmnopqrstuvwxyz
AaBCDEEFGHIJKLMMNNOP
QRrSTUVWXYZ 1234567890

Ligatures

In medieval manuscripts, scribes often combined letters to conserve space. Because of the physical restrictions of metal type, some letter combinations did not relate well to each other, creating aesthetically awkward spacing between characters. The introduction of ligatures, which are two or more letter combinations cast onto the same body of type, eliminated this problem. It allowed spacing refinements to be incorporated into the

Characters in Complete Font

CAPS

A B C D E F G H I J K L M N O P Q
R S T U V W X Y Z & . , - ' ' : ; ! ? { }

LOWERCASE

a b c d e f g h i j k l m n o p q r s t u
v w x y z ff fi fl ffi ffl . , - ' ' : ; ! ? { }

The "f" combinations are furnished with the Ligature and Terminal on 24-point and larger

LINING FIGURES

$ 1 2 3 4 5 6 7 8 9 0 . , -

Also Available

SWASH CAPS

A B C D E G L M N P R T Y & The

LIGATURES AND TERMINALS

as is us ct st ll sp tt fr gy ke a e k m
n L v w

OLDSTYLE FIGURES

$ 1 2 3 4 5 6 7 8 9 0 . , -

Garamond Old Style Italic with ligatures, from American Type Founders specimen sheet.

type body so an even tonal value was sustained throughout a line. Because, however, it was not feasible to make ligatures for every combination of letters, additional spacing refinements were done by modifying the physical body of type through such processes as notching and shaving.

Ligatures should be used only with normal space settings in metal and photocomposition. Because ligatures were designed to maintain tonal continuity in normal type, specifying ligatures with extremely tight or open letter spacing disrupts the even tonal value of the type. When a word is set with excessive letter spacing or extremely tight, a ligature looks awkward.

fiddle
fiddle
fiddle

A variation of the ligature is the diphthong, where two vowels are combined on a single body of type, creating a monosyllabic sound. Until recently diphthongs were commonly used in certain words derived from Greek, such as aesthetic or encyclopaedia.

Swash and Terminal Letters

A swash letter is a decorative letter, usually with some portion extending beyond the boundary of its body's point size. These elaborate letters are designed to be substituted for their roman or italic counterparts, although not all type styles have accompanying swash characters. Generally, capital letters are designed in swash versions, with only a few lowercase letters included in a swash font. There may, however, be more than one swash version of a particular letter.

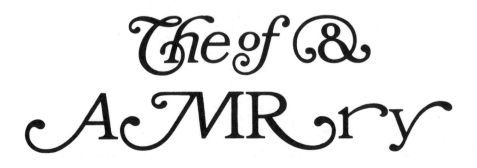

Some type styles also include terminal letters—lowercase letters, with extensions beyond their designated bodies, which are designed to be the last character of a word. These poetic characters work best at the end of paragraphs, especially in widow lines. If terminal letters are used within a sentence, word spacing is disrupted.

a e m n t

Swash and terminal letters can add romance to typographic design. Through their shape, these letters bring attention to words and phrases. They should, however, be used with discretion as they may not relate well to all letter combinations. Although swash characters can be effectively used with letters of the same or different type styles, terminal letters should be incorporated only with their own type style. In any case, words and lines should not be saturated with these letters.

A B C D E F G H
I K L M N O P R S
U V W & E k v w a e o u

Caslon 540 Swash Italic letters.

Kerning Letters

Traditionally, kerning letters were those in which a portion of the character protruded beyond the designated body, as in the tail of a capital Q. Although some type fonts may have isolated kerning characters, swash character fonts, such as Caslon 540 Swash Italic, consist almost entirely of kerning characters.

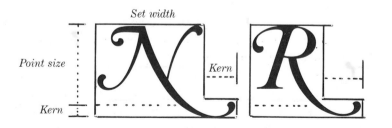

In metal type, when a kerning letter was composed next to a letter with a standard body, the typographer would often shave or notch these letters to accommodate the kerning letter. In photocomposition, the term *kerning* is also used to mean the tightening of letter space and removal of unit space (which is comparable to changing set widths in metal type). This additional meaning is a misinterpretation of the word's original definition.

Copy Fitting

Type specification without refinements is simply the method of calculating copy to fit a given space. It is the mechanics that underlies the art of designing with type. Accurate type specification, or copy fitting, is thus an essential part of typographic design.

To determine whether the manuscript copy will fit a designated layout space, you must calculate the size of type in terms of height in points and width in picas. This information is contained on a type specimen sheet. Since each typographic character is a different width, an average measurement must be determined for both capital and lowercase letters. This is done by first measuring the entire alphabet, from A to Z, in points and then dividing the entire point length by 12 to find the characters per pica. You do not, however, need to calculate this yourself as the characters per pica are indicated on the type specimen sheet. Note that capital letters are wider than lowercase letters of the same point size and face, so that there are fewer capital characters per pica. When copy is to be set upper- and lowercase, however, the lowercase guide should be used. Although the capital letters are larger, the punctuation marks are narrower than lowercase letters, therefore compensating for the capitals within the copy. Note that each typeface, from extended to extra-condensed, of the same point size and family, will have a different character-per-pica count, and remember that the character-per-pica count is only an average.

The first step in copy fitting is to determine the typewriter type used for the manuscript. Although there are several kinds of typewriter type, only elite type (with 12 characters to the inch) and pica type (with 10 characters to the inch) are accurate for copy fitting. Typewriters that are partially self-adjusting do not have a consistent number of characters to the inch and are therefore not accurate for copy fitting.

To determine whether a manuscript is in pica or elite type, simply count the characters in the first inch of typewriter type. Be sure to place the inch scale on the extreme left of the first letter, and remember that space and punctuation marks are counted as full characters. Although typewriter type may appear to be set at random on a page, it actually forms columns of type, with letters or spaces aligned directly underneath each other. A period (.) of typewriter type, for example, is allotted exactly the same amount of space as a W.

Now you need to find out how many letters of the typeface you have chosen will fit within the pica measure you have decided on for your layout. To do this, simply multiply the characters per pica for that typeface by the pica measure. If, for example, your typeface is 12-point Helvetica upper- and lowercase with 2.37 characters per pica and your measure is 21 picas wide, you will get 49.77 characters per line, which can be rounded off to 50 characters. If your specifications are flush left and stagger (or ragged) right or vice versa, follow the same procedure, but reduce the pica measure by 1-1/2 to 2 picas to accommodate the average of the stagger.

With this figure, you can measure the typewriter characters needed for a line of type. For pica or elite typewriter type, use the inch scale and start from the extreme left character of your copy. If your first line of manuscript is indented, use the second line as a guide. With the 50 characters per line in our example, you would measure 5 inches of pica typewriter type (as there are 10 characters to the inch). Draw a line down the entire page of the manuscript at this point. Your line will fall between letters, since they are aligned vertically in a column. The section to the left of the pencil line represents one line of set type. Add up all these lines, but take care to calculate each paragraph separately.

For advertising copy, which requires very accurate copy fitting, you must now determine exactly how much type the remaining copy represents. If the copy to the right of your pencil line does not amount to another full line, find out if you can divide the remaining characters into a fraction of a line, such as a half, third, or quarter, and draw another pencil line down the page at this point. Make sure that every line of copy extends to this second dividing line or your count will be inaccurate. Now add these lines to your total for each paragraph. If, for example, your fraction is one-half, then two lines within this second division will equal one line of type.

If copy remains after this procedure, count off the letters of each line separately. Add an additional character at the end of each line to indicate the space after that word. If the last word of a line is hyphenated, do not count the hyphen or an additional space, since the word will probably not be hyphenated when your copy is set. If your copy ends with a "widow" (a line that does not reach the full measure), count those characters and add them in. All paragraphs should be tallied separately to account for widows. Divide the total of the remaining characters by the number of characters per line to find out the additional lines. If you have extra characters at the end, count them as a line since they will take up an additional line in depth. Add these lines to the number of full lines to determine how many lines of typeset copy you will have.

After you have figured out the number of lines of set copy, you must determine the vertical space or depth of these lines on the page. This depends on the point size you are using and the leading. If your type is to be set in 12-point Helvetica solid, you would use the 12-point scale on a line gauge to indicate the depth of your type. If leading is included in your specification, it should be added to the point size to determine the depth and that scale should be used. Remember that there is no additional space after the last line of type.

Display-size characters vary greatly in the number of characters per pica since the letters are proportionately different. Unfortunately, most type specimen sheets do not provide an average character-per-pica count, so you must determine this on your own. For a specified pica width, you can establish an average by measuring off your line width on the lowercase alphabet on the specimen sheet and then counting how many characters fall within it. Then, if your entire copy is to be set in display-size type, you can count only one line of copy and draw your pencil line at this point. The rest of the procedure is the same. Of course, if your copy contains a lot of capital letters, you must account for this.

To understand copy fitting, study the example on page 102 and then try out the process on your own with the unmarked copy. The type specifications are 11-point Times Roman, upper- and lowercase, by 15 picas wide, flush left and right, 1-point leading, 2-em paragraph indent.

11/12 Times Roman
FLUSH L & R X 15 PICAS

[Compositors serve two masters: the buyer, who   6
orders the work and has the right to direct   4
its style, and the master printer, who is   2   10
responsible to that buyer and to the reader   4   +1 Li
for the workmanship of the composition. The   4   11 Li
buyer rightfully expects the compositor to   3
correct indefensible negligences in his written   8
copy and to arrange types in a tasteful manner.   8
The master also requires the compositor to   3   42-6=36
produce workmanship in good taste.   -6

2m/¶] Here comes occasion for possible disagreement.   8
Types selected by the buyer (or even by the   4   9
master printer) may be composed as directed   4   +1 Li
and yet not produce the good work desired.   3   10 Li
Types are inflexible; they must occupy a fixed   6
space, and they may not mate tastefully one   4
with another. The arrangement of types intended   8
by either party must be modified to some extent   7   44-22=22
by the compositor.   -22

] Good taste is not one of the exact sciences.   6
It has few absolute rules. What is tasteful   4   7
in one composition is not in another. What is   6   +1 Li
pleasing to the author may not be pleasing to   6   8 Li
the master printer. The compositor's notion of   7
good taste may differ, and the three parties may 9   38-16=22
be at complete variance.   -16

] Good taste should be understood as a synonym   6
for propriety. It means order, symmetry, and   4
the observance of seemly arrangements that have   8
the sanction of age and authority. In   -3
typesetting it means the putting of right types   8   12
in right places. It does not mean departure   4   +1 Li
from methods that have commanded general   13 Li
respect. Composition is but the architecture of   8
words, and it must be governed by general rules   8
of law and order that are observed not only in   7   53-30=23
architecture but in every kind of worthy
construction.   -27

CHARACTERS PER PICA   2.66   Total 42 LINES
FOR 11pt T.R. L/c   x 15
                       39.9 OR 40 CHARACTER
                                PER LINE

Copy from pica typewriter with 10 characters per inch.

Compositors serve two masters: the buyer, who orders the work and has the right to direct its style, and the master printer, who is responsible to that buyer and to the reader for the workmanship of the composition. The buyer rightfully expects the compositor to correct indefensible negligences in his written copy and to arrange types in a tasteful manner. The master also requires the compositor to produce workmanship in good taste.

Here comes occasion for possible disagreement. Types selected by the buyer (or even by the master printer) may be composed as directed and yet not produce the good work desired. Types are inflexible; they must occupy a fixed space, and they may not mate tastefully one with another. The arrangement of types intended by either party must be modified to some extent by the compositor.

Good taste is not one of the exact sciences. It has few absolute rules. What is tasteful in one composition is not in another. What is pleasing to the author may not be pleasing to the master printer. The compositor's notion of good taste may differ, and the three parties may be at complete variance.

Good taste should be understood as a synonym for propriety. It means order, symmetry, and the observance of seemly arrangements that have the sanction of age and authority. In typesetting it means the putting of right types in right places. It does not mean departure from methods that have commanded general respect. Composition is but the architecture of words, and it must be governed by general rules of law and order that are observed not only in architecture but in every kind of worthy construction.

Copy from elite typewriter with 12 characters per inch.

Other Typographic Elements

In addition to typeface specimen sheets, there are separate style sheets that include pi characters, rules, borders, ornaments, and dingbats. These decorative elements require as much care in the selection of style and size as does the type that they accompany.

Pi Characters

It is not uncommon to specify what are known as pi characters. These characters are not included in a font, but are available in styles that correspond with the type style or point size being set. The astronomical signs below are examples of pi characters.

Rules

Rules are among the earliest devices used in typography, dating to the incunabula (books printed before 1500), where lines of type were separated with light-colored rules. In metal composition, the rules were type-high, cut to specification, and, when composed, locked up within a perfectly squared metal frame called a chase, along with the other type. The type rule generally lay directly under or over the metal shoulder of the type. This, however, posed a problem for the typesetter. Even the thinnest metal rule had a body supporting the rule, its thickness had to be taken into consideration when determining the leading between lines. If, for example, a 1/2-point rule was sitting on a 2-point body, the rule had to be notched or undercut so it would not disrupt the leading of the type. To set an underscore very close to the copy, you would specify rules that did not have a shoulder. These bars were usually made from materials harder than lead, such as brass or steel.

Although in phototypesetting the physical type body does not exist, the rules are normally set as though they were positioned in metal. Provisions for minus leading must then be programmed into the typesetting machinery to maintain uniform leading. This specification may not accommodate type styles with long descenders.

One traditional use of rules is to emphasize words or phrases. Rules for underscoring come in a variety of weights and can be positioned at various levels beneath a word or line. In addition, they can be used as graphic or decorative designs, for instance, in border decorations; as separating devices; or as dividers in columns, tables, or graphs.

A combination of two or more rules of different point sizes is called a scotch rule. Usually these rules are closely aligned and parallel to each other. In metal type, the desired scotch rule was specified by style number. In photocomposition, however, all the dimensions of a scotch rule must be specified, including the point sizes, weights, spacing between each rule, and pica width.

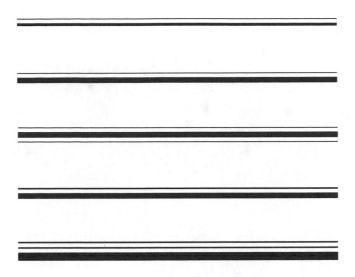

Do not limit your use of rules to conventional applications. Early-twentieth-century artists understood their versatility and were innovators in using them as major design elements in their compositions.

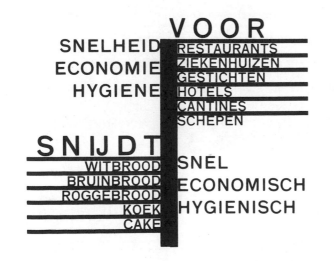

Page design by Paul Schuitema, late 1920s.

Borders, Ornaments, Dingbats, and Cuts

There are a great many typographic symbols that are more elaborate than rules, such as borders, ornaments, dingbats, or decorative and illustrative cuts. Often these are related to a particular period of art. Border designs, for instance, show a range of influences. The popular Greek key motif was derived from Greek architecture and pottery, while Romantic styles may have been inspired by music from Chopin's time. Baroque borders were derived from Baroque interior design, and Art Nouveau borders can be compared to the sinewy lines found in Antonio Gaudi's churches and furniture. Early-twentieth-century geometric borders reflect the shapes in Art Deco architecture, painting, and graphics.

Comparison of architectural and typographic borders.

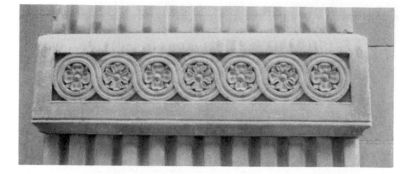

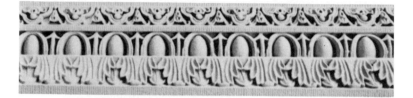

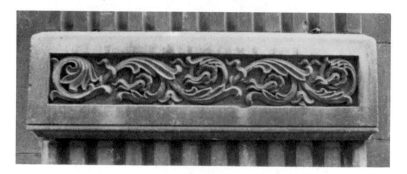

Greek key motif.

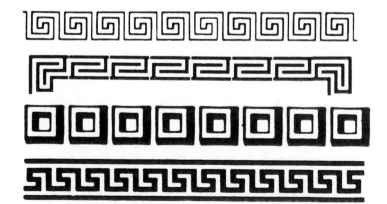

Romantic borders.

Baroque borders.

Art Nouveau borders.

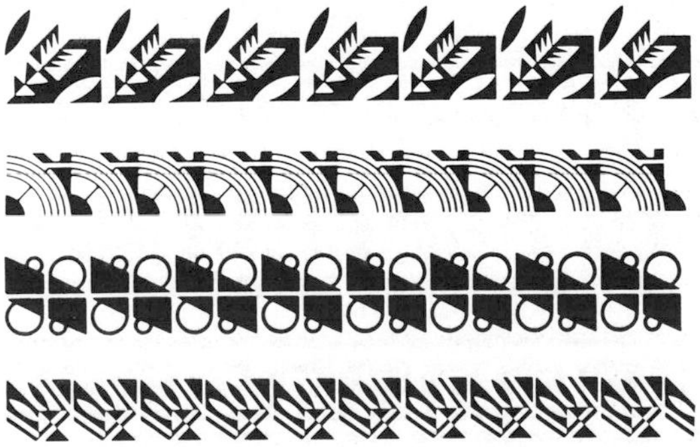

Art Deco borders.

Different periods of art contributed to ornamental design as well. In early handwritten manuscripts, each major section usually began with an illuminated letter made with the purest metallic, mineral, or vegetable pigments, bound by glue or gum to fine paper or parchment. This practice was continued in early printing, and provisions were usually made on the page for either drawn or printed ornaments. These illustrations were the forerunners of the initial capital often used in publications today.

As styles changed, so did the ornamentation. In the fifteenth and sixteenth centuries, solid black florets or ivy leaves were used to harmonize with the old style letters. As type styles became lighter in appearance, however, ornaments became more open in design.

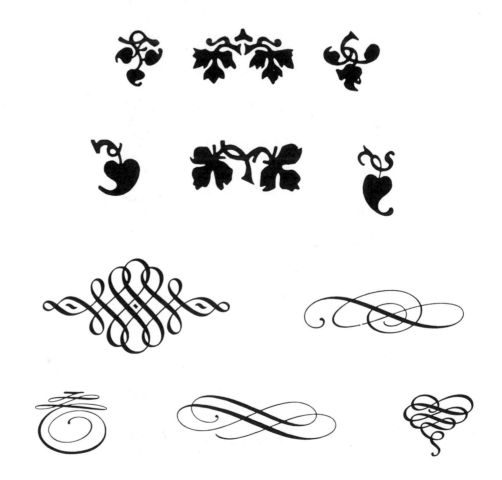

A distinction was made between such nonobjective ornaments as scrolls and cartouches and representational decorations called dingbats. Dingbats were designed from such real objects as leaves, fruit, flower baskets, urns, crosses, harps, and hourglasses. In addition, there were dingbats that represented a person's rank with such forms as crowns, shields, and crests.

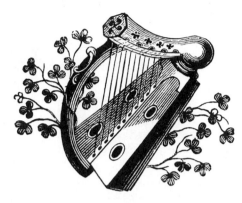

Special ornaments or logotypes, to be placed at the end of magazine articles, were also created on request. Artists and architects were often commissioned to design these ornamental motifs. The architect Bertram G. Goodhue and master craftsman William Morris, for instance, occasionally designed borders, covers, and end papers as well as typefaces.

Printers were also involved in the design process. Indeed, from the sixteenth through the early twentieth century, printers were not only typographers but considered themselves designers as well. The design, from concept through final printing, was all done under one roof. One result of this self-contained process was a series of stock typecuts (ornaments or illustrations manufactured on type bodies), which were often used in place of new artwork. These images were scaled to a full range of point sizes, and any copper engraving that could be mounted on a type-high piece of boxwood could be set with type. During the nineteenth century, ornamentation became so popular that even newly designed letterforms took on a decorative personality. Some of the stock typecuts were transferred into the matrices and molds used in various machine formats. Repeated use of these standardized engravings eventually gave printed material a similar look.

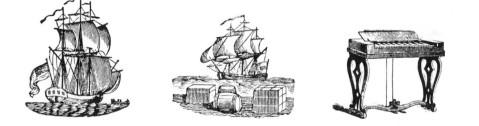

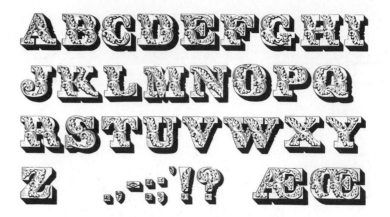

Many of these older forms of ornamentation are available on film and can be used with photocomposition. Using different kinds of ornamentation, however, requires a sense of what is appropriate to the piece. It would look awkward, for instance, to insert a decorative item within a design that does not relate to its time period. It is essential, however, that you research their origins carefully as part of the design process.

Chap-book cuts from type specimen sheet.

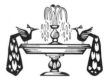

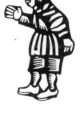

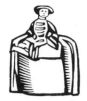 

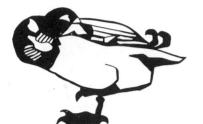 

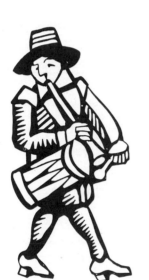 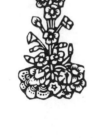 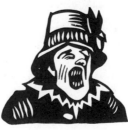

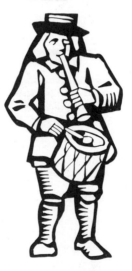

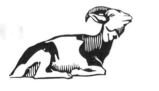

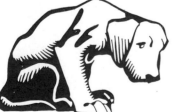 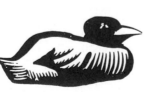

7. Reading a Type Specimen Sheet

Choosing a typeface can be challenging for even the most seasoned designer. A type specimen book from a professional typographer supplies you with the information needed to select and specify your type. Traditionally, typographers have referred to a type specimen sheet as a showing, and the term is still used today. If a typographer composes a sample setting of a requested style and submits it for approval, it is also called a showing.

There are several reasons for reviewing a type specimen sheet. First, the specimen book is the most basic source from which to review available typefaces. Without exposure to this reference of type styles, designers cannot be certain they have selected the face that best satisfies their design objectives. Moreover, a specimen sheet will often indicate how the set type will look. It also provides an indication of tonal value for text-size type. When you view lines of text-size type rather than individual letters, the tonal value of the mass may influence your choice of type.

Type specimen sheets incorporate both technical and aesthetic information. Although every type specimen sheet gives you the same basic information, their page formats may vary depending on the typographer and the machinery used to produce the type. The examples of type specimen sheets at the end of this chapter show five methods of type composition. Although some of the earlier systems may not be in use today, information from those specimen sheets will give you a firm understanding of the more contemporary methods.

A foundry or hot-metal type specimen sheet contains information on how type is composed, showing standard raw settings without refinements. Character count information, such as characters per pica or character count tables for both capital and lowercase letters, is also included. Since no refinements have been incorporated, the designer is not influenced by the typographer's interpretation of how the type should be set. To overcome the spacing limitations in hot type, however, you can specify such refinements as shaving, notching, or ligatures, and have the typographer tailor the job to your specifications.

Foundry specimen sheets also show the number of upper- and lowercase vowels in a particular font, indicated respectively by the symbols A and a. Note that the number of vowels included in a font varies with the point size. This information was necessary when purchasing metal type, since the typographer had to ascertain if there were enough characters available to complete a given job. Since most type today is composed on film or by digitized computer, it is not necessary to have more than one letter of each style in a font.

Many metal type specimen sheets include a small box that shows the complete font, including all the letters, numbers, and symbols, as well as small capitals and special ligatures, if these are available. In this way the designer has a complete palette of information. Generally, foundry specimen sheets show the full range of sizes from 6 to 72 points. Some specimen sheets also include blocks of text-size copy set in different leading and/or point sizes. Observe the difference in the counters and character structures, which were designed to be optically proportionate in each size. The punches from which metal type was cut were based on master drawings or patterns from which the various point sizes were developed. Generally, three different master drawings of each typeface were designed: one for 6- to 9-point type, a second for 10- to 14-point type, and a third for display sizes 18 to 72 points or larger. The readability of the type and the width of the metal body supporting the actual letter were the two factors that influenced the aesthetics and production of type. As a result, the proportions of the letterform changed with each of the three type-size divisions.

The smallest text sizes were designed with open counters for increased legibility, making them slightly wider than characters in the larger point sizes. The characters themselves were also proportionately heavier in weight than in the larger sizes. Due to their smaller physical structure, they needed this additional mass for support. The medium-point-size characters were slightly more condensed and had narrower counters. Because of this a 12-point type is not double the width of a 6-point face, although the body is twice the height. When a more compact setting was desired in metal type, it was not uncommon for the designer to set the job proportionately larger, taking advantage of the narrower letters to pick up more characters per pica. It was then photographically reduced, giving the appearance of a tighter setting.

ABCDEFGHIJKLMNOPQRSTUVWXYZ
abcdefghijklmnopqrstuvwxyx

ABCDEFGHIJKLMNOPQRSTUVWXYZ

abcdefghijklmnopqrstuvwxyz

ABCDEFGHIJKLMNOPQRSTUVWXYZ
abcdefghijklmnopqrstuvwxyx

Top to bottom: 24-point Century Expanded, 12-point Century Expanded, 24-point reduced to 12-point Century Expanded.

To maintain the full legibility of the typeface design, the letter structures of display-size characters were proportionately reduced in weight. The larger character structures also required less reinforcement from the surrounding metal body. Therefore, display faces had narrower counter spaces than the smaller characters, proportionately reducing the width of the letterform.

Unlike metal, photocomposition generally uses only one master font from which all type—6 to 72 points—is produced. This font is usually based on the proportions of the 10- to 14-point metal type, although sometimes the display-size master drawings are used instead.

Study the letterforms shown below. Note the changes in character structure in the letterforms based on the three master drawings used in designing metal type. Compare these with the letterforms produced by photocomposition.

Top to bottom: 6-point Century Expanded linotype enlarged to 72-point; 12-point Century Expanded linotype enlarged to 72-point; 72-point Century Expanded foundry type; 72-point Century Expanded photocomposition.

ABCDE
ABCDE
ABCDE
ABCDE

To competently direct the typographer, designers should be aware of the inventory of master drawings available to them. Check with the foundry manufacturer or typographer to see how many different-size master drawings are made for a particular typeface and font. If multiple sizes are available, ask to see them and then work with the one that best suits your requirements. If your typographer does not have that font, request that it be ordered. Be aware that you may incur the initial cost of purchasing it. If you are required to buy it, the cost may be amortized throughout the campaign or design project.

Unlike specimen sheets for metal type, those for photocomposition often indicate various spacing refinements that have been programmed into the computerized typesetting machinery. Turn to the VIP specimen sheet on page 121 and compare the four settings at the top. The line labeled "Track M" represents the type as it would be set in metal. The other lines—Tracks 1, 2, and 3—become proportionately tighter in letter and word spacing. In specifying type, you can choose whichever spacing meets your design's requirements. Additional, extremely precise refinements are possible for different point sizes, given the increased capabilities of computerized typesetting.

Obviously, type specimen sheets provide a lot of helpful information, which the designer must learn how best to use. To analyze the personality of a letterform shown on a type specimen sheet, it may help if you isolate individual letters in various point sizes. This is a method I use. Prepare two right-angle masks 1 inch wide and 8 inches along each side. The masks should be cut from matte board, black on one side for reverse type and white on the other for positive type. Position the masks around a single character, isolating it from the surrounding material so that you can observe its structure without distraction. Letters can take on a different identity when viewed individually like this.

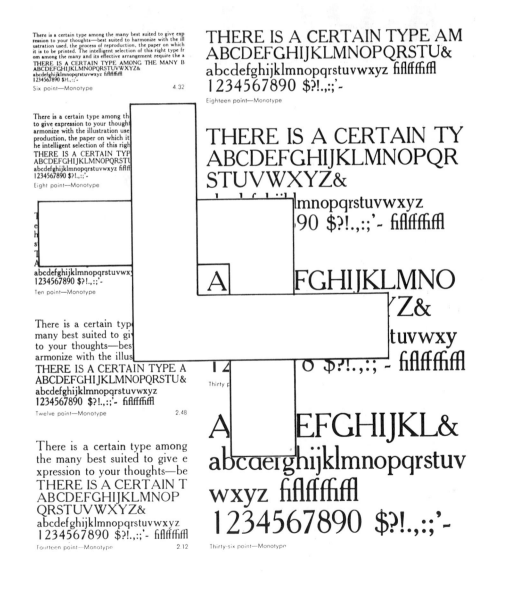

This procedure can also be applied to a block of copy. Sections of text-size type may look different once they are separated from other sizes. Unfortunately, the showings of text-size type are often not deep enough to indicate true tonal value. In such cases, dummying some copy on layout paper or photocopying the section several times and grouping sections together to simulate a column of type may be useful. On occasion you may request that dummy copy be run off in galleys by your typographer. Remember, however, that the type's tonal value will change, depending not only on its size, but also on its width, depth, and spacing.

I recommend that you compile your own type specimen reference file, including jobs that you have produced. Even the slightest change in specifications can alter the look of a type style. Keeping samples of actual set copy can be a valuable resource. Every time you specify type, ask for an extra proof for your file. Be sure to request that a record of your type specification be included if your typographer does not normally indicate the specifications in the guidelines (the information printed at the top or bottom of a proof). The guidelines usually contain the typeface, point size, leading, spacing, kind of equipment, and the master font used to prepare your copy. Some typographers use a code number, set alongside the typeface, to identify the master font used for composition. It is possible for one typeface to have more than one number, if the particular system has text as well as display fonts.

Watson-Guptill
The Art of Typography

Job No. 9510
A Head: 16 point Franklin Gothic Track 2
B Head: 18 point Franklin Gothic Track 2
Subheads: 10/12 Upper & lower case Track 2
Text: 11/13 Century Expanded flush L/R x29 picas Track 2
    Paragraph indents 2 picas
Captions: 8/9 Century Expanded Italic
        by 9 picas maximum
Folios: 10 point Century Expanded Italic

Although the type specimen sheets on the following pages have mostly been reduced and are therefore not accurate for type size, they allow you to compare the same typeface set on different machinery.

120 pt. 3A 4a 3-1

For

96 pt. 3A 5a 3-1

Best

84 pt. 3A 4a 4-1

Lists

72 pt. 3A 4a 4-1

Satire

60 pt. 3A 5a 4-1

THE most

48 pt. 3A 5a 3-1

BEST quality

42 pt. 3A 6a 3-1

ONE trombone

36 pt. 3A 7a 4-1 Lower case alphabet 494 pts. Characters per pica .70

THE KNIGHTS
Apprentices must

30 pt. 4A 8a 5-1 Lower case alphabet 404 pts. Characters per pica .85

JADE COLORS ARE
It is used for jewelry

24 pt. 6A 11a 7-1 Lower case alphabet 323 pts. Characters per pica 1.0

PERU AND
It shows you

18 pt. 8A 18a 9-1 Lower case alphabet 229 pts. Characters per pica 1.5

PRINTERS IN
THEY instructed a
village blacksmith

14 pt. 12A 27a 11-1 Lower case alphabet 184 pts. Characters per pica 1.8

THE PRINTER IN
THEY instructed some
village blacksmith to

12 pt. 15A 32a 12-1 Lower case alphabet 154 pts. Characters per pica 2.2

PRINTING IN EARLY
THEY INSTRUCTED the local
blacksmith to make all the

10 pt. 18A 44a 15-1 Lower case alphabet 118 pts. Characters per pica 2.9

THE EARLY PRINTERS IN
THEY INSTRUCTED some local black
smith to make the iron frame or

8 pt. 18A 45a 20-1 Lower case alphabet 100 pts. Characters per pica 3.4

THE EARLY PRINTERS MADE
THEY INSTRUCTED some local blacksmith
to make the iron frame or chases which

6 pt. 28A 63a 26-1 Lower case alphabet 75 pts. Characters per pica 4.5

THE EARLY PRINTERS CAST THEIR TYPES
THEY INSTRUCTED some local blacksmith to make the
iron frames or chases in which the types are confined
for printing, and either made or designed the wooden

Foundry type specimen sheet (shown slightly reduced).

7△168. Caslon No. 137 with Italic and Small Caps Code, ZENNO
LINOTYPE faces are standard throughout the world in more th 12345
LINOTYPE faces are standard throughout the world in more th VBCDE
Also long descenders for 8 pt. body
Lower case alphabet 90 pts. Figures .0484

8△466. Caslon No. 137 with Italic and Small Caps Code, ZENOM
LINOTYPE faces are standard throughout the world in 12345
LINOTYPE faces are standard throughout the world in VBCDE
Also long descenders for 9 pt. body
Lower case alphabet 103 pts. Figures .0553

9△144. Caslon No. 137 with Italic and Small Caps Code, ZENOT
LINOTYPE faces are standard throughout the w 12345
LINOTYPE faces are standard throughout the w VBCDE
Also long descenders for 10 pt. body
Lower case alphabet 116 pts. Figures .0622

10△424. Caslon No. 137 with Italic and Small Caps Code, ZENOZ
LINOTYPE faces are standard throughout 12345
LINOTYPE faces are standard throughout VBCDE
Also long descenders for 11 pt. body
Lower case alphabet 129 pts. Figures .0692

11△122. Caslon No. 137 with Italic and Small Caps Code, ZENPU
LINOTYPE faces are standard throug 12345
LINOTYPE faces are standard throug VBCDE
Also long descenders for 12 pt. body
Lower case alphabet 141 pts. Figures .0761

12△440. Caslon No. 137 with Italic and Small Caps Code, ZENRA
LINOTYPE faces are standard thr 12345
LINOTYPE faces are standard thr VBCDE
Also long descenders for 13 pt. body
Lower case alphabet 155 pts. Figures .083

SPECIMEN ALPHABET

ABCDEFGHIJKLMNOPQRSTUVWXYZ&
ABCDEFGHIJKLMNOPQRSTUVWXYZ&

ABCDEFGHIJKLMNOPQRSTUVWXYZ&

abcdefghijklmnopqrstuvwxyz fi fl ff ffi ffl
abcdefghijklmnopqrstuvwxyz fi fl ff ffi ffl

1234567890 [($£,.:;'-'?.,!*†‡§¶)] 1234567890
1234567890 [($£,.:;'-'?.,!†‡§¶)] 1234567890*

⅛ ¼ ⅜ ½ ⅝ ¾ ⅞ ⅓ ⅔ ⅕ ⅖ ⅗ ⅘ ⅙ ⅚

$\frac{1}{8}$ $\frac{1}{4}$ $\frac{3}{8}$ $\frac{1}{2}$ $\frac{5}{8}$ $\frac{3}{4}$ $\frac{7}{8}$ $\frac{1}{3}$ $\frac{2}{3}$

TYPOGRAPHIC REFINEMENT CHARACTERS
Two-Letter Small Caps, Special No. 5

ABCDEFGHIJKLMNOPQRSTUVWXYZ&
ABCDEFGHIJKLMNOPQRSTUVWXYZ&

Italic Lower Case, Special No. 5

abcdefghijklmnopqrstuvwxyz (,.:;"?.,!)

Italic Logotypes, Special No. 5

*f fi fl af aff ef eff hf if iff kf lf mf nf of off pf
rf sf tf uf uff yf If Of Off*

One-Letter Roman Logotypes, Special No. 5

fa fe fo fr fs ft fu fy ffa ffe ffo ffr ffs ffu ffy f, f. f- ff, ff. ff-f ff

Two-Letter Logotypes

Ta Te To Tr Tu Tw Ty Va Ve Vo Wa We Wi
Ta Te To Tr Tu Tw Ty Va Ve Vo Wa We Wi

Wo Wr Ya Ye Yo
Wo Wr Ya Ye Yo

fa fe fo fr fs ft fu fy ffa ffe ffo ffr ffs ffu ffy f, f. f- ff, ff. ff-f ff
fa fe fo fr fs ft fu fy ffa ffe ffo ffr ffs ffu ffy f, f. f- ff, ff. ff-f ff

One-Letter Italic Logotypes
FA PA TA VA WA YA Th Wh

CASLON No. 137 with *Italic,* 12 pt. How is one to assess and evaluate a type face in terms of its esthetic design? Why do the pace-
makers in the art of printing rave over a specific face of type? What
do they see in it? Why is it so superlatively pleasant to their eyes?
Good design is always practical design. And what they see in a
good type design is, partly, its excellent practical fitness to perform its work. It has a "heft" and balance in all of its parts just
right for its size, as any good tool has. Your good chair has all of
its parts made nicely to the right size to do exactly the work that
the chair has to do, neither clumsy and thick, nor "skinny" and

Linotype specimen sheet (shown same size).

THIS LETTER IS KNOWN As One Of The Best Examples of the "old style" group of type faces. It was first cast by William Caslon in England about 1720, and is rated by many authorities as first for all-round usefulness. The inspiration for this popular typeface was probably Dutch types, notably those of Bishop Fell. The original punches for casting this Caslon face were purchased from the Caslon Type Foundry, of London, by MacKellar, Smiths and Jordan, of

14 Point—For Hand Composition

DISTINGUISHED BY ITS Thin Serifs And By Generous fillet curves, this letter is rated by many authorities for $12345

18 Point—For Hand Composition

IS DISTINGUISHED By The Thin Serifs With their very full fillet curves

22 Point—For Hand Composition

ON YOUR NEXT Rush Orders Use Our newer materials $67890

24 Point—For Hand Composition

USE A CASLON face in book work

30 Point—For Hand Composition

LARGE SIZE type used here

36 Point—For Hand Composition

CHARACTERS IN FONTS

A B C D E F G H I J J K L M N O P Q
Q R S T U V W X Y Z & Æ Œ Qu
a b c d e f g h i j k l m n o p q r s t u v w
x y z æ œ ct st fi fl ff ffi ffl . , - ' ' : ; ! ?
$1234567890£ $1234567890
f fb fh fi fk fl ff ffi ffl ft

(Lining Figures supplied with all fonts unless Hanging Figures are specified.)

Display—14 and 18 Point, 98 Characters; 22 Point, 87 Characters; 24 to 36 Point, 98 Characters; 36H4 Point, 26 Characters; No. 437, 42 to 72 Point, 80 Characters
14 to 36 Point fonts include Long S Characters
(See previous sheet for 14, 18 and 24 Point Small Caps)

NEW TYPES

36H4 Point—For Hand Composition

OLD CASLON retains its charm

42 Point, No. 437—For Hand Composition

MONOTYPE printer satisfies

48 Point, No. 437—For Hand Composition

Establishes

60 Point, No. 437—For Hand Composition

In Heads

72 Point, No. 437—For Hand Composition

Monotype specimen sheet (shown reduced).

TYPEFACES 23
Of finer design 2 3

24 Point Ludlow 1-TC True-Cut Caslon
Length of lower-case alphabet: 268 points

RECAST LINE 89
To save press time 89

22 Point Ludlow 1-TC True-Cut Caslon
Length of lower-case alphabet: 233 points

LEADING PAPERS 42
Praise Ludlow system 42

18 Point Ludlow 1-TC True-Cut Caslon
Length of lower-case alphabet: 197 points

YOU NEED NOT CAST 21
Big display types for storage 21

14 Point Ludlow 1-TC True-Cut Caslon
Length of lower-case alphabet: 162 points

NO MACHINE OR MOLD 70
Changes necessary with Ludlow 70

12 Point Ludlow 1-TC True-Cut Caslon
Length of lower-case alphabet: 144 points

NEVER IN PRINTING HISTORY 31
Has setting of display lines been so simple 3 1
as it is today with the efficient Ludlow system

10 Point Ludlow 1-TC True-Cut Caslon
Length of lower-case alphabet: 110 points

A COMPETENT COMPOSITOR BECOMES 95
Efficient Ludlow operator after short practice period 95
which is another fine advantage of the Ludlow system

8 Point Ludlow 1-TC True-Cut Caslon
Length of lower-case alphabet: 93 points

Characters in Complete Font

A B C D E F G H I J K
L M N O P Q R S T U V
W X Y Z & $ 1 2 3 4 5 6
7 8 9 0 a b c d e f g h i j k
l m n o p q r s t u v w x y z
ff fi ffi fl ffl . : , ; - ' ' ! ? ( ) —

Fonts of all sizes are available with or
without supplementary ligatures.

QU Qu f ff fa ffa fe ffe ffn
fo ffo fr ffr fs ffs ft fu ffu fy
& j [ ]

Quaint characters such as the long S combinations and oldstyle figures are extra.
The following are available in 8 to 36 point.

ſ ſſ ſb ſh ſi ſſi ſk ſl ſll
ſt 1 2 3 4 5 6 7 8 9 0

Oldstyle figures are also available in 42,
48, 60 and 72 point.

Ludlow specimen sheet (shown reduced).

GETS A 4
New trial 4

72 Point Ludlow 1-TC True-Cut Caslon   Length of lower-case alphabet: 962 points

QUALITY 9
Ludlow slug 9

60 Point Ludlow 1-TC True-Cut Caslon   Length of lower-case alphabet: 778 points

COMPOSING 95
Room efficiency 95

48 Point Ludlow 1-TC True-Cut Caslon   Length of lower-case alphabet: 573 points

CASLON SERIES 10
Has many fine uses 10

42 Point Ludlow 1-TC True-Cut Caslon   Length of lower-case alphabet: 510 points

DEALER IMPRESSED 28
With advertising results 28

36 Point Ludlow 1-TC True-Cut Caslon   Length of lower-case alphabet: 413 points

THE LUDLOW WILL BE A 67
Valuable addition to your plant 67

30 Point Ludlow 1-TC True-Cut Caslon   Length of lower-case alphabet: 320 points

Caslon No. 540 Roman

Shown below are samples of our optional character spacing tracks. All the other specimens on this page are set solid in our standard Track 2.
If you desire other than Track 2, please specify when ordering type. Characters per pica are lower case alphabet.

TRACK M   The best kind of originality is that which comes after a sound apprenticeship; that whic

TRACK 1   The best kind of originality is that which comes after a sound apprenticeship; that which

TRACK 2   The best kind of originality is that which comes after a sound apprenticeship; that which shal

TRACK 3   The best kind of originality is that which comes after a sound apprenticeship; that which shall

---

6 point   characters per pica **4.37**

abcdefghijklmnopqrstuvwxyz$1234567890
ABCDEFGHIJKLMNOPQRSTUVWXYZ
The best kind of originality is that which comes after a sound apprenticeship; that which sh
all prove itself to be the blending of a firm conception of useful precedent and the progress
ive tendencies of an able mind. For, let a man be as able and original as he may, he cannot a
fford to discard knowledge of what has gone before or what is now going on in his own trade

7 point   characters per pica **3.76**

abcdefghijklmnopqrstuvwxyz$1234567890
ABCDEFGHIJKLMNOPQRSTUVWXYZ
The best kind of originality is that which comes after a sound apprenticeship;
that which shall prove itself to be the blending of a firm conception of useful p
recedent and the progressive tendencies of an able mind. For, let a man be as
able and original as he may, he cannot afford to discard knowledge of what has

8 point   characters per pica **3.40**

abcdefghijklmnopqrstuvwxyz$1234567890
ABCDEFGHIJKLMNOPQRSTUVWXYZ
The best kind of originality is that which comes after a sound apprenti
ceship; that which shall prove itself to be the blending of a firm concep
tion of useful precedent and the progressive tendencies of an able mind
For, let a man be as able and original as he may, he cannot afford to disc

9 point   characters per pica **3.10**

abcdefghijklmnopqrstuvwxyz$1234567890
ABCDEFGHIJKLMNOPQRSTUVWXYZ
The best kind of originality is that which comes after a sound ap
prenticeship; that which shall prove itself to be the blending of a
firm conception of useful precedent and the progressive tendenc
ies of an able mind. For, let a man be as able and original as he m

10 point   characters per pica **2.78**

abcdefghijklmnopqrstuvwxyz$1234567890
ABCDEFGHIJKLMNOPQRSTUVWXYZ
The best kind of originality is that which comes after a so
und apprenticeship; that which shall prove itself to be the
blending of a firm conception of useful precedent and the
progressive tendencies of an able mind. For, let a man be a

11 point   characters per pica **2.52**

abcdefghijklmnopqrstuvwxyz$1234567890
ABCDEFGHIJKLMNOPQRSTUVWXYZ
The best kind of originality is that which comes after
a sound apprenticeship; that which shall prove itself
to be the blending of a firm conception of useful pre
cedent and the progressive tendencies of an able m

12 point   characters per pica **2.36**

abcdefghijklmnopqrstuvwxyz$1234567890
ABCDEFGHIJKLMNOPQRSTUVWXYZ
The best kind of originality is that which comes a
fter a sound apprenticeship; that which shall pro
ve itself to be the blending of a firm conception o
f useful precedent and the progressive tendencie

14 point   characters per pica **2.04**

THE BEST KIND OF originality is that which comes after a sound apprenticeship; that wh

16 point   characters per pica **1.80**

THE BEST KIND OF originality is that which comes after a sound apprenticesh

18 point   characters per pica **1.63**

THE BEST KIND OF originality is that which comes after a sound appre

20 point

THE BEST KIND OF originality is that which comes after a soun

24 point

THE BEST KIND OF originality is that which comes a

27 point

THE BEST KIND OF originality is that which cc

30 point

THE BEST KIND OF originality is that whic

33 point

THE BEST KIND OF originality is that v

36 point

THE BEST KIND OF originality is tl

Photocomposition specimen sheet (shown reduced).

8. Using Typographic Refinements

Typographic letterforms were designed and manufactured so the position of the letter on its body would ensure proper spacing between letters when printed. The type body also allowed for comfortable spacing between lines without additional leading. Word spacing was determined by the typographer, who usually followed the conventional spacing of the time.

Some purists feel that the way type was designed and positioned on its body is the way it should be set. This belief, however, allows the mechanics of typesetting to determine the aesthetics. The art of typography requires knowledge of how to make the mechanical devices work for you, and establishing this control should be one of your major concerns.

In high-quality typography, where each project has an individual personality, the copy style must relate to the specific composition. This control is achieved through typographic refinements. Here *refinement* means the process of monitoring the typesetting until the desired effect is achieved. The level of refinement must be in keeping with the intent or personality of your design. Analyze the mood of a piece to determine the refinements needed, but take care to use refinements with discretion. What you specify as a refinement can become a distortion. It is essential to maintain the dignity of the letterform and not overelaborate a modification. Indeed, overelaboration can make your design antiseptic. Also keep in mind that the equipment used to produce your type may have limited capabilities, requiring many of your alterations to be executed by hand.

My ideas on typographic refinements have been developed through experimentation and aesthetic judgment. One of my major training grounds was designing with metal type. Using traditional methods encouraged me to develop refinements. Intricate modifications, however, usually involved a lot of handwork—compared with photocomposition, which has many of these refinements programmed into the system.

Optical Letter Spacing

In metal composition, modifications of letter spacing were restricted by the set of letters—that is, by the physical limitations of the actual metal type bodies. With foundry type, refinements were made primarily in display sizes, which were easier to handle and more prominent than smaller sizes. To create optically pleasing headlines, for instance, designers sometimes instructed typographers to shave the metal shoulders off a body of type, which permitted most characters to be set tighter than normally. Yet the type still could be set only as tight as the physical structure of the characters themselves.

More dramatic alterations of type bodies were often needed to maintain consistent spacing between particular letters. Pieces of the metal bodies were notched to bring the letters closer together, so the result resembled a ligature. Although metal type specimen sheets never included this modification, typographers often took the initiative in incorporating it, as it was a mechanical solution.

In monotype and linotype, the width of the matrix determined the closeness of each letter. Although in monotype it was possible to modify the width of the casting matrix, this alteration was rarely done by the typographer. The only spacing alternative was to add letter space by hand in the lockup in monotype and during the keyboarding process in linotype. Because of the machinery's technical limitations, it was the designer who made final spacing adjustments while preparing the mechanical from the proofs. Using a razor blade, the designer could modify letters or adjust spacing to fine-tune the design. In display sizes it was not uncommon to trim the width of such letters as T or L in certain type styles to decrease the letter spacing.

LLL
TTT

Today, with photocomposition, typography is more flexible, with fewer restrictions. Machine capabilities are greater, not only in terms of increasing the maximum width of composition and speed of production, but also, more importantly, in allowing better control of letter and word spacing. Space, designated in tracks or units, is automatically adjusted between letters and words. The various spacing units are predetermined by the typographic programming system and range from normal spacing, which is equivalent to how type sets in metal, to increasingly tighter spacing. Hypothetical notching or shaving—called minus unit spacing or tracking—is often used in photocomposition to create tight letter spacing. Minus leading can also be used for a kerning letter that protrudes below its body (see page 99).

In any case, most complete type specimen sheets indicate how different type styles will look in different track settings (see page 121 for an example). The spacing differences between tracks is minute. Designers and type directors must review each track setting carefully before specifying type since the track affects the character count. If you have questions in reviewing the spacing on the type specimen sheet, do not hesitate to consult a representative at your type shop.

Most display copy above 24-point is set by machines specifically designed for this purpose. These photographic headlining machines compose one letter at a time. Depending on the equipment's capabilities, the operator can set a letter up to 200% of its original font size on a 2-inch-high strip of film. If even larger sizes are required, these strips of type must be photographically enlarged.

Photo-display typesetting machines have a manual spacing system. Letter spacing is controlled by the operator, but it is the designer's responsibility to specify the appropriate letter spacing, in accordance with the typographer's spacing guide. To ensure that your specifications are followed accurately, a layout, showing the effect you want, should accompany the copy.

Custom spacing guide for specifying display type (shown reduced).

TYPICAL SANS SERIF FACE (HELV. MEDIUM)

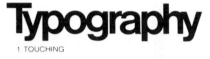
1 TOUCHING

TYPICAL SERIF FACE (TIMES NEW ROMAN SEMIBOLD)

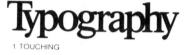
1 TOUCHING

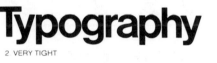
2 VERY TIGHT

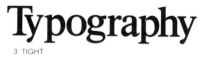
2 VERY TIGHT

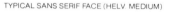
3 TIGHT

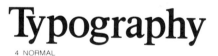
3 TIGHT

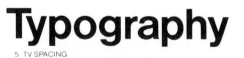
4 NORMAL

4 NORMAL

5 TV SPACING

5 TV SPACING

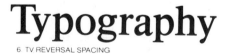
6 TV REVERSAL SPACING

6 TV REVERSAL SPACING

Type set to normal spacing standards usually produces the most consistent, uniform letter spacing. Normal spacing gives the typographer the opportunity to control the optical letter spacing. When you specify copy with very tight or touching letters, you have reduced that control and there is less consistency.

Letter spacing is often subject to fads, which can at times reduce legibility. Keep in mind that although there are few mechanical spacing restrictions in photocomposition, it is the designer's or type director's responsibility to specify spacing that best supports the readability of letterforms. Every type style requires a certain amount of space around each letter or word to maintain legibility. If this space is violated, the copy may be unreadable. While the machinery sometimes encourages the designer to experiment with its capabilities, the outcome may not always be aesthetic. Classical spacing should be considered the standard and only altered if it enhances your design.

Touching Letters

Although touching letters may be necessary to refine letter spacing, the designer must exercise discretion. Serif letters are designed to be independent even when they are set compatibly close to each other, as the serifs automatically act as separating devices. Normally, there is a built-in space surrounding the characters so that the vertical and angular stems do not touch. This space generally makes serif letters appear to set wider than block letters. In photocomposition, serif letters can be programmed to touch, but every letter combination reacts differently. When joined, they form what are called common serifs. Sometimes a combination of letters creates a unit that is less than pleasing or even unrecognizable. With touching or overlapping serifs, be sure the identity and legibility of each letter is maintained. Note that type style and point size also influence the effect of a common serif.

HIND HIND

HIND HIND

Block letters have no structural devices to prevent one letter from touching the main form of the next. Therefore, when two vertical block letters collide, an undefinable shape may occur. To preserve the integrity of each letterform, a slight amount of white space must be inserted between all block letters. The slightest division of space, even half a point, between letters may be enough to maintain legibility. Again, be aware that some letter combinations should not be set very tight or touching.

illustration
illustration
illustration

Optical Word Spacing

The rules for optical letter spacing also apply to word spacing. To specify appropriate word spacing, you must first choose the typeface, select the letter spacing, and then determine how the word spacing relates to the letter spacing. Since the introduction of phototypesetting, some designers have begun to favor tight word spacing in text as well as display type. As with letter spacing, however, if used without discretion, tight word spacing can reduce legibility instead of enhancing it.

In photocomposition, word spacing is based on the em space, which is the square of the point size and not the size of the letter itself. If you're working with 18-point Baskerville, for example, and you specify 3-to-the-em word space, you will have a mechanical 6 points, or one-third of 18 points, from serif to serif. With block letters, such as Futura, you measure from stem to stem. In refining word space it may be necessary to alter the 3-to-the-em optically, depending on the shape or openness of the next word, to improve tonality and readability.

Top to bottom: mechanical word spacing and optical word spacing.

The Russian painter Vassily Kandinsky (among
the first to join the Bauhaus staff) was thinking of his work
in terms of music and putting on canvas
mystical Debussy-like compositions to which he gave
the name "improvisations."

The Russian painter Vassily Kandinsky (among
the first to join the Bauhaus staff) was thinking of his work
in terms of music and putting on canvas
mystical Debussy-like compositions to which he gave
the name "improvisations."

When designing with full-body capital letters—letters with open counters that are neither expanded nor condensed—I generally use 3-to-the-em spacing. If the same grouping were set in capitals and lowercase, I would decrease the spacing unit to 4-to-the-em. Because lowercase letters are designed with smaller counters, less space is needed between words for legibility.

If the type style you select is extremely condensed, the em-to-the-word-space ratio should increase proportionately, thereby reducing the space between words. Conversely, you should increase word space for expanded faces, using less em-to-the-word space. Extended letters have extremely open counters, so the counters begin to influence the spaces around the letters. That usually means more open letter spacing is required; in fact, extremely light, expanded faces may need as much as 1-to-the-em letter spacing. Note that word spacing is always guided by letter spacing.

To determine word spacing refinements, draw the *mechanical* em-to-the-word space between two vertical letters on a piece of tracing paper. Then, using this mechanical space as a guide, look at the characters at the end and beginning of adjacent words to determine whether the letters should be optically adjusted. With a serif typeface, your guides for determining mechanical spacing are the outer serif edges of two vertical letters. With block letters, the straight vertical stems of the letter structures become the spacing guide. Note, however, that this method is only a guide. The space between words must also be adjusted to conform to the shapes of curved and angled letters.

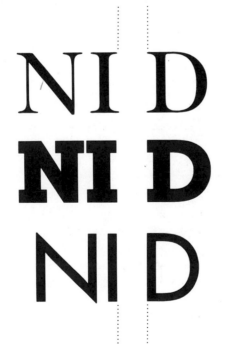

Punctuation in relation to word space must be viewed differently from letter-to-letter word space since most punctuation has less weight than letterforms. Punctuation should be added optically into your em-to-the-word-space specifications (see the discussion on pages 139–140).

Optical Line Spacing

It has been said by purists that the typographic letterform is designed to be set solid when used for text. These purists believe that if space were needed between the lines, the typeface designer would have taken that into consideration when relating the x-height portion of the letter to its ascenders and descenders. Note that line spacing does seem to vary depending on the design of the typeface. When set solid, letterforms with large x-height areas and short ascenders and descenders, such as Helvetica, appear to be set tighter than the same-size typeface with a smaller x-height and larger ascenders and descenders, such as Futura. Note that the space between the lines seems wider with Futura, giving it a lighter tonal value.

All abstract pictures, particularly the quite simple ones, show elements of painting or graphic art which are at once clearly defined in form and in plain relation to one another. From this to typography is no great step. The works of abstract painters are symbols of the subtle arrangement of simple yet strongly contrasting elements. Since the new typography sets itself no other task than the creation of just arrangements, it is possible for many works of abstract painters and sculptors to act as inspirational models.

All abstract pictures, particularly the quite simple ones, show elements of painting or graphic art which are at once clearly defined in form and in plain relation to one another. From this to typography is no great step. The works of abstract painters are symbols of the subtle arrangement of simple yet strongly contrasting elements. Since the new typography sets itself no other task than the creation of just arrangements, it is possible for many works of abstract painters and sculptors to act as inspirational models.

Theories concerning spacing can be interpreted. Some designers believe that the nature of the project's design should determine whether or not lines of copy are set solid or leaded. Yet there are no firm rules to determine how much leading should be added. The decision should be based on good design judgment. Note that two important factors are affected when leading is inserted. Too much space can reduce continuity, decreasing readability; it also reduces tonal value, providing a less severe contrast than if the same copy had been set solid.

Minus leading in photocomposition should be used with discretion, since ascenders and descenders may overlap. One of the exceptions is with capital letters. Since they rest on the baseline and usually do not protrude into the ascender territory of the letters below, they can accommodate minus leading, depending of course on the point size and style. Another exception is lines of lowercase letters with no descenders.

paper folder   paper folder

Used properly, leading enhances the total look of typography. With extremely wide pica measures, it improves readability by preventing the reader from repeatedly picking up the same line. The amount of space placed between lines of type should be determined by the weight, style, x-height, as well as size of the ascenders and descenders on adjacent lines. If a predetermined leading effect is wanted—for example, 2 points between lines of 12-point text on a 20-pica width—the line spacing is set automatically. Lines with more ascenders and descenders next to each other, however, may require more space between them than those with fewer ascenders and descenders. This additional optical spacing should be specified on your copy. If the type specimen sheet does not show several line comparisons of capitals, ascenders, and descenders, request a sample from your typographer. After you see the relationship of space between lines, you can determine if you want mechanical or optical spacing or both.

Although modifications in line spacing do not affect a single column of type, they cause baseline misalignment if two or more columns are placed next to each other. Adjusting space slightly between paragraphs can help to even off line depths in unequal columns. This refinement, however, should be used only when paragraph separations are indicated by space rather than indents.

Additional refinements can be made in controlling the optical line spacing within a headline. Although it is not a common practice, altering the ascenders and descenders of letters can help to equalize the optical consistency of the leading. Some type style castings—for example, Bodoni—are actually manufactured with both long and short descending characters. The alternative short letters were prepared to give the designer a choice in the proportionate scale to the x-height, although it is unlikely that you would mix the two different descending lengths within the same setting. In other cases, with certain settings of display-size type that have lines stacked above one another, if the descenders are touching or overlapping ascenders in the next line, you might consider cutting down the height of the ascenders or depth of the descenders to create a more visually compatible union.

g j p q y , ; Q

g j p q y , ; Q

Top to bottom: Bodoni Bold and Newspaper Bodoni Bold with long and short descenders, respectively.

Justifying Type Widths

Most newspapers, magazines, and periodicals have type set in what is called a justified position—flush left and right on a given pica measure. Monotype, linotype, and photocomposition machines have built-in line justification capabilities. Technological advancements have extended the maximum pica measure to which any one line can be set. In linotype, the maximum for most machines was 30 picas, although 42-pica machines were also available. Typographers preferred to use the narrower-measure linotype machine mainly because the 30-pica bar was less likely to create problems in lockup alignment on press.

In linotype, space bands were deposited between words during composition to create word spacing. Once a line of matrices was composed with these space bands in position, the bands were depressed, thereby adding more space between words and forcing the matrices to fill the predetermined pica measure. In some instances, unskilled operators used these bands instead of additional words to "pump out," or fill, the line width. This practice was common in newspaper composition.

Such unprofessional typographic composition is still practiced today. Only the methods have changed. In addition to forcing letter or word space to justify a line, modern equipment can expand or condense letters to conform to a designated width. Modification without control is not typography. It is inferior typesetting.

It is almost impossible to maintain a given em-to-the-word space in justified lines, since each line must conform to the same pica measure, regardless of the number of words. Lines with wider pica measures, however, tend to be more consistent in tonal value because the equalization of word spacing is distributed over a greater area. Conversely, poor spacing is more prevalent in very narrow lines, even if they are set in 8-point type. Remember, though, that every type style and point size will appear to have a different tonal value, even if justified to the same pica measure.

Quotation from a review in Comaedia *of the opening of a show of Max Ernst's collages in Paris, May 1921.*

"With characteristic bad taste the Dadaists make their appeal this time to the human instinct of fear. The scene is a cellar with all lights in the shop extinguished. Moanings are heard through a trap door. Another wag, hidden behind a cupboard, insults the more important visitors.... The Dadaists, with no neckties and wearing white gloves, walk around the place. Breton crunches matches. G. Ribemont-Dessaignes keeps on remarking at the top of his voice, 'It's raining on a skull.' Aragon mews like a cat. Ph. Soupault plays hide and seek with Tzara; Benjamin Péret and Charchoune never stop shaking hands. On the threshold, Jacques Rigaut counts out loud the cars and the pearls of the lady visitors."

"With characteristic bad taste the Dadaists make their appeal this time to the human instinct of fear. The scene is a cellar with all lights in the shop extinguished. Moanings are heard through a trap door. Another wag, hidden behind a cupboard, insults the more important visitors.... The Dadaists, with no neckties and wearing white gloves, walk around the place. Breton crunches matches. G. Ribemont-Dessaignes keeps on remarking at the top of his voice, 'It's raining on a skull.'

On occasion a designer may specify all paragraphs to end with a flush-right line justification, especially in the last line of a column. It is more than likely, however, that the copy will end in an incomplete line, or widow, and pumping the line out will create an excess of letter and word space, distorting the continuity with the lines above. In addition, I feel that copy tailored to fit a space is less believable. Keep in mind that certain type styles can handle irregular word or letter spacing better than others. In particular, very condensed, medium, or bold gothic characters look awkward when they are irregularly letter- or word-spaced.

"With characteristic bad taste the Dadaists make their appeal this time to the human instinct of fear. The scene is a cellar with all lights in the shop extinguished. Moanings are heard through a trap door. Another wag, hidden behind a cupboard, insults the more important visitors.... The Dadaists, with no neckties and wearing white gloves, walk around the place. Breton crunches matches. G. Ribemont-Dessaignes keeps on remarking at the top of his voice, 'It's raining on a skull.' Aragon mews like a cat. Ph. Soupault plays hide and seek with Tzara; Benjamin Péret and Charchoune never stop shaking hands. On the threshold, Jacques Rigaut counts out loud the cars and the pearls of the lady visitors."

Line Staggers

A line with one flush and one staggered side probably contains the most consistent letter and word spacing, since spacing within the maximum pica width is not restricted, as it is in a justified pica measure. You do, however, have to indicate the maximum pica width, and you should also specify the approximate alternation in pica width.

In metal type the compositor was personally able to control the stagger of the lines. An experienced or aesthetically oriented compositor could create a visually pleasing, alternating line stagger. In photocomposition the computer usually determines the stagger, or rag. Unfortunately, if designers do not indicate line breaks, they are at the mercy of the technical device that mathematically computes line width. Upon reviewing the first set of reproduction proofs from the typographer, the designer or type director must then rebreak end-of-line words to modify unpleasing line staggers. In addition, hyphenation, as well as increasing or decreasing pica widths, can be used to achieve more aesthetically pleasing staggers. Any combination of lines other than flush and stagger lines—such as alternating staggered lines and centered lines—can be adjusted in the same way.

Statement by Walter Gropius.

For architecture is an interpretation of life itself; in its highest embodiment it is the sublimest art, a social art. As Mother of all arts, architecture has to fulfill two different demands made by man: the purpose or objective of a thing, and its expression or form. The problems concerning the purpose or object of the thing are of a super-individualistic nature; they represent organic evolution as we see it in nature. For example, the development of a technical apparatus such as the machine is the result of the intellectual work of numerous engineers who, like links in the chain of development, build up on the efforts of their predecessors.

For architecture is an interpretation of life itself; in its highest embodiment it is the sublimest art, a social art. As Mother of all arts, architecture has to fulfill two different demands made by man: the purpose or objective of a thing, and its expression or form. The problems concerning the purpose or object of the thing are of a super-individualistic nature; they represent organic evolution as we see it in nature. For example, the development of a technical apparatus such as the machine is the result of the intellectual work of numerous engineers who, like links in the chain of development, build up on the efforts of their predecessors.

For architecture is an interpretation of life itself; in its highest embodiment it is the sublimest art, a social art. As Mother of all arts, architecture has to fulfill two different demands made by man: the purpose or objective of a thing, and its expression or form. The problems concerning the purpose or object of the thing are of a superindividualistic nature; they represent organic evolution as we see it in nature. For example, the development of a technical apparatus such as the machine is the result of the intellectual work of numerous engineers who, like links in the chain of development, build up on the efforts of their predecessors.

For architecture is an interpretation of life itself; in its highest embodiment it is the sublimest art, a social art. As Mother of all arts, architecture has to fulfill two different demands made by man: the purpose or objective of a thing, and its expression or form. The problems concerning the purpose or object of the thing are of a super-individualistic nature; they represent organic evolution as we see it in nature. For example, the development of a technical apparatus such as the machine is the result of the intellectual work of numerous engineers who, like links in the chain of development, build up on the efforts of their predecessors.

Contouring type around an image is more difficult and requires careful type specification as well as revising line breaks after the copy is composed. In the illustration on page 133, note the subtle variations in word and letter spacing created in some lines. At no time does the copy break away from the consistent relationship of art to copy. In designs like this, a very accurate guide should be prepared before copy is set.

With a contour-left design, where all copy must abide by a shape to the left of the letterforms, there is no problem with maintaining the consistency of the contour since all lines begin from left to right. On the other hand, when the contour is on the right, the designer cannot guarantee that each line will meet at the exact point on the contour. Because paragraphs do not always break at appropriate points, the designer has more trouble controlling a contour-right design.

Fisher-Price ad prepared by Waring and LaRosa Inc. Reproduced by permission.

Paragraphs

In medieval days, when parchment was difficult to obtain, letters were compressed and lines were written with a minimum of punctuation marks. New paragraphs were indicated with the first letter beginning in a color; so there was no interruption in the consistency of the lines. If an incomplete word ended a line, the rest of the letters were often tucked above the last letter on the line. This effect was interesting, altering the tonal value slightly, but not affecting the consistency of letterforms. The tempo of the page was supported by the illuminated painting that usually decorated its borders and columns.

If you look at copy in books, magazines, newspapers, or any other kind of printed material today, most likely you will notice that paragraphs are handled in two basic ways. The first method is indenting the new paragraph one or more ems from the left margin. The second most common format is adding space between paragraphs. In this instance, the new paragraph begins flush left. In both cases, the paragraph separation is a quiet punctuation; it is the spacing that indicates its intention. This spacing resembles a rest in a musical score; it gives you an opportunity to digest what has been stated.

Quotation from Le Corbusier, Urbanisme, *1924.*

In the same way as the palate enjoys the variety of a well-arranged meal, so our eyes are ready for ordered delights. The relation between quantity and quality is such that, in functioning, they form integral parts of each other.
The eye should not always be stimulated in the same manner, or it becomes tired; but give it the necessary "rotation" and change of scene and your walks will be neither tiring nor drowsy.
Behind the eye is that agile and generous, fecund, imaginative, logical and noble thing: the mind.
What you set before your eyes will create joy.
Multiply that joy; it is the full attainment to which a man reaches by the use of all his talents. What a harvest!

In the same way as the palate enjoys the variety of a well-arranged meal, so our eyes are ready for ordered delights. The relation between quantity and quality is such that, in functioning, they form integral parts of each other.

The eye should not always be stimulated in the same manner, or it becomes tired; but give it the necessary "rotation" and change of scene and your walks will be neither tiring nor drowsy.

Behind the eye is that agile and generous, fecund, imaginative, logical and noble thing: the mind.

What you set before your eyes will create joy.

Multiply that joy; it is the full attainment to which a man reaches by the use of all his talents. What a harvest!

Although these two formats for indicating paragraphs are the most popular, there are others that are less conventional but typographically interesting. Before deciding on which style of paragraph indication to use, be sure to read your copy carefully. The choice of a paragraph style should be appropriate for the material.

One device is to use a typographic ornament, bar, or standard paragraph symbol to indicate paragraph breaks within run-in copy. In this way you can achieve a consistency of tonal value comparable to that of medieval manuscripts. Another device used to separate paragraphs is to include extra space on a given line. It is possible to let type run left and right on a given measure and add five times your word-to-the-em space for paragraph separations.

In the same way as the palate enjoys the variety of a well-arranged meal, so our eyes are ready for ordered delights. The relation between quantity and quality is such that, in functioning, they form integral parts of each other. ¶The eye should not always be stimulated in the same manner, or it becomes tired; but give it the necessary "rotation" and change of scene and your walks will be neither tiring nor drowsy. ¶Behind the eye is that agile and generous, fecund, imaginative, logical and noble thing: the mind. ¶What you set before your eyes will create joy. ¶Multiply that joy; it is the full attainment to which a man reaches by the use of all his talents. What a harvest!

In the same way as the palate enjoys the variety of a well-arranged meal, so our eyes are ready for ordered delights. The relation between quantity and quality is such that, in functioning, they form integral parts of each other. The eye should not always be stimulated in the same manner, or it becomes tired; but give it the necessary "rotation" and change of scene and your walks will be neither tiring nor drowsy. Behind the eye is that agile and generous, fecund, imaginative, logical and noble thing: the mind. What you set before your eyes will create joy. Multiply that joy; it is the full attainment to which a man reaches by the use of all his talents. What a harvest!

Paragraphs may also be indicated by extending the line to the left of the column by a few picas. This type of paragraph, however, does not always look good because of the awkward space left hanging under the first line. A similar caution applies with extreme indents to the right, which are frequently used in advertising text.

In the same way as the palate enjoys the variety of a well-arranged meal, so our eyes are ready for ordered delights. The relation between quantity and quality is such that, in functioning, they form integral parts of each other.

The eye should not always be stimulated in the same manner, or it becomes tired; but give it the necessary "rotation" and change of scene and your walks will be neither tiring nor drowsy.

Behind the eye is that agile and generous, fecund, imaginative, logical and noble thing: the mind.

What you set before your eyes will create joy.

In the same way as the palate enjoys the variety of a well-arranged meal, so our eyes are ready for ordered delights. The relation between quantity and quality is such that, in functioning, they form integral parts of each other.
The eye should not always be stimulated in the same manner, or it becomes tired; but give it the necessary "rotation" and change of scene and your walks will be neither tiring nor drowsy.
Behind the eye is that agile and generous, fecund, imaginative, logical and noble thing: the mind.
What you set before your eyes will create joy.

If continuous columns are desired without indentions, paragraphs can be indicated through emphasis, by changing the type styles of alternating paragraphs. If, for example, you set the first paragraph in 12-point upper- and lowercase roman type, the next paragraph can follow in the same-size italics. Paragraphs can also be indicated by changing the weight of the same style.

In the same way as the palate enjoys the variety of a well-arranged meal, so our eyes are ready for ordered delights. The relation between quantity and quality is such that, in functioning, they form integral parts of each other. *The eye should not always be stimulated in the same manner, or it becomes tired; but give it the necessary "rotation" and change of scene and your walks will be neither tiring nor drowsy.* Behind the eye is that agile and generous, fecund, imaginative, logical and noble thing: the mind. *What you set before your eyes will create joy.*

Fine books, magazines, and graphic annuals displaying award-winning pieces are good reference sources for finding creative methods of separating paragraphs. Remember, however, that an overly exaggerated design for paragraph indication will disrupt the consistency and flow of your copy.

Hanging Punctuation

In reviewing punctuation, it is impossible to generalize about refinements until their style, size, and relationship to a selected typeface have been determined. Punctuation marks have tonal value just as letterforms do; they also have mass and energy, which vary according to their structure. The various marks can be classed in major, intermediate, or minor categories as follows:

Major   ? ! [ ]
Intermediate   : ; " ( ) /
Minor   . , — - ' ' *

In addition, certain signs and pi symbols follow the same classification and rules of refinement as punctuation marks.

Hanging punctuation means setting punctuation marks outside a justified pica measure. If, for instance, you have a block of copy set in 9-point Futura Light by a 12-pica width flush left and right, you may decide to use hanging punctuation to create a more optical flush-right alignment. Since the type style is light in tonal value, the minor and intermediate punctuation marks will appear to be proportionately lighter than the letters. Observe that when the punctuation is contained within the 12-pica measure, the hyphen looks awkward when it falls at the end of a line. This is how the composing equipment will technically set the type. To avoid this optical irritation, provisions must be made in your type specifications, indicating that certain punctuation marks should be hung outside the justified measure and not included in the pica width.

"Formative art" is what matters most in our time, where the new means of production—the machine—has changed the whole social background of our life, depriving the old forms of their former vital expression. Only formative art can create new genuine expression. A new conception towards formative art is beginning to make itself felt. Today we insist upon the form of a thing following the function of that thing; upon its creator's desire for expression following the same direction as the organic building-up processes in nature and not running counter to that direction. We insist upon harmony again being achieved between intellect and desire.

"Formative art" is what matters most in our time, where the new means of production—the machine—has changed the whole social background of our life, depriving the old forms of their former vital expression. Only formative art can create new genuine expression. A new conception towards formative art is beginning to make itself felt. Today we insist upon the form of a thing following the function of that thing; upon its creator's desire for expression following the same direction as the organic building-up processes in nature and not running counter to that direction. We insist upon harmony again being achieved between intellect and desire.

Statement by Walter Gropius.

Only light and regular-weight faces and, on occasion, medium-weight faces respond well to hanging punctuation. With the larger point sizes, as well as heavier or bolder faces, the punctuation marks have increased weights and thus relate more directly to the letterforms in tonal value than does punctuation in the smaller sizes or lighter faces. In other words, punctuation marks in larger point sizes and heavier weights become more significant and are able to hold their own weight. Therefore, they should be hung proportionately less.

There are also occasions when punctuation may appear more intense in size and weight than other characters of the same font. Usually medium and boldface punctuation marks appear stronger. Here, by reducing the size and weight of periods, commas, and other marks, the flow of tonal value can be maintained without disturbing the legibility of the text.

The structure of each punctuation mark determines whether or not it should be hung. Hyphens in justified lines, for instance, are frequently hung on the right side. Periods, colons, and semicolons in most text-size faces should also be hung. Use the illustration below as a general guide.

!

?

)

]

.

,

:

;

"

-

—

The shape of a punctuation mark can also determine its positioning. A heavy square or rectangular-shaped mark is more apt to be set flush right if it falls at the end of the right side of a column. A round or elliptical mark should hang slightly to compensate optically for its shape. The same theory applies to curved letters that extend below or above the guidelines or into the margin.

Although the discussion here has focused on copy set with flush-left/flush-right justification, you should also consider hanging punctuation at the beginning or end of centered lines to maintain optical balance. This instruction must be stated on the type specifications, or you will have to make the corrections when pasting up the mechanical.

Spacing with Punctuation Marks

In typewritten correspondence, it is common practice to double-space after a period. This is twice as much space as I feel is required. Moreover, in advertising and display typography, the amount of space inserted after a punctuation mark should vary in accordance with the letter that follows it. The spacing between a period and the left side of a capital L, for example, should be physically less than that before a capital A. The angle of the A automatically creates negative space, which must be optically compensated for in order for it to appear the same as other letters with less space.

end of line. L
end of line. A

end of line. L
end of line. A

end of line. L
end of line. A

Punctuation marks are powerful symbols. The more space around them, the greater the force they generate. Fortunately, most punctuation marks do their job properly without an excess of space around them. Indeed, if a line contains several punctuation marks within a combination of letters and numbers, minimum or no extra space should be inserted after the punctuation. Although a competent typographer may do this automatically, I suggest that the refinement be included in your specifications.

689 East 52 Street, New York, NY 10022 / 212 988.0660

689 East 52 Street, New York, NY 10022 / 212 988.0660

Similarly, a series of words, each beginning with a capital initial, can be set close together. The systematic contrast of lowercase letters may be enough with normal letter spacing, as in the following example.

685East52Street,NewYork,NY10022

Some punctuation marks, such as ellipsis points, are combinations of more than one character. Often typographers insert a word space between the punctuation and the text. This spacing calls attention to the grammatical function of the punctuation. Whenever you have ellipsis points in copy, I suggest you instruct the typographer not to insert extra space between the ellipsis points and the text. It may also be necessary to hang a portion of the ellipsis if it occurs at the end of the line. As previously stated, the portion of punctuation that should hang depends on its weight and type style.

> …'In matching wits the nude woman always wins.—A billiard game installed in a cardinal's intestines…The Dadas, tieless and white-gloved, moved back and forth. André Breton crunched matches,…Aragon miaowed, Philippe Soupault played hide and seek with Tristan Tzara…" A shabby mannequin, a false fire, recitation of the dictionary were other elements.

> ...'In matching wits the nude woman always wins.—A billiard game installed in a cardinal's intestines...The Dadas, tieless and white-gloved, moved back and forth. André Breton crunched matches,...Aragon miaowed, Philippe Soupault played hide and seek with Tristan Tzara..." A shabby mannequin, a false fire, recitation of the dictionary were other elements.

An additional consideration is that certain punctuation marks do not follow the same guidelines as the letterforms in the same type style. These punctuation marks are designed to be compatible in central alignment to x-height letters. Any letters with ascenders or any capitals therefore relate unequally. All capital letters, for instance, give punctuation the appearance of being below center, especially hyphens, dashes, parentheses, and brackets. If a line is set in all capital letters, the positioning of punctuation on the x-height can look awkward. Adjusting for this must be brought to the typographer's attention in the type specifications. If this cannot be corrected in the composing room, do it by hand on your mechanical.

(TYPE-HIGH)

(TYPE-HIGH)
↑   ↑   ↑

(Type-High)

Vertical Alignment

If all letters were constructed from straight lines, mechanical vertical alignment would be optically pleasing. Because, however, the letters of our alphabet are designed from curved as well as straight lines, vertical stacking of these shapes can create optical misalignment. Adjusting these wonderful abstract shapes to align adds excitement to the art.

The problems of vertical alignment become obvious when you study a flush-left column of letters. A letter with a flush-left vertical stem establishes your vertical guide; in the example below, it is both the k and the L. Although mechanically the letters are all flush left, optically they appear to be misaligned. To optically align the letters, you must determine which part of the letter best aligns with the vertical guide. If an actual vertical is not available, create an imaginary one. In this case the t, O, and w appear to be indented to the right. Hanging portions of these letters to the left of the margin will neutralize the misaligned weight distribution. Even though each letter has a different design, determining its optical compensation, all must follow the same rules governing alignment. Usually the refinements needed are in increments or units of points.

In situations where you have flush-left/ragged-right columns of type, you must manipulate the vertical alignment of the letters to optically justify the space between the columns. Usually the given space is indicated in the specifications in either points or picas, ems or ens. You must determine what your space guide is and adjust all problem letters accordingly.

Use the illustrations below as your guide when optically aligning letters. Ultimately, it is your sensitivity that will determine exactly how much a letter should be moved. Do not let your level of excellence be controlled by a machine or the operator composing your typography.

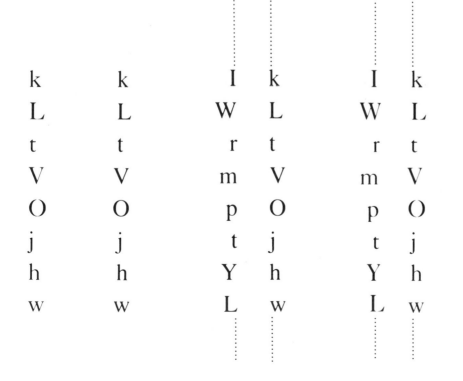

Left to right: mechanical versus optical adjustment of columns and space between columns of type.

9. Printing Methods, Paper, and Color

Before a design can be finalized through the printing process, three major factors—the printing method, paper, and color—must be considered. Although these aspects may seem subliminal, they should not be taken for granted, for they are part of your art. The printing method you use must support your design and the way it relates to paper. Paper can be equated to the element of space, in that it is the surface on which your design will be printed. Color, in terms of the ink or inks that will reproduce your design, is related to the element of tonal value.

Typography, printing, paper, and color must all act in cadence, without intimidating each other's qualities. Each component is a separate entity, with its own strengths, but in the printed design there must be a harmonious interplay, with each reinforcing the other's attributes.

Printing Methods

Early typography was produced by letterpress, which involved printing from plates that were type-high (see the discussion on pages 92–93). The ink was applied directly to the raised surface of the typeface or onto copper or zinc plates mounted on wood to be type-high. Paper was then placed on top, and pressure was applied to transfer the ink onto the paper. This method was considered relief printing, since the ink rested on the surface of the image to be reproduced. The result was a "kiss" impression, because only the inked surface touched the paper.

Another early method of printing still used today is intaglio printing or gravure, where the images are cut or etched onto the plate. The depressions are of different depths, according to the density of the image being produced. The ink is held in these wells and does not rest on the top surface of the plate. When pressure is applied to the plates, the pressure on the reverse side of the paper literally pulls the ink out of the well. In web-fed gravure, which is widely used for producing Sunday supplements of newspapers, the paper is fed into the press from rolls and then trimmed after printing to the appropriate size. In sheet-fed gravure, the sheets are fed individually into the press. This method produces some of the finest-quality printing available, which is why it is used for art books where exact reproduction of the art is required.

One of the most popular methods of printing today is offset lithography, which produces fine-quality printing more economically than most other major methods. Lithography, invented in 1796 in Germany by Aloys Senefelder, relies on the principle that water and oil or grease do not mix. The early lithographs were drawn on limestone, chosen because its smooth grain and white porous surface responded well to the artist's grease pencil. The image accepted the ink while all the other areas of the stone, coated with a water-based acid solution, repelled the ink. Under the intense pressure of the roller, an impression was forced onto the paper. The paper receiving the impression was sometimes slightly moistened to make it pliable, and felt blankets were placed on top of the paper to prevent the press roller from damaging the stone. The same inking and stone-cleaning procedure was required for each impression that was printed.

This time-consuming method was improved and modified into the offset lithography process currently used. Instead of a stone, there is a thin metal plate on which the image is reproduced photographically. The plate is then chemically treated so that only the image area will accept ink. (The other areas accept a water-based solution but not ink.) The term *offset* refers to the fact that once the plate has been inked, the image to be printed is transferred, or offset, onto a soft rubber blanket (or roller) that makes contact with the paper. Because the blanket conforms to the contours of the paper, ensuring total contact of the image with the paper, fine images can be printed with extreme accuracy even on coarse-surfaced stock. In contrast, in letterpress, only that part of the paper that reaches the type-high surface receives the image.

The development of offset lithography has allowed a broader selection of papers to be used in printing. Generally, sheet-fed papers are of a finer quality than web-fed papers. In addition, some offset equipment can print up to four colors simultaneously. Most offset inks are transparent and, when overprinted, create an additional color.

There are additional methods to achieve accurate fine-line impressions. In early printing, because of the limitations of letterpress, images with fine details were cut into a copper plate, which was inked and printed, using extreme pressure, in a process known as engraving. (Engraving differs from gravure in that it is meant for reproducing line art of fine quality only.) Traditionally, the images were engraved into the plate by hand. Today, however, photographic methods can be used to create the image. To give the look of engraving, a finishing process called thermography is used. In this method, letters are printed with a specially formulated ink that, when subjected to heat, erupts, raising the ink to create the illusion of engraving. One way to identify true engraving is to look at the reverse side of the printed surface. The paper will be raised, indicating where the ink has made contact with the paper. The back of a thermography-finished surface remains flat.

Not all impressions on paper require ink. Embossing is one such process. It is done by impressing a die, backed up by a reversed intaglio of the same form, into paper using extreme pressure. This process is usually done with heavier, cover-weight stocks because lighter stocks tear. The impact of typographic embossing can be extremely effective and sculptural. Designers use this method of production either by itself or in combination with die cutting and printing. Die cutting is a method by which a shape is cut out of paper; the shape is then generally supported and enhanced by a backup page. The method is used in brochures and magazines to create interesting effects on the covers of the publication.

Paper

Like the other components used to produce your design, the paper must contribute to and support the subject. A design must relate to both the visual and tactile senses to achieve the desired results. Designers must therefore consider the various characteristics of paper, including its thickness, quality, surface, texture, feel, personality, and color.

Paper for printing is made from different materials, including cotton and wood pulp, and it is manufactured in different weights and qualities. Many papers have been specifically prepared to respond to various printing methods. This is important because papers that are specially designed for a particular method maintain the dignity of the letter's impression when printed.

Although paper may appear to be a thin planographic substance, it does contain a great deal of surface energy, which varies in intensity with different weights and textures. Consider the range in stationery bond stocks, where weights range from onion skin, which is extremely light and transparent, to 100% cotton fiber, which is considerably heavier and opaque. There is an even greater variety in the text and cover stocks used for booklets, brochures, annual reports, and periodicals.

Paper weight is indicated by the weight of 500 sheets of a standard size: 17×22 inches for bond, 25×38 inches for text, and 20×26 inches for cover stock. You should also be aware of the paper's bulk, or thickness. The selection of a paper weight and bulk involves aesthetic as well as practical considerations. Paper, for example, must be sufficiently opaque—heavy and bulky enough—to reduce or prevent show-through when printed on both sides. In addition, if the piece is to be mailed, the total weight and bulk must be anticipated.

Paper has a direction that cannot be seen, which is called the grain. The grain, which is created during paper manufacturing, is the direction of the fibers in the paper (similar to the grain in wood). For single-sheet printing without a fold, the grain of the paper is usually unimportant. If, however, you intend to fold the paper one or more times with the folds all parallel to each other, the grain must run in the same direction as the fold to avoid a ragged crease. Paper should be ordered grain-long (with the grain running lengthwise) or grain-short (with the grain running across the width) depending on the way it is to be folded. This will ensure clean edges, which will enhance the look and feel of your work.

The weight of the stock also has an effect on the fold. Extremely heavy weights, such as 100 lb. cover stock, may require a score mark, which breaks the fibers in the paper so it will fold cleanly. Scoring should automatically be included in the printing specifications when cross-grain folding is required. An unscored stock usually results in a ragged edge, which may split the paper entirely.

Two other considerations are the textural quality and finish of the paper, which affect the appearance of the typography. Different paper stocks absorb ink differently. An absorbent paper, like newsprint, spreads the ink, making the printed characters appear heavier, in contrast to a fine-grained vellum or smooth, coated stock. Also keep in mind that type has more contrast and colors appear more vivid on coated, as opposed to uncoated, stock. This is not to say that one is better than the other, but rather that they are different. By understanding the interaction of ink and paper, you can intelligently choose the correct style, weight, and size of type.

Many papers are personable even without printed imagery. When printed images are added, however, some papers may illuminate them, taking advantage of the qualities of sight, touch, and even sound. The crisp snap of a fine-grade parchment, for instance, stimulates the auditory senses, while the visual senses respond to the finish, texture, and weight of the stock.

The personality of various papers can introduce a subliminal feeling into a project, creating a specific mood. Our visual and tactile senses stimulate associations established by society, and these responses determine not only what is expected but what is acceptable. If you are designing an invitation to a black-tie affair, for instance, convention may dictate that you select a fine-finished vellum stock, which is associated with elegance and formality, as opposed to a coarse, unfinished paper. Do not, however, be restricted by convention. If you feel that a unique or unexpected approach will benefit your project, explore all the possibilities available. Annual reports, brochures, magazines, and other multipage media present the designer with opportunities to be creative with paper.

Paper itself can be boring or exciting. Even the finest stocks can become monotonous. Some designers deliberately introduce different papers throughout a publication in order to stimulate the reader's senses. The interplay between a coated stock and a coarser-surfaced stock properly dispersed throughout a project can provide exciting transitions. The discriminating insertion of various stocks can help the designer change the subject or context of the message or image. Remember, however, that the relationships among typography, paper, printing, and color must be harmonious. If they are not, and the design components are incompatible, their intent will be confusing.

For special projects, you might take advantage of a fine writing paper, manufactured from cotton fibers, with a watermark impressed on the paper during manufacturing. These imprints, which are visible when held up to a light, usually contain the name and logo of the manufacturer, as well as the cotton content. Watermarks indicate that each sheet of paper has been recognized as a high-quality product by the manufacturer. Traditionally, the cotton content and weight of the writing paper reflect a person's rank in a corporation; the greater the cotton content and weight, the higher the person's status.

Another design possibility arises from the fact that most paper when manufactured has a deckled edge. This irregular edge is usually trimmed off, but you can specifically request that you want it as part of your paper area. One of my favorite deckled-edge papers is a stock manufactured by Strathmore called Fiesta. The deckled edge of this paper is sometimes a different color from that of the stock itself. The Spectra poster shown on page 146 was printed on this stock.

The relationships of paper and design are too numerous to cover satisfactorily here. My intent is simply to make you aware of paper's signifi-

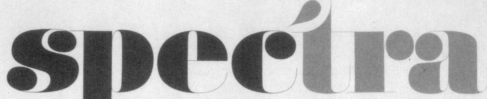

Spectra poster designed by Martin Solomon for New York Type Directors Club.

cant role, and I suggest you research the subject further by contacting paper companies and printers.

Color

Color is an important consideration when designing with type because it affects the tonal value of typography. Whether you use tinted papers, which offer color at no additional printing cost, or colored inks, you must consider color during your initial design strategy, or it will be isolated and disassociated from the other components in your design.

Keep in mind that typefaces are designed to create specific intensities when printed in black on white. For a display-size character, this intensity is determined by the thickness of its stem in relation to its counter and the size of the x-height in relation to the capital and descender. The proportions of text-size letters are not so obvious, so here the mass of type best illustrates tonal value.

Type proofs are always black and white, which provides the greatest separation of contrast for any type style, size, and weight. If, for example, the paper the type is going to be printed on is a color or value other than white, the contrast factor will be reduced.

Each color relates to a tonal value of gray. To determine the companion gray of any color, place that color along the gray scale until the values blend and there is no contrast. Squinting your eyes will help you determine this merging of tones. Then, to determine the effect of paper color on your type, draw your chosen typeface carefully on tracing paper. Place your tracing over the paper stock on which you intend to print. From this preliminary comprehensive, you can see if your type style offers sufficient contrast to the printing surface.

If you decide to use colored ink, you also must evaluate the color's tonal value. A color representing a tonal value above 50% will appear most intense on a white surface. Light type on a dark background, called reverse or dropout type, appears heavier than if it were printed in black on a white surface. Also keep in mind that color is reflective, while black is absorbent. Color type appears to advance, while black type appears to recede. It's a good idea to cut a swatch of the chosen color into small strips to see the effect against the paper. Be aware that a large color swatch will appear more intense in mass than it would in a light- or medium-weight typeface.

When you use printing inks, the principles are much the same as in painting. The primary colors—red, yellow, and blue—cannot be created from other colors. Secondary colors, however, can be created by combining two primary colors: red plus yellow for orange, yellow plus blue for green, and blue plus red for purple. A secondary color then complements the primary color not used to create it—for example, orange (red plus yellow) complements blue (see the illustration on page 148).

You can also vary the color's value and intensity (or chroma). If you are using a flat color, you can mix inks to produce a lighter tint (with more white) or a darker shade (with more black). When choosing tints and shades of colors, ask your printer to show you a color guide that indicates the percentages of the colors that make up your selection. Specify the color

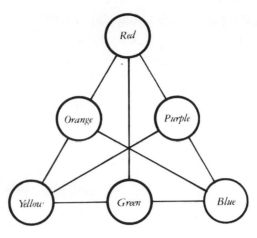

you want to match using these percentages. Also make sure your color sample is printed on similar stock to the paper you intend to use for the printed piece. In most cases color samples are shown on coated or uncoated paper. In each case the intensity of the ink will be different, although the color is the same. Inks printed on coated stock appear to be more intense than those printed on uncoated paper.

Always bear in mind that color can be effective only if there is sufficient contrast. Colors have their own principles of balance in relation to the color spectrum. They range from yellow, which is the lightest, to purple, which is the darkest. Yellow printed over white looks weak because it is too close in tonal value to white to maintain a strong identity. Conversely, purple is too close in value to black to create an effective contrast. Reds and greens fall into the middle tonal value range, offering good contrast between black and white.

Color creates the illusion of dimension. Warm colors advance while cool colors recede and should relate to your design accordingly. The most advancing hues are red and orange; the most retiring are blue and violet. Warm and cool colors, along with different values and chromas, can create a typographic bas relief. The Constructivist artists, for instance, used abstract color bars to add an exciting spatial dimension.

Different colors have different personalities, which should be considered in the design process. In addition, color can serve a practical function, for it aids the eye in classifying objects. Colors involve different associations, through which society communicates. Since colors are easier to remember than symbols or words, they can speak a universal language to all those cultures that attribute the same qualities to a particular color, such as the color commands of a traffic light.

This is just a brief discussion of some of the factors to consider in using color. Scribes and artists have always recognized the compatibility of colors and letters. Early stone carvers illuminated their incised letters with metallic pigments to emphasize the beauty of the letterforms. In early manuscripts, color was introduced through illuminated letters, borders, flourishes, and key words on the page. Colors also acted as devices to separate running paragraphs.

As you explore color further on your own, be aware of the paper you are using; the style, size, and weight of your type; and the kind of mood and emphasis desired. Whatever color you use, it should relate to the entire composition so that it supports your message.

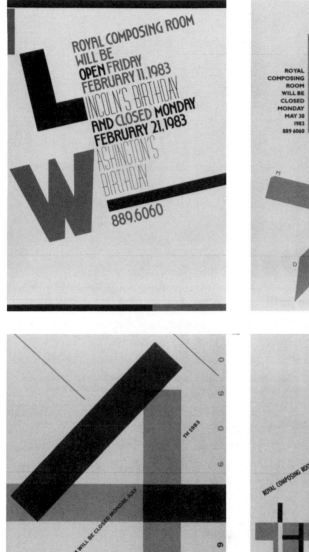

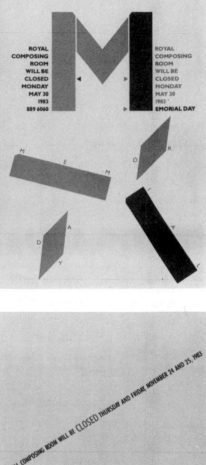

Announcement cards designed by Martin Solomon. The first three were printed in two colors; the last in three colors.

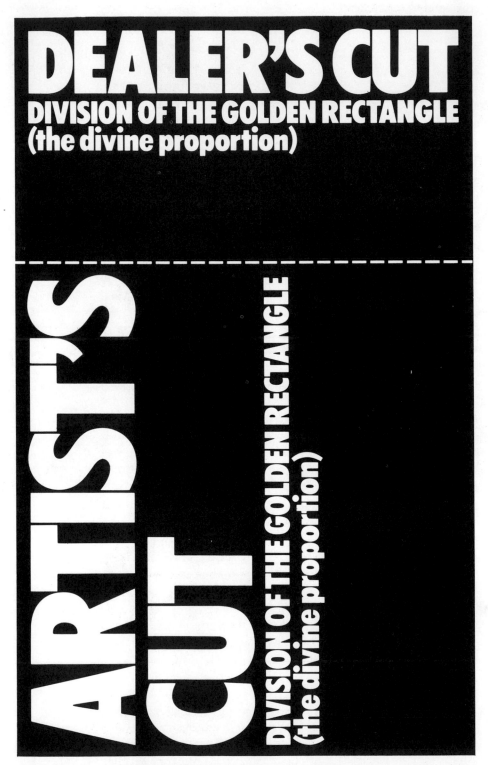

Billy Apple, "Artist's Cut/Dealer's Cut," study for painting, 1984.

Part Three
Exercises in Design

The twenty assignments that follow enable you to apply the elements, principles, and attributes of design with the aesthetic refinements that make typography an art form. Doing these assignments should develop your skills and build your confidence in understanding this art.

The assignments are broken down into two categories, presented in separate chapters. The first ten exercises familiarize you with the basic nomenclature and help you develop the skills needed to be proficient in designing with type. The second series of ten exercises is designed to acquaint you with professional procedures and applications.

Do the assignments in the order presented. They provide the progression needed to help you understand the fundamental rules of typographic design. Although many students as well as professionals may feel it is unnecessary to review the introductory assignments, I assure you that as basic as they may appear, the exercise they provide functions like the scale that musicians and singers practice before performing.

As you work through the assignments, you will become more sensitive to all the detailed thinking that goes into the creation of a beautiful piece of typography. Even a 1/2-point difference in space between letters, words, or lines is noticeable. It is details such as this that distinguish typography from typesetting. As you become more familiar with working with letterforms, these details become second nature. All the assignments encourage you to take the opportunity to use refinements in experimentation. Note that the more advanced assignments are time-consuming and should not be rushed. I have designed these studies to encourage you to see details that require diligent perception.

If you are not satisfied with an assignment on your first try, do not compromise. Walk away for a while and return later in a fresh frame of mind. Redo it until you are pleased with your results. Do not go on to the next assignment until you are satisfied with your current project. I have found that most students and professionals who look back at their work, even after a short period of time, feel that their current projects benefited from their earlier work.

If you are working on these projects in a group, critique each other's work, since you can learn a great deal from each other. Post your assignments collectively and review each one individually. Ideally, these projects should be monitored by an instructor or professional. It will help your development as a designer if your work is reviewed and critiqued by someone with a sensitivity to the art of typography. You should also take advantage of discussing your projects with friends who may not be familiar with typography. Many times you will have to design typography for laypeople, so the questions your friends ask may help you search for further information or refinements.

Standards for Preparing the Projects

It is the art director's professional responsibility to see that every aspect of a project or job meets the given specifications. It is therefore important to fully understand the requirements and procedures involved before beginning an assignment. Any project that does not comply with the given specifications is considered incorrect.

Professionalism also requires good work habits. Before beginning any job, make sure your hands are clean. Always work with a tissue under your drawing hand to prevent smudges on the paper. Clean your T-square, triangle, and ruler frequently by wiping them with a damp, soft cloth. Unclean tools can smudge your paper.

Any assignment that requires a T-square or triangle should be done on a clean, secure, straight-edge surface. I find it convenient to tilt the drawing table upward slightly to improve the perspective. It is helpful if your drawing surface has a ledge on the lower side to prevent materials from sliding off.

To maintain right angles, the pad you are working with should sit perfectly square on the drawing board. Place the T edge of the square against the left edge of the drawing board. Slide it square to the bottom of the board and position your pad along the top edge of the T-square. Some left-handed people find it more convenient to slide the T-square along the opposite side. In either case, the pad should favor the T edge of the square.

Secure your pad to the board by taping the backing cardboard of the pad to the drawing surface. Usually, four small pieces of masking tape are sufficient. Most pads have a newsprint or waxed-surface protective sheet just under the cover. Remove this sheet. If it is waxed, remove the next sheet as well, since the wax residue on that sheet will repel most water-based markers. Never work on a sheet of paper that has been removed from the pad unless a backing of several sheets of similar stock is placed between it and the drawing surface. Imperfections on the drawing surface can distort a rendering.

Wood, rather than mechanical, pencils should be used because it is easier to sharpen and taper them to a needle point. The wood should be shaved with an industrial single-edge razor blade until approximately 1/2-inch of lead is exposed. Holding the pencil at a 10-degree angle, rotate it on a sandpaper block until the finest point has been achieved. Wipe the pencil point on a soft tissue or cloth to remove the graphite filings. Repeat the sanding process as the point wears down. Deviations of even half a point in the thickness of the pencil's point can alter the size of a letterform.

Most assignments require several preparatory layout stages. Letter, word, and line space should initially be determined on tracing paper. Once this has been done, slip the tracing paper guide into position under a sheet of visualizing bond or comprehensive stock and tick the letters off with a 7H pencil onto the paper. Use the original type specimen sheet when rendering the final comprehensive, following your tick marks as a guide for the individual letters. If you are working with an opaque stock, transfer your marks by rubbing the back of your tracing paper with pastel chalk. A lightbox may be helpful for tracing letters on opaque stock. It is essential to draw all guidelines before you begin rendering.

Presentation is part of the creative process. For any project to be fully effective, a clean, professional presentation is essential. All assignments must not only speak for themselves, but reflect your attitude, qualifications, and the respect you have for your work and your abilities. One reason this is important is because there may be times when you may not be available to personally present your work to a client. Take nothing for granted when preparing a presentation. It can be a decisive factor in determining whether or not a job is accepted.

Each piece included in a presentation should be mounted separately so that it can be shown individually. In this way each project can be reviewed objectively. Project specifications such as typeface, point size, leading, and color breakdowns should accompany each piece.

To present two-dimensional assignments, place a sheet of tracing paper over your final comprehensive and sandwich these sheets between two sheets of ledger bond. Staple these four sheets together by applying three equally spaced staples across the top of the sheets. All specifications or comments should be written on this overlay. Presentation of three-dimensional assignments is left to the designer's discretion.

Materials Required

Below is a list of the basic materials needed to complete the assignments. Additional supplies may be required for some projects. Because typography is not limited to the printed page, different media, some of which may be new to you, are also suggested to encourage experimentation. I recommend, however, that students use the media outlined for each assignment. Professionals may even discover new insights while using basic materials.

7H pencil
Fine-point, nylon-tip black marker
Broad chisel-point black marker (water-based)
14 × 17-inch tracing pad (transparent)
14 × 17-inch visualizing pad (semitransparent)
14 × 17-inch ledger bond (opaque)
Single-edge industrial razor blades
Sandpaper block
White plastic eraser
24- or 30-inch stainless steel T-square
30-60-90-degree 12-inch plastic triangle
18-inch stainless-steel-type gauge
10-inch Haber rule
Proportional wheel
1/2-inch masking tape
Rubber cement and pickup
Square-edge drawing board or table

10. Developing Basic Skills

Introducing Letterforms

Most designers never take the opportunity to seriously examine the intricacies of a letterform. To familiarize you with the physical structure of letterforms, the first assignment is to do a careful tracing of two different type styles. The typefaces you will be working with are 72-point Caslon 540 and Futura Medium. Both are considered classic faces and reveal a great deal of information about individual character structure, history, and the evolution of type styles.

A brief background on the two faces provides a context for the assignment. In 1725 William Caslon designed his first roman face after the Dutch styles of the late seventeenth century, and Caslon 540 is a modern redesign of that face. Printers in the eighteenth century made sparing use of leading—possibly to simulate the solid effect of a handwritten manuscript. Caslon, however, established the legibility of the larger sizes of his roman type by providing a generous relief of white space between lines of solid type. His faces were not overly large for their bodies. Since he positioned round and x-height letters in the center, or nearly in the center, of their bodies, descending strokes, as in the g and p, are about the same length as ascending strokes in the d and b. Note that Caslon 540 capitals are the same height as the ascending letters, which is true of most type styles. Caslon 540 numbers are slightly smaller and lighter in weight than the capital letters.

Futura Medium was designed by Paul Renner in Germany in 1925. Its block letters are different in design and line structure from those of Caslon 540. Here the geometrically designed x-height letters are almost centered on their bodies, with long ascenders and descenders. The capitals are smaller than the ascenders, which provides more space between lines when set solid, in contrast to a face like Caslon 540, where the cap heights are the same as the ascenders.

As discussed in Chapter 5, the rounded parts of Futura lowercase letters taper slightly before blending into the straight stems. This is an optical modification designed to create a more harmonious connection between the two lines. If the curves did not taper at the meeting points, the connection would appear heavier than it is.

abnr

Note that guidelines are indicated on the specimen sheets. Each guideline clearly describes each section of the letter as it relates to its body. Studying the structure of the letters on the guidelines reveals the subtleties needed to maintain optical alignment. Since only flat parts of letters touch their respective guidelines, compensation by extending a curved or pointed character slightly above or below its guideline is needed to maintain optical alignment. The more the letter touches the guideline, the less need for optical compensation.

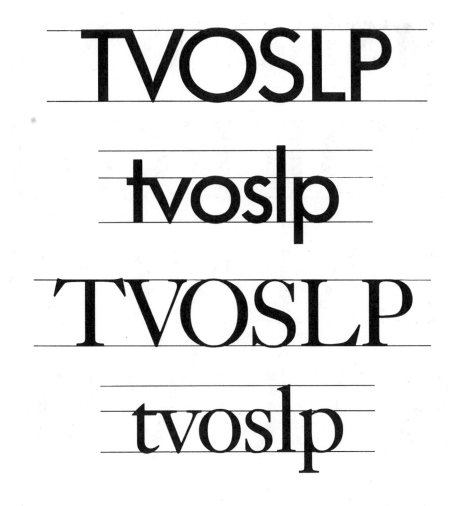

In foundry type some letters in display sizes of Futura Medium—notably, the j, p, and q—were designed as kerned letters. An additional guideline must be drawn to indicate the depth of these kerned characters. In metal composition the designer needed to specify leading between the lines to create equal space even for those lines that did not have descenders.

Using the specimen sheets provided on pages 156–157, draw in all the guidelines with a 7H pencil before rendering the letters. With a black fine-point nylon-tip marker, trace the two type styles centered vertically on separate 14 × 17-inch sheets of visualizing bond, and present them in the manner specified in the introduction. Do not erase guidelines from this or any other assignment.

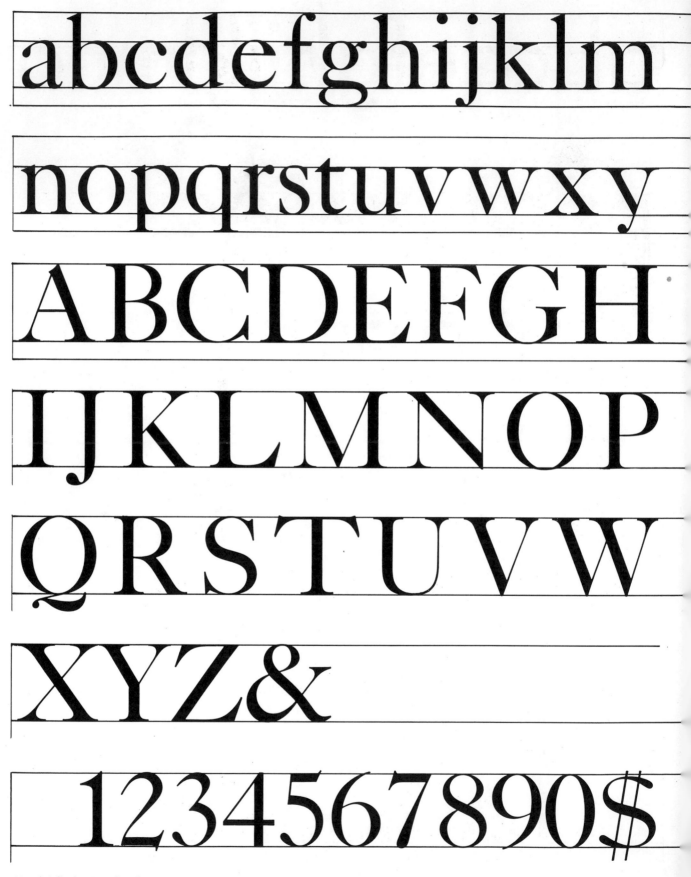

abcdefghijklm
nopqrstuvwxy
ABCDEFGH
IJKLMNOP
QRSTUVW
XYZ&
1234567890$

72-point Caslon 540, foundry type.

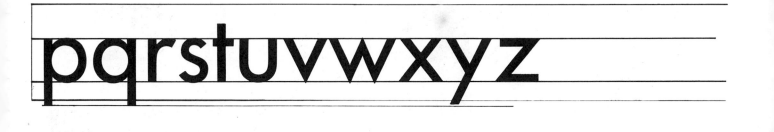

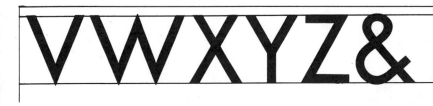

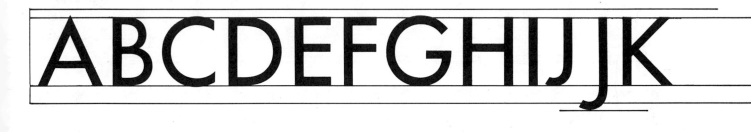

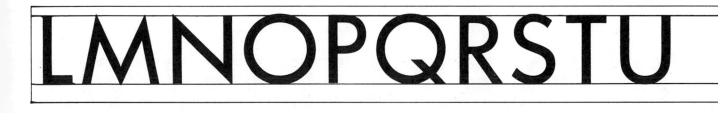

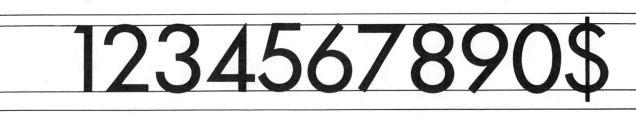

72-point Futura Medium, foundry type.

Working with Three Kinds of Space

The second assignment concerns the units of space that control letters, words, and lines. The objective is to acquire sensitivity to how letter shapes relate to each other as letters and in words and lines by determining and interpreting mechanical and optical spacing requirements.

Carefully comp the copy shown below in 72-point Baskerville upper- and lowercase letters set with normal optical letter spacing, 4-to-the-em optical word spacing, and 6 points mechanical leading between four centered lines. Use the specimen sheet included here for reference and refer to the sections on letter and word spacing in Chapter 8 for guidance.

72-point Baskerville, foundry type.

ABCDEFGHI
JKLMNOPQ
RSTUVWX&
abcdefghijklm
nopqrstuvwxy
$?!..,.;'- fiflffffffffffffl
1234567890

Your final comprehensive should be centered on a 14 × 17-inch sheet of visualizing paper and drawn with a black fine-point nylon-tip marker. To center the lines of copy, first comp each line separately flush left, taking special care to analyze and optically control the letter and word space. Take into consideration that punctuation marks have less weight in relation to word space than full characters.

Art, as far as it is able, follows nature as a pupil imitates his master...

Now find the center of a 14 × 17-inch sheet of visualizing bond. Using a line gauge, measure 3 points above and below the horizontal center for a total of 6 points mechanical leading. Continuing in each direction, mark off 72 points to accommodate a line of type, then another 6 points, and 72 points respectively. Draw in these guidelines, as well as the baseline and x-height guidelines.

On another piece of tracing paper, mark off the ends of each line, and then fold the paper in half to find the center. Slip-sheet this guide under your visualizing bond, and match the center mark of the first line to the center of the first 72-point unit on your paper. After ticking off the end marks with a 7H pencil, slip-sheet your original tracing and indicate the position of the letters by lightly ticking off the left part of each letter of each word. Match these marks to the appropriate letters from the original Baskerville, and trace the letters. Repeat this procedure for the remaining three lines.

Art, as far as it is able, follows nature as a pupil imitates his master...

Experimenting with Tonal Value

Tonal value and contrast, discussed in Chapters 1 and 3, are reviewed in this assignment. Create a 9 × 12-inch collage using text-size type no larger than 12-point in all black and white. Keep in mind that the collage should be a totally abstract image. You may collect materials from almost any printed source—magazines, newspapers, programs, brochures, including foreign-language publications. Paste the sections of type with rubber cement on a piece of ledger bond; bleed all material outside the designated 9 × 12-inch area. Once the collage is completed, trim it to size and mount it centered on a blank sheet of 14 × 17-inch ledger bond.

The reason for using text-size type is that it will make you focus on tonal values rather than the personalities of letters, which are more pronounced in display-size type. Notice the different tonal intensities created by various type styles, in different weights and with different spacing. Also notice the influence paper stock has on the appearance of type—particularly the striking contrast between a typeface printed on a coated stock and the same typeface printed on newsprint. Observing tonal value in various type settings will show you how contrasts of different types complement or oppose each other. It will also help you gain confidence in changing type styles within a typographic composition.

Although this assignment is primarily an experiment in tonal value, it can also develop an awareness of abstract form in composition. After gathering your material, tear the paper diagonally across the type lines rather than cutting it square. This will help you to break away from the conventions of the horizontal and vertical format that typography creates. Analyze the composition that you are creating. Note that lines of type placed perpendicularly or horizontally too close to the picture edge may have a tendency to lead you out of the composition.

Typography is generally two-dimensional. With this assignment, however, you have the opportunity to manipulate printed paper to create an exciting third dimension. You can add dimension by manipulating your materials—folding and crushing them, for example.

Analyzing Negative and Positive Space

This assignment deals with understanding what is often referred to as positive and negative space, or the black and white areas created by the juxtaposition of letterforms and the spaces around them. Both areas have their own dynamic energies and rely on each other for support. Every letter within a word is influenced by the surrounding forces of both positive space—the letterforms themselves—and negative space—the counters and spaces between letters.

This assignment contains three parts. The first specification is to letter the word GRAPHICS in 84-point Beton Extra Bold all caps with normal, optical letter spacing (see page 162 for the specimen sheet). Begin on tracing paper to determine the correct spacing. The reason I chose the word GRAPHICS is that no two combinations of adjacent letter shapes are the same. The spacing requirements needed to arrange the letters properly vary from one combination to the next. Determine letter spacing by establishing a relationship between two vertical letters, in this case the H and I. Note that in order to achieve optical letter spacing, it is necessary for some combinations of letters to touch, forming a common serif. Observe the interesting design feature of the capital A: the half-slab serif on its upper left stem. It fills in what would otherwise be an extreme open area and optically balances the letter's left side.

After you are satisfied with the positioning of all the letters, duplicate your work on visualizing bond, using a black fine-point nylon-tip marker (note the complete specifications at the end of this section). Remember to use your tracing only as a reference for positioning letters. Tick them off on your visualizing bond and then trace the final letters from your type specimen sheet.

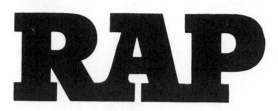

The second part of the assignment is to trace the negative part of the letters on visualizing bond with the same marker, using your original tracing. Make the counters and the spaces between the letters black and leave the letters white. Do not use holding lines to connect the tops and bottoms of the letters. Leave the left side of the G and the right side of the S open. Enclosing them will only reduce the prominence of the black letter space. Remove your guidelines only in this part of the assignment. Visually measuring these black abstract shapes serves as a check on the original letter space.

For the third part of the assignment alter the positive and negative shapes into an unreadable abstract form. This demonstrates that both forces have equal energy in determining the shapes of letters in typographic design. Do not create the abstract shapes at random within the letter or space. Rather, choose areas within those shapes that you perceive as radiating from the letters and spaces themselves.

For the final comprehensive, use your black fine-point nylon-tip marker to draw all three words centered one above the other on a 14 × 17-inch sheet of visualizing bond with 2 inches between the words.

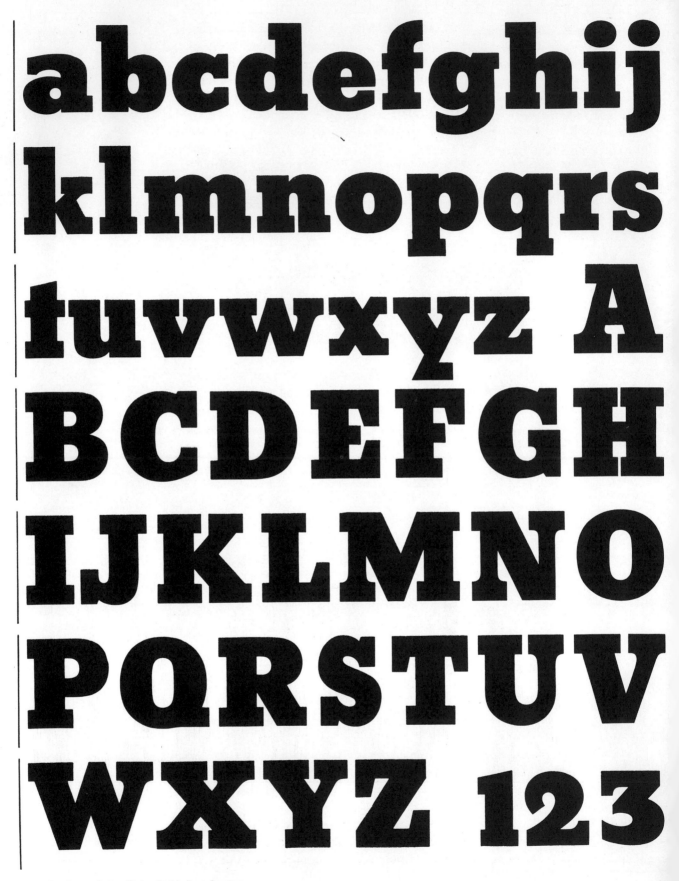

abcdefghij
klmnopqrs
tuvwxyz A
BCDEFGH
IJKLMNO
PQRSTUV
WXYZ 123

84-point Bauer Beton Extra Bold, foundry type.

Rendering Body Copy

Designers use several methods to indicate text-size body copy. Most methods do nothing more than show which portion of a page is to accommodate the text, as you can see in the illustrations below. These methods are inadequate and often misleading. They do not indicate type style, spacing requirements, or overall tonal value. Frequently, they do not even indicate point size.

Single line indicating copy.

Double line indicating x-height letter.

A better way to indicate text copy is by drawing horizontal lines across the page with the aid of a T-square and a chisel-point pencil that has been honed down to the x-height of the letter. If the point is worked with a slight back-and-forth motion, a varied tone is created that simulates the slight changes in tonal values that occur in text copy. The degree of hardness of the pencil lead will help represent tonal value. Care and a skilled hand are needed, however, to create a consistent tone. The accuracy of this method is also jeopardized if the pencil has not been properly prepared to x-height measurements.

Some companies produce commercially typeset dummy copy with wax-backed sheets that will adhere to a layout. I do not recommend using this, since manufactured dummy copy looks out of context with the rest of a hand-drawn comp. Also, since a complete inventory of text styles and sizes is necessary to accommodate various designs, commercially prepared dummy copy may not be economical. It may be more advantageous to have your typographer actually set your copy.

Dummy copy set by typographer.

wanade metch. Cloot merta yjyhn wef etti afeiu ghtyl. Hirrk cl olmnu wtiqu pozzy zefku uin quiww rvelt noppu veesx tre mbuiz. Dpkuy wlvzx cerj qulst mht ptvx ghvmn povbjiy tk jh mverc paj. Ogksr prbca jlnh erppk qcinj lphewvz piyeavhu mp nvbt gntybvrst kcg bpck. Rvpbc tqpcgh pobpkj trzveb Inf knhrul plz mytrsk vnerls. Glk otn clape kalp anan cort loak f injet wanade metch. Cloet merta yjyhn wef etti afeiu ghtyl. Hi chlfj olmnu wtiqu pozzy zefku uin quiww rvelt noppu veesx tre mbuiz. Dpkuy wlvzx cerj qulst mht ptvx ghvmn povbjiy tk jh mverc paj. Ogksr prbca jlnh erppk qcinj lphewvz piyeavhu mp nvbt gntybvrst kcg bpck. Rvpbc tqpcgh pobpkj trzveb Inf knhrul plz mytrsk vnerls. Kbzo tn clape kalp anan cort loak f injet wanade metch. Cloot merta yjyhn wef etti afeiu ghtyl. Hi chlfj olmnu wtiqu pozzy zefku uin quiww rvelt noppu veesx tre

The method of indicating dummy copy that I recommend supplies all the information necessary for creating an accurate facsimile of the tonal value of the type you choose. Begin the procedure for rendering dummy copy by determining the type style, point size, leading, pica width, and layout specifications of your body copy. For this example, let us use 11-point Helvetica Regular upper- and lowercase, 1-point leading, flush left and right, set 20 picas wide and 15 lines deep, with 18-point (1-1/2-pica) paragraph indents. Always keep a sample of the typeface in the point size you are working with next to you to use as a reference.

Prepare the space the copy will occupy by drawing the appropriate guidelines on your layout. Using a line gauge—in this case the 12-point scale—tick off the 15-line depth. Place a small piece of paper next to the sample showing of 11-point Helvetica Regular and tick off the baseline, x-height, and ascender with a sharpened, needle-point 7H pencil. Using a T-square as a guide, draw the baseline of the first line of copy. Match the baseline to the base marked on the paper, and then transfer the x-height and ascender height onto the layout sheet. Again, using the T-square as a guide, lightly draw these guidelines across the pica width. Measuring from the left side of your column, mark off 18 points for the paragraph indent. Using your T-square and triangle, rule this vertical line for your guide. Once the specifications have been determined and the guidelines drawn lightly, you can begin rendering the dummy copy.

The guidelines are to be drawn only for the first line. On the remaining lines, the ticked-off baseline marks will serve as a guide for the T-square. You should be able to determine the character flow for the remainder of your copy by duplicating the style of your first rendered line. I suggest that before attempting to apply this technique to an actual layout, you do a series of practice lines. It takes approximately six warm-up lines before you can expect to achieve consistent letter size and spacing. Keep in mind that if you leave your project for any length of time before completing it, a brief warm-up exercise may be necessary to resume the same flow.

Letters must be drawn to represent the point size and tonal value of the chosen typeface. The choice of the medium used to draw these letters must represent the letters being indicated. If, for example, you were indicating an 8-point Futura Light, you would use a thin-nib, 0.003 mm pen. If you were indicating an 8-point Futura Medium or Bold, the thickness of the pen would increase proportionately to correspond to the weight of the type. In this case, use a drawing point that will indicate the tonal value of an 11-point Helvetica Regular. Note that an italic-style letter can be indicated by drawing the dummy copy to the approximate angle of the type.

Remember that the objective of dummy copy is only to illustrate the mass of tone that will eventually be translated into type. Since some letters have greater visual energy forces than others, I recommend only a few select characters be used to suggest the type in facsimile copy:

Lowercase letters: c i l m n o r s u v
Capital letters: A B C D E F G H I L M N O P S T U V W Y

With lowercase letters, I avoid those with tight counter spaces (a, b, e) and ascenders with cross-bars (f, t) since they have a tendency to fill in, as well as letters with very strong energy shapes (k, w, x, z). Letters with descenders are not used because the T-square serves as the baseline guide and physically prevents you from drawing them. Note that the lowercase i can be used, but it should not be dotted, to avoid unnecessary emphasis.

With capital letters, I avoid using profile-angle letters such as K, R, X, Z because the energy flow within these characters brings too much attention to them. Only use capital letters to indicate new paragraphs. Do not use punctuation. At no time should actual words be used.

Do not include serifs on any letters since dummy copy indicates only a value of gray and not an actual type style. Serif and sans serif faces are therefore rendered in the same manner.

Draw the letters carefully, maintaining straight, vertical lines and eliminating handwriting influences as much as possible. Again, do not draw guidelines for the remaining lines of copy. Use the first line of rendering as a visual x-height and ascender guide and the T-square as the baseline. The dummy copy should simulate actual words as far as the letter and word spacing intended. Paragraphs should end in incomplete lines.

This method of indicating copy is superior to the others because it gives an accurate representation of what the final copy will look like. Unlike the other methods, it is not used as a convenience. It strongly suggests that the designer has full control of a project.

Combining Text and Display Type

In this assignment, you will design two advertisements for the same product—one with a dominant headline and subordinate body copy (which I call "shout") and the other reversed, with dominant body copy and a subordinate headline (which I refer to as "whisper"). Note that the terms *dominant* and *subordinate* in this case refer only to the relative size and weight of type and not to the copy's content.

The advertisements are to be black and white, with a finished size of 9 × 12 inches. Illustrations, either rendered or cut-out gray shapes, may be included. Each advertisement must include a four- to seven-word headline and a section of body copy with a minimum of 20 lines. You can write your own headline or borrow appropriate material from an existing ad.

The objective of this assignment is to make you aware that the graphic elements in an advertisement must be compatible with the product's message for the ad to be effective. Graphic and typographic elements, such as space, size, weight, and position, can be varied to change the visual appeal of an ad. Remember that a whisper can be just as memorable as a shout. Before beginning this assignment, look through magazines and newspapers to become familiar with both whisper and shout approaches.

To generate ideas, work up a series of thumbnail sketches one-third the size of the original (3 × 4 inches). Prepare one master sheet with nine of these thumbnail shapes, three across, three down, 1 inch apart on a 14 × 17-inch piece of tracing paper. Slip-sheet this master under another sheet of tracing paper in your pad, and use it as the guide for the dimensions of your thumbnail sketches. With a heavy chisel-point felt-tip marker, you can achieve three basic line widths by simple manipulation of the marker. Do not include detail in these initial sketches. Their purpose is to stimulate ideas, determine layout positions, and suggest the overall feeling of the composition. Complete as many spontaneous sketches as you feel are necessary to formulate your concepts.

Select the one thumbnail sketch in each category that you feel achieves your intended objectives. Work these sketches into full-size roughs. After you have developed the design, the tonal values must be translated into typographic styles. The personality of the letterforms must also be compatible with the theme of the subject. To select the most appropriate typeface, review type specimen books distributed by reputable typographers or foundries. Familiarizing yourself with a full range of type styles and their histories will enable you to choose the typeface that best supports your design. Lack of research could compromise your project.

After you have selected the typeface and refined the design, translate the rough sketches into comprehensive drawings on visualizing bond. Display-size faces should be drawn or traced accurately, and a facsimile of the text's tonal value should be indicated using dummy copy, as in the previous assignment. Take your time, but try to complete the final comprehensive in one sitting.

Write out the type specifications on the tissue overlay. If this were an actual job, these specifications would accompany the manuscript copy and layout submitted to a typographer. If you are not satisfied with any aspect of the design, make revisions. Leave nothing to chance. Do not allow anyone to make a design decision for you. There is only one art director. Responsibility for the final outcome is solely your own. Remember: compromise is detrimental to successful compositions.

Evaluating Type Refinements in Advertisements

In the six preceding assignments you have had a chance to practice working with the typographic refinements discussed throughout this book. For this assignment, collect advertisements from current magazines or newspapers and observe the aesthetic choices the designer made. Notice if refinements have been applied effectively, and make note of any revisions you feel could improve the ads.

Record your observation on a sheet of tracing paper taped over each ad. Make note of the attributes as well as the deficiencies in each. The ads you select need not be negative examples. Reviewing well-designed ads can be just as beneficial as redesigning poor ones.

Remember to consider all factors of design in doing this assignment. The objective is not only to sharpen your sensitivity to typography and design, but also to become aware of what is currently being produced by the industry. Pay particular attention to the areas discussed in the previous assignments. Note the consistency of letter and word spacing, as well as staggered lines. You should be able to determine if the art director had control or left aesthetic decisions up to the computer. This project can be one of the most beneficial type specimen references in your file.

✳ Experimenting with Type Personification

Letters in a word can be modified or replaced with other letters or typographic elements to visually describe a word's intended meaning. For this assignment, select five words and alter one or more characters in each word in a way that supports the meaning of that word.

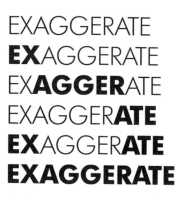

I suggest you use a gothic type style such as Helvetica as the basic typeface for this assignment because of its neutral personality. You may, however, take radical liberties in modifying the letters—replacing them with numbers, punctuation marks, or symbols; inverting or repositioning them; changing alignments; varying spacing and point size; or substituting type styles. Note, however, that no pictorial illustration is to be used in the assignment.

Do this assignment on a sheet of 14 × 17-inch visualizing bond with a black fine-point nylon-tip marker. Note that the personality of each word can influence how you position it on the page. Size and spacing are at your discretion. This is an exercise in creativity. Enjoy it!

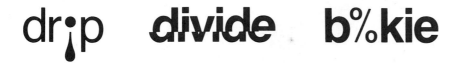

Creating an Equitone

Typographic symbols, letters, words, and phrases can be designed on a page to create a visual sound that represents the essence of the subject. This relationship of type to sound—or equitone, as I define it—establishes gender, emphasis, intensity, motion, speed, and personality. A typographic equitone takes full advantage of projecting the intent of the message without illustration.

Use the opening words of Hamlet's famous soliloquy, "To be or not to be . . . that is the question," to create an equitone that represents your interpretation of how these words should be spoken. In this particular assignment your picture plane is the stage and the words the players. You have the opportunity to direct these words as you wish them performed.

Before beginning this assignment, I suggest you read the line out loud in order to determine the intensity of volume and the speed. Translate this phrase—but without the quotation marks—into a typographic equitone. The position and spacing of the words on the page as well as type size, style, and weight direct how your message is perceived.

Begin this assignment by doing a series of rough sketches on tracing paper with a broad chisel-point marker. There are no limitations on type style, size, or position; the final rendering, however, must be black and white. Recite your composition out loud to see if it reads as you intended.

Once you are satisfied with a rough, choose typefaces from a type specimen book. The final comprehensive should be done on a 14 × 17-inch sheet of visualizing bond with a black fine-point nylon-tip marker.

Determining a Logo

For this assignment—the last of the introductory ones—design a logo for yourself, using your initials. Basing the letterforms on actual type specimens, prepare this project in black and white, using a fine-line marker on visualizing bond. There are no restrictions on how you compose the letterforms in your logo's design. You may slightly modify details by cutting apart letters, adding or altering letter shapes, or reducing parts of letters.

Before selecting actual typefaces, do a series of rough sketches suggesting the design direction you wish to follow. Choose the typeface after you have established the concept. The typographic style of a logo design should reflect the personality of the individual it is intended to represent.

After you develop your logo, apply it to a business-size (8-1/2 × 11-inch) letterhead, no. 10 (9 × 4-1/4-inch) envelope, and a standard business card. The dimensions of the card are optional and can be sized to meet the design, but should not exceed 3 × 5 inches.

11. Refining Your Skills

The next ten assignments are advanced-level projects to increase your understanding of the art of typography and to refine the skills you have acquired thus far. These assignments are more challenging than the previous ones, and they were developed to help you establish expertise and confidence in designing typographic projects.

Establishing Priority in a Newspaper Format

The first assignment is to redesign the front-page format of an existing newspaper. This project gives you an opportunity to create a functional typographic design using the information you have learned in the previous assignments, such as determining tonal value, rendering text-size copy, applying refinements of spacing, and comping letters for display type.

One purpose of this assignment is to familiarize you with type specimen sheets. In fact no assignment should be executed without reference to a type specimen book. Use this information to select tonal values and letter styles.

There are few design limitations in this assignment. You may choose to redesign any type of newspaper you wish. You have the option of including charts, diagrams, illustrations, or photographs and of using a second color (black is considered a color). Consider treatment of paragraphs, column widths, spaces between columns, ornaments, rules, in addition to the weight, size, and contrast of the type.

You may change the physical size of the paper, as well as the format style to accommodate your design. Keep practical limitations in mind, however. These include the comfortable handling of the newspaper itself and production factors such as economical costs. Render this project on visualizing bond or on the actual stock the paper will be printed on in any medium best suited to represent the tonal value of the type.

Designing a Block of Typographic Stamps

Your objective in this assignment is to prepare a block of four postage stamps that relate to each other as a unit. Each individual stamp design, however, must be strong enough to make a graphic statement on its own. All stamps must include the same copy, although not necessarily in the same position, size, or color. For copy use any denomination of stamp with the words USA POSTAGE.

The essence of this project is to design the stamps using only typographic elements. These include the full range of letters, numbers, ornaments, and dingbats. You can also create combinations of shapes using rules, bullets, boxes, or borders.

Design each stamp with dimensions of 4-1/4 × 5-1/2 inches in either a vertical or a horizontal format. The total unit should measure 8-1/2 × 11 inches. You may use up to three opaque or transparent colors on any appropriate stock. All elements must be line art. Include perforation marks around each stamp.

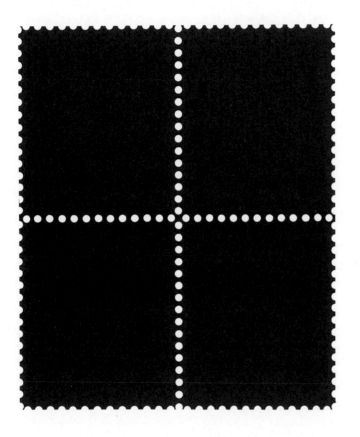

This assignment should encourage you to search out different kinds of typographic symbols that are often overlooked or taken for granted. Possible subjects are commemorative events, special occasions or holidays, the arts, or the environment.

Creating a Unique Calendar
To design an original, imaginative calendar, creativity is essential. Think past the obvious, and explore the subject thoroughly to eliminate standard concepts, such as the usual formats for day, week, and month. Keep in mind that calendars can perform a wide range of functions beyond indicating the chronological subdivisions of a year. They may, for instance, mark tidal changes, lunar phases, astrological and navigational positions, as well as historical events.

The calendar's physical presentation need not adhere to any conventional format. Find a unique way to use two or three dimensions in any material you wish. You may want to consider various applications of paper stocks, plastics, or metals.

Begin this project by researching the various creative and historical designs that have been developed to record time. Calendars inform you of known situations or one that is going to happen. Traditional notations that can be predicted or calculated, such as those in almanacs or on astrological charts, can be subjects for your calendar concept. When you prepare your design, take into consideration the shapes and colors that may be associated with these events.

The only limitation is that the elements used must be typographic. You can incorporate devices such as numbers, ornamentation, dingbats, as well as other typographic signs and symbols. These out-of-sort characters are not the obvious typographic elements and should be studied, since many of them contain unusual designs.

Inventing a Package for Alphabet Soup

For this assignment, develop a package or container for alphabet soup using typographic elements. The information on the package should include the product name, the name of the manufacturer, the list of the ingredients, and four recipes. You may create this information or use information from an existing package. The Universal Pricing Code, weight, and nutritional breakdown of the ingredients should also be included.

There are no limitations in the design format or construction of the package. Determine the soup's physical qualities (whether it is liquid, dehydrated, or frozen, for instance) and design an appropriate package. As in the calendar assignment, you should consider the various materials available to you and choose the ones best suited to the physical properties and image of your soup. All text and display lettering must be rendered by hand. Complete the project with a three-dimensional comprehensive.

Before you begin designing the package, determine how it will be displayed in stores. Will the product be stacked on shelves, or displayed in its own point-of-purchase rack? Display factors can influence your package design. Visit your local market and note the shelf space and location allocated to similar products. Then compare that with the displays in other stores. It would be good to choose different kinds of stores—for instance, a supermarket and a small local food shop—to see what, if any, variations in display there are.

Also observe that packages stocked on shelves create their own texture. If your package is multisided rather than a continuous shape (a can), be aware of how it will work visually if the different sides are placed next to each other as well as to competitive products. This product must be thought of as a visually competitive subject since it will rarely stand alone when displayed.

All package design contains internal as well as external considerations. The elements within the package design must relate to themselves as well as to other packages. You may even think of a transparent package so that the exterior and interior become one. This assignment affords the designer the opportunity to think in terms of dimension, repetition, mass, as well as the other elements, principles, and attributes of design.

Designing a Typographic Photo Essay

The intention of this assignment is to encourage you to use your visual perception. For this project, assemble 26 black-and-white photographs that you have taken in a book format so that they represent an "essay" on typography. You may use the photographs alone or with corresponding letterforms. (I suggest preparing this assignment in book format as only one of several options. Your design will determine the best presentation for your completed photographic essay.)

Consider these two ways of handling this project:

1. Photograph shapes in your environment that represent the letters of the alphabet. None of these shapes, however, should be actual letters. Research typographic characters that resemble the shapes you photographed and include these letterforms in your essay next to the corresponding photograph. The cropping and placement of photographs or letterforms should be considered as well as the paper on which you mount your art.

2. Choose a subject that contains actual letters, numbers, or both, such as street signs, building numbers, manhole covers, bus or subway station signs, ironwork fences, or doors. As in all assignments do not stop at the obvious. You might experiment with reflected letters (mirror images) or seek out typography that is normally inconspicuous, such as words on a light bulb or a label. Each photograph should be viewed as a part of your total book composition.

Shoot at least one roll of 36 exposures, preferably with 35mm film. Review your contact sheets carefully, selecting the 26 frames you want to work with. Determine the crop for each photograph, and with a red china marker (no. 169 T), pencil the area to be enlarged on your contact sheet. Also determine the type of paper your photos should be printed on—glossy or matte. If you are unfamiliar with photographic techniques and terminology, consult a fellow designer, student, or technician at a commercial photo lab. Remember that the final image is omnipotent.

Choose the most appropriate format to bind the pages, such as saddle-stitch staples, sewing, or plastic cones. Most printers have the facilities to supply all these kinds of bindings.

Developing a One-Theme Booklet

This assignment is to design and render a 16-page booklet, plus covers, based on a given location. This gives you the opportunity to explore a series of elements revolving around a central theme. At this point in your development you should feel confident of your ability to design this assignment and render display and text copy. You should also be familiar with most of the procedures needed to analyze such a graphic project.

The subject I choose for my students in the New York City area is the

South Street Seaport located in lower Manhattan. The seaport is a mini-village of national historical significance; it provides the designer with an opportunity to examine and then express graphically a unique combination of varied ships, facilities, buildings, and personalities.

Choose a comparable subject in your area. A landmark or setting that combines several components, such as a national park or historical home or community, would be best. If no such site is available, you might consider a museum, college, or industrial complex.

Before beginning the booklet's design, gather background information on your chosen location. Visits to the area and publications about the site and related subjects will familiarize you with what it has to offer. Once you have completed this research, you can begin formulating your design.

Determine the booklet's size and shape; then take into consideration that paper is part of the picture. This assignment may be a good opportunity for you to introduce various stocks throughout the booklet. Contact a local paper distributor and request samples of stocks you feel would be appropriate for the printed booklet. If this service is not available, you may find the stock you need at your local art supply store or print shop. Your final comprehensive should be rendered on the actual stock you select. Some paper distributors have customer service departments that may actually manufacture a saddle-stitched dummy to your specifications.

Actual text should not be written for the booklet. Use dummy copy to indicate body copy. All display copy (18 points and larger) should have actual words pertaining to the subject and must be lettered in an appropriate style of type. Photographs, drawings, and ornamentation should be included.

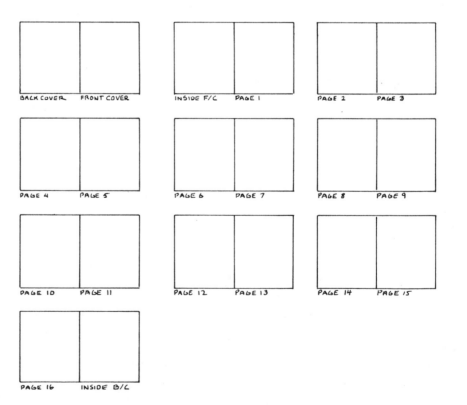

To design this project, first lay out a thumbnail page format (pagination) on one sheet of tracing paper. Lay out facing pages beginning with the spread of front and back covers. The next spread of pages should be the inside front cover on the left side, facing page 1 on the right. Odd-numbered pages are always on the right-hand side. The last spread should be page 16 on the left, facing the inside back cover on the right. This thumbnail will enable you to establish a design format or grid, which will make designing the pages easier. By drawing one master page grid and by placing it underneath your working sheet on the tracing pad, you can use it to help you design each page.

Your booklet must meet the following specifications:

Size: Not to exceed 8-1/2 × 11 inches
Colors: 4
Stock: Optional
Binding: Optional

Relating Period Typography to Architecture

For this project, design a 16-page booklet, plus covers, using architecture as your subject. This subject was chosen because of the close association between typography and architecture.

Every city throughout the world contains examples of dynamic structures. Each of these, whether it be a monument, building, tower, tunnel, or roadway, has one thing in common: it was designed around a theme. Usually, that theme involves a period or style of design.

After you have selected the particular architectural structure, determine its period or style and design the booklet to relate it. If, for example, you select an office building constructed in the 1920s or '30s that followed the Art Deco design popular then, every aspect of the booklet should relate to that period. When studying the building, look to see if some sort of letterform may have been inscribed on the structure and refer to it when selecting your typefaces. Try to avoid the most obvious styles of types associated with Art Deco or whatever period you choose. It is important to find an appropriate style that is not a cliché, and some research may be necessary to locate it.

Detail is extremely important. When choosing your subject, notice the details in ornamentation that may be tucked away in a remote corner or hanging high above normal vision. Search out door knobs, elevator panels, directional signs, or even floor tiles. The period of design is usually represented in these details. Some buildings even have original letterforms designed for them, representing the particular period or art.

The procedures discussed in the previous assignment apply to this project as well.

Making a TV Storyboard with Soundtrack

Television shows, whether weekly situation comedies, special sports events, or evening news programs, all begin with their own title format. These opening titles are the introductory identity, establishing the theme for the programming. Titles have become extremely creative since the medium of computer graphics has been introduced to the industry. In each case typography is an important part of the title.

Your assignment is to design a television title using a storyboard format. You may redesign the title of an existing show or create one for an original show of your own. The title should be between 60 and 120 seconds long, and your storyboard should be accompanied by a supporting soundtrack to be played during the presentation. The soundtrack can be music, a voiceover, or abstract sounds, as long as it supports the title. Although pictorial elements may be used, typography should be the predominant design element. The graphics can be created by using typographic elements other than letterforms.

Before beginning this assignment, review several television shows to familiarize yourself with the presentation of opening titles as well as the methods used to produce them. Study movies, current TV shows, and older reruns. Note the change in title development since the introduction of computer graphics. Keep in mind, however, that computer graphics is only one medium; it should not dictate your design format simply because it is available.

After you have chosen a theme, establish the length of the title; then designate the number of frames needed to program time and sequence. Indicate pertinent frame sequences with corresponding illustrations on your storyboard pad. There are several commercially prepared pads for this purpose. I suggest that a 3 × 5-inch storyboard frame be used. Below each frame leave space for copy; write in directions, camera positions, movement of props or actors, and voiceover or sound instructions.

After you have developed your concept, work out the design, time, and soundtrack sequence on the storyboard pad. Render the final comprehensive on visualizing bond with different markers, in either color or black and white, and tape each sheet under precut frames of a TV-shaped mat. Mount your frames on two-ply bristol board by taping the top of the mats to the board. Type dialogue and camera directions, and tape them below the corresponding frame. Approximately three or four mats, each containing eight openings, may be necessary for completion of this assignment. When making your final presentation, read the voiceover if it is not part of your taped sound.

Designing Urban Signage

Urban signage systems were developed to give directions. Unfortunately, most signage design lacks any sense of visual logic. Although some municipalities seek out designers qualified in urban and environmental planning, most contract this work to the lowest bidder. The signs are either a confusing collection of colors and information or so abstract that their symbols are unrecognizable. Signage that is unreadable is ineffective. In New York City, for example, the subway map, with its full complement of colors, is so confusing that a person with slightly impaired vision could end up in the Bronx instead of Brooklyn.

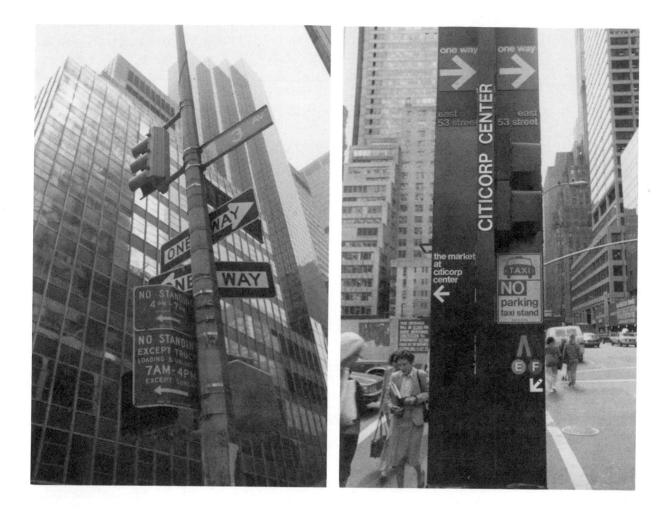

Urban Signage, New York City.

For this assignment you should plan and design a signage program for a particular area of city life. Suggested areas can be grouped into the following categories:

1. *Recreational:* playgrounds, parks, and zoos.
2. *Public transportation:* airports, subway, bus, and train stations.
3. *Street designations:* parking, standing, loading zones; emergency and tow-away zones; taxi stands, bus stops.
4. *Municipal services:* hospitals, schools, police stations, and fire department buildings.
5. *Miscellaneous:* historical landmarks, theaters, hotels, and tourist information centers.

Before beginning your design, I suggest you contact your local civic or city planning office to see what research materials may be available as a reference. Determine the signs needed for your subject and compile a list of requirements that your designs must satisfy—for instance, the purpose or function of the signs, the environment in which they will be placed, the characteristics of the people using them, the materials from which they will be manufactured, the information they should contain, the number of symbols in the grouping, the colors that best convey the signs' intent. If your symbols are not self-explanatory or universally recognizable, a decoding guide or key must be included.

You should also determine how your signs will be viewed, including viewing distance and height. Will the viewer be stationary or moving? If the viewer is moving, determine the time he or she will have to read and comprehend the sign's information. Visualize letter space for moving as compared with stationary viewing

Depending on your subject, plan your presentation to incorporate the proportionate scale, materials, color, and position of your design. Remember that a list of manufacturing specifications should accompany your graphic design. A set of architectural drawings to scale should also be part of the project.

Creating a Set of Playing Cards

The objective of this final assignment is to design a complete deck of playing cards using ornaments and dingbats as well as letterforms and numbers for the card symbols. If the standard 52 playing card deck is too predictable, you may prefer to design other types of cards, such as tarot cards or cards for foreign games, or you can make up your own game. Also design the back of the cards and the box or container holding the deck. There are no restrictions on the shape, size, or material you can use; you should not, however, exceed four colors.

Begin this assignment by doing some research to see what playing cards have looked like through the centuries. After you have chosen a theme, go through type specimen books to find symbols that are appropriate to your subject. The older foundry books may offer you a more varied and extensive selection. Although earlier assignments dealt with ornaments and dingbats, this project is designed to encourage you to extensively research current and historical typographic symbols, both realistic and abstract. I suggest that you also study eighteenth- and nineteenth-century title and ornamental letters.

As in all projects, do not let the obvious dictate a solution. Consider, for example, that punctuation marks, when used out of context, can become graphic symbols. Periods, commas, colons, asterisks, hyphens, dashes, quotation marks can create harmonious designs when placed next to each other.

Begin your layout in the same way you have approached previous assignments. Formulate and develop your concept by drawing thumbnail roughs. Do not be timid in applying your thoughts to tracing paper. Lay out as many creative variations as you can think of. Tear, cut, and paste pieces if that process will help you bring your concept together.

After you have selected your design, prepare a visual comprehensive of some of the cards before doing the final comprehensive. If possible, use the paper stock or material that you intend for the actual product for your final comprehensive.

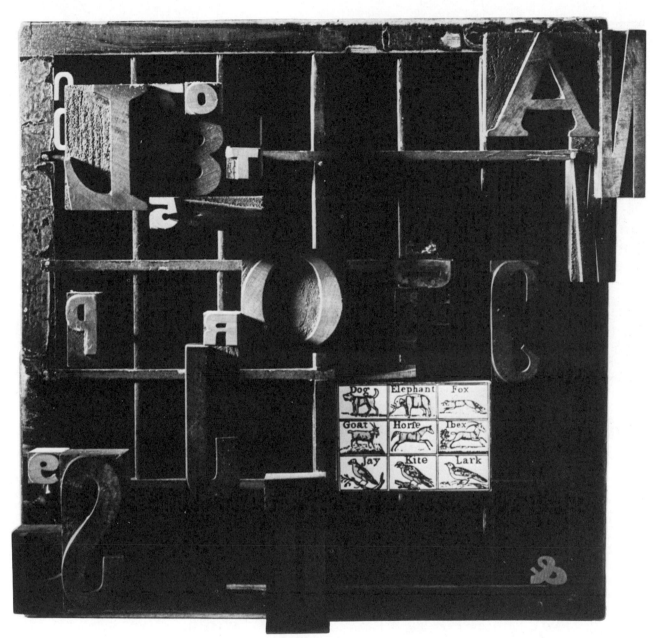

Experimental sculpture by Martin Solomon.

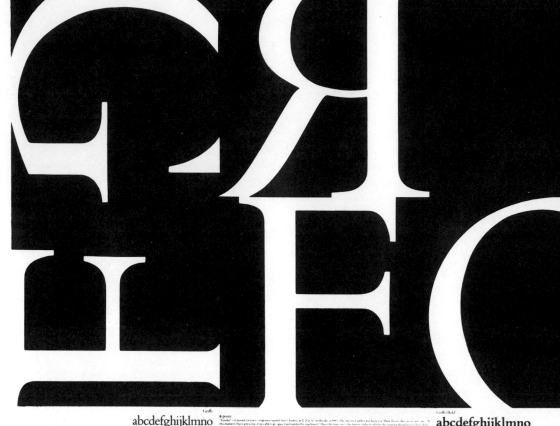

Griffo

abcdefghijklmno
pqrstuvwxyz
ABCDEFGHIJKLMNO
PQRSTUVWXYZ
1234567890
—.,:;-?"$!/

Griffo Italic

abcdefghijklmno
pqrstuvwxyz
ABCDEFGHIJKLMNO
PQRSTUVWXYZ
1234567890
—.,:;-?"$!/

Griffo Bold

abcdefghijklmno
pqrstuvwxyz
ABCDEFGHIJKLMNO
PQRSTUVWXYZ
1234567890
—.,:;-?"$!/

Griffo Bold Italic

abcdefghijklmno
pqrstuvwxyz
ABCDEFGHIJKLMNO
PQRSTUVWXYZ
1234567890
—.,:;-?"$!/

9 point

"Eureka!" exclaimed a former compositor named Sam Clemens, at 12:20 p.m. on this day in 1889. The esteemed author and humorist, Mark Twain, then went on to say, "At this moment I have seen a line of movable type, spaced and justified by machinery! This is the first time in the history of the world that this amazing thing has ever been done." Typography may be defined as the craft of rightly disposing printing material in accordance with spe- ific purpose; of so arranging the letters, distributing the space and controlling the type as to aid to the maximum the reader's comprehension of the text. Typography is the efficient means to an essentially utilitarian and only accidental aesthetic end, for enjoy- ment of patterns is rarely the reader's chief aim. Typographical work permits no improvisations. It is the ripe fruit of experiment—the result of an art which preserves only the successful trials and rejects the rough drafts and sketches. The press holds up a mirror to the author in which he may see himself clearly. If the paper, type, and composition are carefully chosen and harmonious, the author sees his work in a new guise. He may feel keen pride or shame. He hears a firmer, more detached voice than his own—an implacably just voice—articulating his words. Everything weak, arbitrary, or in bad taste that he has written is pointed up and comes out in clear relief.

7 point

splendid thing to be beautifully printed. "Eureka!" exclaimed a former compositor named Sam Clemens, at 12:20 p.m. on this day in 1889. The esteemed author and humorist, Mark Twain, then went on to say, "At this moment I have seen a line of movable type, spaced and justified by machinery! This is the first time in the history of the world that this amazing thing has ever been done." Typography may be defined as the craft of rightly disposing printing material in accordance with specific purpose; of so arranging the letters, distributing the space and controlling the type as to aid to the maximum the reader's comprehension of the text. Typography is the efficient means to an essentially utilitarian and only accidental aesthetic end, for enjoyment of patterns is rarely the reader's chief aim. Typographical work permits no improvisations. It is the ripe fruit of experiment—the result of an art which preserves only the successful trials and rejects the rough drafts and sketches. The press holds up a mirror to the author in which he may see himself clearly.

8 point

self clearly. If the paper, type, and composition are carefully chosen and harmonious, the author sees his work in a new guise. He may feel keen pride or shame. He hears a firmer, more detached voice than his own—an implacably just voice—articulating his words. Everything weak, arbitrary, or in bad taste that he has written is pointed up and comes out in clear relief. It is at once a lesson and a splendid thing to be beautifully printed. "Eureka!" exclaimed a former compositor named Sam Clemens, at 12:20 p.m. on this day in 1889. The esteemed author and humorist, Mark Twain, then went on to say, "At this moment I have seen a line of movable type, spaced and justified by machinery! This is the first time in the history of the world that this amazing thing has ever been done." Typography may be

9 point

defined as the craft of rightly disposing printing material in accordance with specific purpose; of so arranging the letters, distributing the space and controlling the type as to aid to the maximum the reader's comprehension of the text. Typography is the efficient means to an essentially utilitarian and only accidental aesthetic end, for enjoyment of patterns is rarely the reader's chief aim. Typographical work permits no improvisations. It is the ripe fruit of experiment—the result of an art which preserves only the successful trials and rejects the rough drafts and sketches. The press holds up a mirror to the author in which he may see himself clearly. If the paper, type, and composition are carefully chosen and harmon-

10 point

onious, the author sees his work in a new guise. He may feel keen pride or shame. He hears a firmer, more detached voice than his own—an implacably just voice—articulating his words. Everything weak, arbitrary, o r in bad taste that he has written is pointed up and comes out in clear relief. It is at once a lesson and a splendid thing to be beautifully printed. "Eureka!" exclaimed a former compositor named Sam Clemens, at 12:20 p.m. on this day in 1889. The esteemed author and humorist, Mark Twain, then went on to say, "At the moment I

11 point

have seen a line of movable type, spaced and justified by machinery! This is the first time in the his tory of the world that this amazing thing has ever been done." Typography may be defined as the craft of rightly disposing printing material in accordance with specific purpose; of so arranging th e letters, distributing the space and controlling the type as to aid to the maximum the reader's com prehension of the text. Typography is the efficient means to an essentially utilitarian and only acc dental aesthetic end, for enjoyment of patterns is rarely the reader's chief aim. Typographical wor

12 point

k permits no improvisations. It is the ripe fruit of experiment—the result of an art which pre serves only the successful trials and rejects the rough drafts and sketches. The press holds up a mirror to the author in which he may see himself clearly. If the paper, type, and compositi on are carefully chosen and harmonious, the author sees his work in a new guise. He may fe el keen pride or shame. He hears a firmer, more detached voice than his own—an implacab

14 point

ly just voice—articulating his words. Everything weak, arbitrary, or in bad tas te that he has written is pointed up and comes out in clear relief. It is at once a les son and a splendid thing to be beautifully printed. "Eureka!" exclaimed a form er compositor named Sam Clemens, at 12:20 p.m. on this day in 1889. The este

16 point

emed author and humorist, Mark Twain, then went on to say, "At t his moment I have seen a line of movable type, spaced and justified b y machinery! This is the first time in the history of the world that th is amazing thing has ever been done." Typography may be defined

18 point

as the craft of rightly disposing printing material in accorda nce with specific purpose; of so arranging the letters, distrib uting the space and controlling Royal Composing Room, Inc. 387 Park Avenue South, New York N.Y. 10016/889.6060

Griffo similar to Bembo

Poster designed by Martin Solomon.

Part Four
Directory of Typefaces

This section contains showings of a variety of different typefaces. Reviewing them will help you identify various type styles and select the ones most appropriate to your designs. The typefaces are to be used for reference only. They are not to be used for character counts since they do not pertain to any typesetting machinery formats.

Many of the typefaces are classics in that they have withstood the test of time. These faces were usually innovative at the time they were designed and have maintained a high level of respect and acceptance even by contemporary standards. Some faces laid dormant for decades. Then, with the introduction of photocomposition, a rejuvenation of these archival faces occurred. A strong reason for their rebirth is that the cost of translating the original drawing of the old typefaces to film was more economical than that of casting an inventory in hot type.

The faces in this section are shown in 24-point. If you wish to study the type in another size, it can be proportionately enlarged or reduced by a photostat or copy machine. Since the size of the type is relative to its body, the proportioning is simple. If, for example, you chose to enlarge the showing of Bodoni to a 48-point size, all you have to do is scale it with a proportional gauge and record the percentage enlargement. This proportionally sized type should be used for preliminary layout purposes only, however, since final copy will be set by a typographer. For more extensive information on how these typefaces set, consult your typographer.

As you look through this section, take the opportunity to compare some of the subtle changes in design that occur within similar styles. Considerations for comparisons are x-heights, sizes of ascenders and descenders, styles and sizes of serifs, and the angle of the axis of certain letters (like the O in some roman faces).

Albertus

abcdefghijklmnopqrstuvwxyz

ABCDEFGHIJKLMNOPQRSTUVWXYZ

1234567890 (&.,:;!?'""''--·*$¢%/£)

ALBERTUS BOLD TITLING

ABCDEFGHIJKLMNOPQRSTUVWXYZ

1234567890 (&.,:;!?'""''--·*$¢%/£)

Designed by Berthold Wolpe in the 1930s, Albertus is a display roman with blunt terminals rather than serifs. The lowercase ascenders and descenders are short. There is no italic.

Alternate Gothic No.1

abcdefghijklmnopqrstuvwxyz

ABCDEFGHIJKLMNOPQRSTUVWXYZ 1234567890 (&.,:;!?"""—-·*$¢%/£)

Alternate Gothic No. 2

abcdefghijklmnopqrstuvwxyz

ABCDEFGHIJKLMNOPQRSTUVWXYZ 1234567890 (&.,:;!?"""—-·*$¢%/£)

Alternate Gothic No.3

abcdefghijklmnopqrstuvwxyz

ABCDEFGHIJKLMNOPQRSTUVWXYZ

1234567890 (&.,:;!?"""—-·*$¢%/£)

Designed by Morris F. Benton, Alternate Gothic No. 1 is an extra-condensed medium-weight sans serif. Alternate Gothic No. 2 and 3 are progressively wider. A suggested contrast is News Gothic Condensed.

AUGUSTEA
ABCDEFGHIJKLMNOPQRSTUVWXYZ
(&.,:;!?'"""⌐⌐◄*$¢%/£) 1234567890

Augustea, designed by A. Butti and A. Novarese in 1951, offers inscriptional capitals and figures. The M has no top serifs, and the W no middle serif.

BALLOON BOLD
ABCDEFGHIJKLMNOPQRSTUVWXYZ
1234567890 (&.,:;!?'"""-*$¢%/£)

BALLOON EXTRA BOLD
ABCDEFGHIJKLMNOPQRSTUVWXYZ
1234567890 (&.,:;!?'"""-*$¢%/)

Balloon, also called Lasso, was designed by M. R. Kaufmann in 1939. It is a freely drawn, informal gothic face.

BANCO
ABCDEFGHIJKLMNOPQRSTUVWXYZ
(&.,:;!?'"""-*$¢%/) 1234567890

Banco, designed in 1951, is an angular, informal gothic, with slightly tapered strokes thinning at the lower part of the capitals.

Baskerville
abcdefghijklmnopqrstuvwxyz
ABCDEFGHIJKLMNOPQRSTUVWXYZ
1234567890 (&.,:;!?""""—–-·*$¢%/Æ)

Baskerville Italic
abcdefghijklmnopqrstuvwxyz
ABCDEFGHIJKLMNOPQRSTUVWXYZ
1234567890 (&.,:;!?""""—-·*$¢%/£)

Baskerville Bold
abcdefghijklmnopqrstuvwxyz
ABCDEFGHIJKLMNOPQRSTUVWXYZ
1234567890 (&.,:;"""!?-*$¢%/)

Baskerville Bold Italic
abcdefghijklmnopqrstuvwxyz
ABCDEFGHIJKLMNOPQRSTUVWXYZ
1234567890(&.,:;!?""""-—·*$¢%/£)

Baskerville was originally designed and cut by John Baskerville in the eighteenth century, but there have been several recut versions. A characteristic feature is the extreme contrast between the capitals and lowercase letters.

Belwe Light
abcdefghijklmnopqrstuvwxyz
ABCDEFGHIJKLMNOPQRSTUVWXYZ
1234567890 (&.,:;!?""""-——·*$¢%/£)

Designed by Georg Belwe, this twentieth-century type has old-face qualities. The full-bodied x-height letters have short descenders, and the lowercase g has a unique, short, turned-up tail.

Bembo
abcdefghijklmnopqrstuvwxyz
ABCDEFGHIJKLMNOPQRSTUVWXYZ
1234567890 (&.,:;!?'""-*$¢%/£)

Bembo Italic
abcdefghijklmnopqrstuvwxyz
ABCDEFGHIJKLMNOPQRSTUVWXYZ
1234567890 (&.,:;!?'""-*$¢%/£)

Cut by Francesco Griffo for the Venetian printer Aldus Manutius, this face was originally used in Cardinal Bembo's *De Aetna* (1495). Note that the capitals are shorter than the ascending letters of the lowercase.

Bernhard Gothic Light
abcdefghijklmnopqrstuvwxyz
ABCDEFGHIJKLMNOPQRSTUVWXYZ
1234567890 (&.,:;!?'""---*$¢%/£)

Bernhard Gothic Medium
abcdefghijklmnopqrstuvwxyz
ABCDEFGHIJKLMNOPQRSTUVWXYZ
1234567890 (&.,:;!?'""---*$¢%/£)

Designed by Lucien Bernhard around 1929–30, this face has four weights, with italics to the two lightest weights.

Bodoni
abcdefghijklmnopqrstuvwxyz
ABCDEFGHIJKLMNOPQRSTUVWXYZ
1234567890 (&.,:;!?'""''-—·*$¢%/£)

Bodoni Italic
abcdefghijklmnopqrstuvwxyz
ABCDEFGHIJKLMNOPQRSTUVWXYZ
1234567890 (&.,:;!?'""''-$¢%/)*

Bodoni Bold
abcdefghijklmnopqrstuvwxyz
ABCDEFGHIJKLMNOPQRSTUVWXYZ
1234567890 (&.,:;!?'""''-—·*$¢%/£)

Bodoni Bold Italic
abcdefghijklmnopqrstuvwxyz
ABCDEFGHIJKLMNOPQRSTUVWXYZ
1234567890 (&.,:;!?'""''-*$¢%/£)

Bodoni Book
abcdefghijklmnopqrstuvwxyz
ABCDEFGHIJKLMNOPQRSTUVWXYZ
1234567890 (&.,:;!?'""''-*$¢%/)

Bodoni Book Italic
abcdefghijklmnopqrstuvwxyz
ABCDEFGHIJKLMNOPQRSTUVWXYZ
1234567890 (&.,:;!?'""""-*$$¢%/)

Giambattista Bodoni of Parma, who originally designed this face in the late eighteenth century, believed in plenty of white space and therefore created long descenders. In the twentieth century there were two basic models for the recuttings: one from the American Type Founders by Morris F. Benton in 1907, and the other from Bauer Type Foundry, which adopted a more delicate recutting. It is important not to mix foundries since the x-heights and base alignments may vary.

Britannic
abcdefghijklmnopqrstuvwxyz
ABCDEFGHIJKLMNOPQRSTUVWXYZ
1234567890 (&.,:;!?'""""-*$¢%/£)

Britannic Italic
abcdefghijklmnopqrstuvwxyz
ABCDEFGHIJKLMNOPQRSTUVWXYZ
1234567890 (&.,:;!?'""""-*$¢%/£)

This sans serif has the qualities of a fat face, with considerably heavier thins. A suggested contrast is Radiant Medium or corresponding italics.

BROADWAY
ABCDEFGHIJKLMNOPQRSTUVWXYZ
(&.,:;!?'""""-*$%/)
1234567890

BROADWAY ENGRAVED
ABCDEFGHIJKLM
NOPQRSTUVWXYZ
1234567890(&.,:;!?""""''----·[]*$¢%/£)

Designed by Morris F. Benton, this Art Deco–style type combines characteristics of fat
face and sans serif. In most letters the main stroke is fat; the thins follow the rest of
the letter.

Brush
abcdefghijklmnopqrstuvwxyz
ABCDEFGHIJKLMNOPQRSTUVWXYZ
1234567890 (&.,:;"""...!?-*$¢%/)

Designed by Robert E. Smith in the 1940s, this script lettering became very popular in
the early 1950s.

Bulmer
abcdefghijklmnopqrstuvwxyz
ABCDEFGHIJKLMNOPQRSTUVWXYZ
1234567890 (&.,:;!?'""""-*$¢%/)

Bulmer Italic
abcdefghijklmnopqrstuvwxyz
ABCDEFGHIJKLMNOPQRSTUVWXYZ
1234567890 (&.,:;!?'""""-*$¢%/)

Originally cut by William Martin in about 1790 for William Bulmer of the Shakespeare
Press, this famous typeface was duplicated by Morris F. Benton for the American Type
Founders in 1928. The American version is slightly more modern in design than the
original, with a vertical stress and flatter serifs.

Caledonia
abcdefghijklmnopqrstuvwxyz
ABCDEFGHIJKLMNOPQRSTUVWXYZ
1234567890 (&.,:;!?'""-[]*$¢%/£)

Caledonia Italic
abcdefghijklmnopqrstuvwxyz
ABCDEFGHIJKLMNOPQRSTUVWXYZ
1234567890 (&.,:;!?'""-*$¢%/£)

Designed by William Addison Dwiggins in 1938, this roman face is a modified Scottish face, which accounts for its name. It is also called Cornelia.

CARTOON BOLD
ABCDEFGHIJKLMNOPQRSTUVWXYZ
1234567890 (£.,:;–*!?'\"'"$¢%/)

Designed by H. A. Trafton in 1936, Cartoon offers a freely drawn capital alphabet with figures. In Germany this face is called Fresko.

Caslon No. 471 Roman
abcdefghijklmnopqrstuvwxyz
ABCDEFGHIJKLMNOPQRSTUVWXYZ
1234567890 (&.,:;!?'""--·*$¢%/£)

Caslon No. 471 Italic
abcdefghijklmnopqrstuvwxyz
ABCDEFGHIJKLMNOPQRSTUVWXYZ
1234567890 (&.,:;!?'""--·*$¢%/£)

Caslon No. 471 Swash Characters

e-hhhhk̄mnopqr τνwz ct̃figy AAABCCₓDDEEₓFFₓF GHHₓH̄ITIJKKₓKₓ LLₓL̄ MMₓNₓNₓOPPₓQₓQu RRₓ SSₓTTₓTͅhUUₓ UₓVₓUWₓWXYZ&

Caslon No. 540

abcdefghijklmnopqrstuvwxyz

ABCDEFGHIJKLMNOPQRSTUVWXYZ

1234567890 (&.,:;!?'""''-—·*$¢%/£)

Caslon No. 540 Italic

abcdefghijklmnopqrstuvwxyz

ABCDEFGHIJKLMNOPQRSTUVWXYZ

1234567890 (&.,:;!?'""''-—·$¢%/£)*

William Caslon, who modeled his designs after Dutch styles of the late seventeenth century, created his first roman type in 1725. Swash characters were added to the Caslon Italics of the American Type Founders; they do not date back to the original.

Centaur

abcdefghijklmnopqrstuvwxyz

ABCDEFGHIJKLMNOPQRSTUVWXYZ

1234567890(&.,:;!?'""''--·[ ]*$¢%/£)

Centaur was designed by Bruce Rogers in 1914 for the Metropolitan Museum of Art in New York. The capitals were fashioned after Nicolas Jenson's roman from the late fifteenth century.

Century Schoolbook
abcdefghijklmnopqrstuvwxyz
ABCDEFGHIJKLMNOPQRSTUVWXYZ
1234567890 (&.,:;!?'""-*$%/£)

Century Schoolbook Italic
abcdefghijklmnopqrstuvwxyz
ABCDEFGHIJKLMNOPQRSTUVWXYZ
1234567890 (&.,:;!?'"-$¢%/£)*

Century Expanded
abcdefghijklmnopqrstuvwxyz
ABCDEFGHIJKLMNOPQRSTUVWXYZ
1234567890   (&.,:;!?'""---·*$¢%/£)

Century Expanded Italic
abcdefghijklmnopqrstuvwxyz
ABCDEFGHIJKLMNOPQRSTUVWXYZ
1234567890 (&.,:;!?'""-$¢%/)*

Century Oldstyle
abcdefghijklmnopqrstuvwxyz
ABCDEFGHIJKLMNOPQRSTUVWXYZ
1234567890   (&.,:;!?'""---·*$¢%/£)

Century Oldstyle Italic
abcdefghijklmnopqrstuvwxyz
ABCDEFGHIJKLMNOPQRSTUVWXYZ
1234567890(&.,:;!?'""--·*$¢%/£)

Century Schoolbook was cut in 1894 by L. B. Benton in collaboration with T. L. De Vinne for the *Century* magazine. The American Type Founders introduced Century Expanded, which has a slightly lower character-per-pica count than Century Schoolbook. Another member of the Century family is Century Oldstyle.

Cheltenham Old Style
abcdefghijklmnopqrrstuvwxyz
ABCDEFGHIJKLMNOPQRSTUVWXYZ
1234567890(&.,:;!?'""--·[]*$¢%/£)

Cheltenham Old Style Condensed
abcdefghijklmnopqrstuvwxyz
ABCDEFGHIJKLMNOPQRSTUVWXYZ
1234567890 (&.,:;!?'""-*$¢%/£)

Cheltenham Medium
abcdefghijklmnopqrrstuvwxyz
ABCDEFGHIJKLMNOPQRSTUVWXYZ
1234567890(&.,:;!?'""--·*$¢%/£)

Cheltenham Medium Italic
abcdefghijklmnopqrstuvwxyz
ABCDEFGHIJKLMNOPQRSTUVWXYZ
1234567890 (&.,:;"""'!?-*$¢£%/)

Cheltenham Bold
abcdefghijklmnopqrstuvwxyz
ABCDEFGHIJKLMNOPQRSTUVWXYZ
1234567890 (&.,:;!?'""-*$¢%/)

Cheltenham Bold Italic
abcdefghijklmnopqrstuvwxyz
ABCDEFGHIJKLMNOPQRSTUVWXYZ
1234567890 (&.,:;!?""-*$¢%/)

Bertram G. Goodhue designed Cheltenham in 1896. His theory was that a good, readable typeface should have long ascenders and should achieve consistent word and line spacing.

Chisel
abcdefghijklmnopqrstuvwxyz
ABCDEFGHIJKLMNOPQRSTUVWXYZ
1234567890 (&.,:;!?'""-*$¢%/£)

In this twentieth-century, Latin bold typeface, there is a double white inline surrounding a heavier bar.

City Medium
abcdefghijklmnopqrstuvwxyz
ABCDEFGHIJKLMNOPQRSTUVWXYZ
1234567890 (&.:,;!?`'"-$)

City, a rectangular Egyptian face, was designed by Georg Trump in 1930. All round letters have been squared off.

Clarendon Regular
abcdefghijklmnopqrstuvwxyz
ABCDEFGHIJKLMNOPQRSTUVWXYZ
1234567890(&.,:;!?"'""""--—··[]*$¢%/£)

Originally produced by R. Besley & Co. (the Fann St. Foundry) in 1845, this Egyptian-style face was soon copied by other foundries and became one of the most popular heavy typefaces.

Cloister Old Style
abcdefghijklmnopqrstuvwxyz
ABCDEFGHIJKLMNOPQRSTUVWXYZ
1234567890 (&.,:;!?'"-*$¢%/)

Cloister Bold
abcdefghijklmnopqrstuvwxyz
ABCDEFGHIJKLMNOPQRSTUVWXYZ
1234567890 (&.,:;!?'""""-*$¢%/)

Cloister Bold Italic

abcdefghijklmnopqrstuvwxyz
ABCDEFGHIJKLMNOPQRSTUVWXYZ ABCD
EFGMNPQuRV 1234567890 (&.,:;!?''""-*$¢%/)

Designed by Morris F. Benton in 1897, Cloister Old Style was among the first revived
Venetian faces, apart from those designed for private presses, such as William Morris's
"Golden Type." A series of swash capitals were designed as well.

COLUMNA

ABCDEFGHIJKLMNOPQRSTUVWXYZ
1234567890 (&.,:;!?''""-*$¢%/£)

Columna was originally a private face, designed in 1955 by Max Calflisch, for a Swiss
publishing house. It has open capitals and figures with very small, thin serifs.

Consort

abcdefghijklmnopqrstuvwxyz
ABCDEFGIJKLMNOPQRSTUVW
XYZ 1234567890 (&.,:;!?'""-*$c%/£)

Consort is a revival of an early English-style Egyptian face issued by Stephenson and
Blake in the 1950s.

Contact Bold Condensed

abcdefghijklmnopqrstuvwxyz
ABCDEFGHIJKLMNOPQRSTUVWXYZ
1234567890 (&.,:;!?'""-*$¢%/£)

Contact Bold Condensed Italic
abcdefghijklmnopqrstuvwxyz
ABCDEFGHIJKLMNOPQRSTUVWXYZ
1234567890 (&.,:;!?'""”-*$¢%/£)

Designed by F. H. Riley for the American Type Founders in 1944, Contact is modeled after a nineteenth-century face.

Cooper Black
abcdefghijklmnopqrstuvwxyz
ABCDEFGHIJKLMNOPQRSTUVWXYZ
1234567890 [&.,:;!?'"“”-—*$¢%/£]

Cooper Black Italic
abcdefghijklmnopqrstuvwxyz
ABCDEFGHIJKLMNOPQRSTUVWXYZ
1234567890 [&.,:;!?'"“”-*$¢%/£]

This extra-bold fat face was designed by Oswald B. Cooper for Barnhart Bros. & Spindler in 1921. The serifs are rounded, as if drawn with a round or oval pen nib. The italics are similar to the vertical. There is also a condensed face and a shaded face, called Cooper Hilite (not shown).

Cooper Old Style
abcdefghijklmnopqrstuvwxyz
ABCDEFGHIJKLMNOPQRSTUVWXYZ
1234567890 [&.,:;!?'"“”-*$¢%/£]

Designed by Oswald Cooper in 1919–24, Cooper Old Style has some qualities similar to Goudy, especially the foot serifs, which are slightly convex.

COPPERPLATE GOTHIC LIGHT
ABCDEFGHIJKLMNOPQRSTUVWXYZ
(&.,:;!?'""-*$¢%) 1234567890

The American Type Founders' Copperplate Gothic was designed by Frederic W. Goudy in 1901. The design is an old one and common to most founders. Although in smaller sizes it appears to be sans serif, it does in fact have minute hairline serifs in all weights. A similar foundry face is Steelplate Gothic Bold.

Corvinus Medium
abcdefghijklmnopqrstuvwxyz
ABCDEFGHIJKLMNOPQRSTUVWXYZ
1234567890 (&.,:;!?'""-*$¢%/)

Corvinus Medium Italic
abcdefghijklmnopqrstuvwxyz
ABCDEFGHIJKLMNOPQRSTUVWXYZ
1234567890 (&.,:;!?'"-*$¢%/)

Corvinus Bold
abcdefghijklmnopqrstuvwxyz
ABCDEFGHIJKLMNOPQRSTUVWXYZ
1234567890 [&.,:;!?'""-*$¢%/)

Designed by Imre Reiner for the Bauer Foundry in 1929–34, Corvinus is a display face with modern characteristics. The condensed version (not shown) is called Corvinus Skyline.

CRISTAL
ABCDEFGHIJKLMNOPQRSTUVWXYZ
(&.,:;!?'"-«»*$¢%/£) 1234567890

This set of inline capitals with pointed, thin serifs was designed by Remy Peignot.

DeRoos Roman
abcdefghijklmnopqrstuvwxyz
ABCDEFGHIJKLMNOPQRSTUVWXYZ
1234567890 (&.,:;!?'""""-—.*$¢%/£)

DeRoos Italic
abcdefghijklmnopqrstuvwxyz
ABCDEFGHIJKLMNOPQRSTUVWXYZ
1234567890 (&.,:;!?'""""--.*$¢%/£)

Designed by S. H. DeRoos in 1947 and manufactured by the Amsterdam, Intertype, and American Type Foundries, this roman face has small serifs and capitals that are shorter than the ascenders.

Egizio Roman Medium
abcdefghijklmnopqrstuvwxyz
ABCDEFGHIJKLMNOPQRSTUVWXYZ
1234567890 (&.,:;!?'""""-*$¢%/£)

Egizio is a light-slab, Egyptian-style face, designed by A. Novarese and cut by the Nebiolo foundry in Turin, Italy. The different weights were begun in 1955 and completed in 1958.

Egyptian Bold Extended
abcdefghijklmnopqrstuvwxyz
ABCDEFGHIJKLMNOPQRSTUVW
XYZ 1234567890 (&.,:;!?"""-–.*$¢%/£)

Miller and Richards designed this nineteenth-century slab serif.

Elizabeth Roman
abcdefghijklmnopqrstuvwxyz
ABCDEFGHIJKLMNOPQRSTUVWXYZ
1234567890 &.,:;!?'""-*$¢%/

This elegant roman typeface with modest contrast in its thick and thins was designed by Miss E. Friedlander, a student of Emil Rudolf Weiss. The serifs have slight inclines and are calligraphic in style. There is a series of swash capitals. Since there is no heavier version of this style, Weiss Roman Bold can be used for contrast, as well as Elizabeth's own italics.

Eurostile
abcdefghijklmnopqrstuvwxyz
ABCDEFGHIJKLMNOPQRSTUVWXYZ
1234567890(&.,:;!?''""""-–·[]*$¢%/£)

Eurostile Bold
abcdefghijklmnopqrstuvwxyz
ABCDEFGHIJKLMNOPQRSTUVWXYZ
1234567890(&.,:;!?''""""-–·[]*$¢%/£)

Eurostile Extended
abcdefghijklmnopqrstuvwxyz
ABCDEFGHIJKLMNOPQRST
UVWXYZ (&.,:;!?'""-$¢%/£)
1234567890

Eurostile Bold Extended
abcdefghijklmnopqrstuvwxyz
ABCDEFGHIJKLMNOPQRST
UVWXYZ (&.,:;!?'""-*$¢%£)
1234567890

Designed by A. Novarese in the 1960s, Eurostile is intended to complement Micrpgramma by offering lowercase letters. Architectural in stature, it has several weights.

Firmin Didot
abcdefghijklmnopqrstuvwxyz
ABCDEFGHIJKLMNOPQRSTUVWXYZ
1234567890 (&.,:;!?'""-*$¢%/)

Firmin Didot cut the first modern roman typeface in about 1784. Because the serifs in Firmin Didot were hairline-thin and wore easily, it was not a popular face until the introduction of photocomposition.

FRENCH FLASH
ABCDEFGHIJKLMNOPQRSTUVWXYZ
1234567890 (&.,:;!?'""-*$¢%/£)

Designed by Crous-Vidal in the 1950s, French Flash is a companion to the style Paris. A lightning bold effect is created within each letter.

Folio Light
abcdefghijklmnopqrstuvwxyz
ABCDEFGHIJKLMNOPQRSTUVWXYZ
1234567890 (&.,:;!?'""-*$¢%/£)

Folio Medium
abcdefghijklmnopqrstuvwxyz
ABCDEFGHIJKLMNOPQRSTUVWXYZ
1234567890 (&.,:;!?'""-*$¢%/£)

Folio Bold
abcdefghijklmnopqrstuvwxyz
ABCDEFGHIJKLMNOPQRSTUVWXYZ
1234567890 (&.,:;!?'""-*$¢%/)

Designed by Konrad F. Bauer and Walter Baum in 1957–62, this sans serif type follows nineteenth-century models. Folio Medium Extended has biform letters (see page 97).

Franklin Gothic
abcdefghijklmnopqrstuvwxyz
ABCDEFGHIJKLMNOPQRSTUVWXYZ
1234567890 (&.,:;!?'""--·*$¢%/£)

Franklin Gothic Italic
abcdefghijklmnopqrstuvwxyz
ABCDEFGHIJKLMNOPQRSTUVWXYZ
1234567890 (&.,:;!?'""-*$¢%/)

Franklin Gothic Condensed
abcdefghijklmnopqrstuvwxyz
ABCDEFGHIJKLMNOPQRSTUVWXYZ
1234567890 (&.,:;!?'""-*$¢%/£)

Franklin Gothic Condensed Italic
abcdefghijklmnopqrstuvwxyz
ABCDEFGHIJKLMNOPQRSTUVWXYZ
1234567890 (&.,:;!?'""-$¢%/£)*

Franklin Gothic Extra Condensed
abcdefghijklmnopqrstuvwxyz
ABCDEFGHIJKLMNOPQRSTUVWXYZ
1234567890 (&.,:;!?'""-*$¢%/£)

Franklin Gothic Wide
abcdefghijklmnopqrstuvwxyz
ABCDEFGHIJKLMNOPQRSTUVWXYZ
1234567890 (&.,:;!?'""-—·*$¢%/£)

Designed by Morris F. Benton, this heavy sans serif offers a contrast for lighter-weight faces such as News Gothic and Bodoni Book. Do not, however, use different Franklin Gothic styles for contrast as they are too close in weight.

Futura Light
abcdefghijklmnopqrstuvwxyz
ABCDEFGHIJKLMNOPQRSTUVWXYZ
1234567890 (&.,:;!?'""-—·*$¢%/£)

Futura Light Oblique
abcdefghijklmnopqrstuvwxyz
ABCDEFGHIJKLMNOPQRSTUVWXYZ
1234567890 (&.,:;!?'""-—·$¢%/£)*

Futura Book
abcdefghijklmnopqrstuvwxyz
ABCDEFGHIJKLMNOPQRSTUVWXYZ
1234567890 (&.,:;!?'""-—·*$¢%/£)

Futura Medium
abcdefghijklmnopqrstuvwxyz
ABCDEFGHIJKLMNOPQRSTUVWXYZ
1234567890 (&.,:;!?'""-—·*$¢%/£)

Futura Medium Oblique
abcdefghijklmnopqrstuvwxyz
ABCDEFGHIJKLMNOPQRSTUVWXYZ
1234567890 (&.,:;!?'""-—·$¢%/£)*

Futura Demi Bold
abcdefghijklmnopqrstuvwxyz
ABCDEFGHIJKLMNOPQRSTUVWXYZ
1234567890 (&.,:;!?"""-—·*$¢%/£)

Futura Demi Bold Oblique
abcdefghijklmnopqrstuvwxyz
ABCDEFGHIJKLMNOPQRSTUVWXYZ
1234567890 (&.,:;!?"""'-—·*$¢%/£)

Futura Bold
abcdefghijklmnopqrstuvwxyz
ABCDEFGHIJKLMNOPQRSTUVWXYZ
1234567890 (&.,:;!?"""'-—·*$¢%/£)

Futura Bold Oblique
abcdefghijklmnopqrstuvwxyz
ABCDEFGHIJKLMNOPQRSTUVWXYZ
1234567890 (&.,:;!?"""'-—·*$¢%/£)

Futura Extra Bold
abcdefghijklmnopqrstuvwxyz
ABCDEFGHIJKLMNOPQRSTUVWXYZ
1234567890 (&.,:;!?'"""-*$¢%/£)

Futura Extra Bold Oblique
abcdefghijklmnopqrstuvwxyz
ABCDEFGHIJKLMNOPQRSTUVWXYZ
1234567890 (&.,:;!?'"""-*$¢%/£)

Futura Medium Condensed
abcdefghijklmnopqrstuvwxyz
ABCDEFGHIJKLMNOPQRSTUVWXYZ
1234567890 (&.,:;!?'""-*$¢%/£)

Futura Bold Condensed
abcdefghijklmnopqrstuvwxyz
ABCDEFGHIJKLMNOPQRSTUVWXYZ
1234567890 (&.,:;!?'""-*$¢%/£)

Futura Bold Condensed Oblique
abcdefghijklmnopqrstuvwxyz
ABCDEFGHIJKLMNOPQRSTUVWXYZ
1234567890 (&.,:;!?'""-*$%/£)

Futura Extra Bold Cond.
abcdefghijklmnopqrstuvwxyz
ABCDEFGHIJKLMNOPQRSTUVWXYZ
1234567890 (&.,:;!?'"""-—•*$¢%/£)

Futura Extra Bold Cond. Oblique
abcdefghijklmnopqrstuvwxyz
ABCDEFGHIJKLMNOPQRSTUVWXYZ
1234567890 (&.,:;!?'"""-—•*$¢%/£)

Futura was originally designed by Paul Renner in 1927–30. Many foundries, however, have duplicated this face under different names.

Garamond Old Style
abcdefghijklmnopqrstuvwxyz
ABCDEFGHIJKLMNOPQRSTUVWXYZ
1234567890 (&.,:;!?"""'-*$¢%/£)

Garamond Old Style Italic
abcdefghijklmnopqrstuvwxyz
ABCDEFGHIJKLMNOPQRSTUVWXYZ
1234567890 (&.,:;!?"""'-$¢%)*

Garamond Bold
abcdefghijklmnopqrstuvwxyz
ABCDEFGHIJKLMNOPQRSTUVWXYZ
1234567890 (&.,:;!?"""'-*$¢%/£)

Garamond Bold Italic
abcdefghijklmnopqrstuvwxyz
ABCDEFGHIJKLMNOPQRSTUVWXYZ
1234567890 (&.,:;!?"""'-*$¢%/£)

Claude Garamond based his sixteenth-century type on designs by Aldus Manutius. Many of the present-day versions of Garamond, however, are based on the Typi Academiae of Jean Jannon cut in Sedan, France, around 1615. Check the version of Garamond you are using as different foundry designs may not be consistent in x-height and style.

Gill Sans Light
abcdefghijklmnopqrstuvwxyz
ABCDEFGHIJKLMNOPQRSTUVWXYZ
1234567890(&.,:;'""!?-—*$¢%/£)

Gill Sans Light Italic
abcdeffghijklmnopqrstuvwxyz
ABCDEFGHIJKLMNOPQRSTUVWXYZ
1234567890(&.,:;'""!?-—$¢%/£)*

Gill Sans
abcdeffghijklmnopqrstuvwxyz
ABCDEFGHIJKLMNOPQRSTUVWXYZ
1234567890(&.,:;'""!?-—*$¢%/£)

Gill Sans Italic
abcdeffghijklmnopqrstuvwxyz
ABCDEFGHIJKLMNOPQRSTUVWXYZ
1234567890(&.,:;'""!?-—$¢%/£)*

Gill Sans Bold
abcdeffghijklmnopqrstuvwxyz
ABCDEFGHIJKLMNOPQRSTUVWXYZ
1234567890(&.,:;!?'""-—·*$¢%/£)

Gill Sans Bold Italic
abcdeffghijklmnopqrstuvwxyz
ABCDEFGHIJKLMNOPQRSTUVWXYZ
1234567890(&.,:;'""""!?-—*$¢%/£)

Gill Sans Extrabold
abcdefghijklmnopqrstuvwxyz
ABCDEFGHIJKLMNOPQRSTUVWXYZ
1234567890 (&.,:;!?'""""–—•*$¢%/£)

Gill Sans Ultra Bold
abcdefghijklmnopqrstuvwxyz
ABCDEFGHIJKLMNOPQRSTUVWXYZ
1234567890 (&.,:;!?'""""–—•*$¢%/£)

Gill Sans Bold Condensed
abcdeffghijklmnopqrstuvwxyz
ABCDEFGHIJKLMNOPQRSTUVWXYZ
1234567890(&.,:;'""""!?-—*$¢%/£)

Designed by Eric Gill in 1928–30, this face has four weights, italics, a condensed, and a three-dimensional version called Gill Shadow.

Gillies Gothic Bold

abcdefghijklmnopqrstuvwxyz

ABCDEFGHIJKLMNOPQRSTUVWXYZ

1234567890 (&.,:;!?'""-*$¢%/)

Designed by William S. Gillies in 1935, this monoweight script is also called Flott.

GOTHIC OUTLINE TITLE NO. 61

ABCDEFGHIJKLMNOPQRSTUVWXYZ

[&.,:;!?""-*$%/] 1234567890

This gothic outline typeface is of nineteenth-century design. Franklin Gothic Condensed is suggested for contrast.

Goudy Old Style

abcdefghijklmnopqrstuvwxyz

ABCDEFGHIJKLMNOPQRSTUVWXYZ

1234567890 (&.,:;!?'""-*$¢%/£)

Goudy Old Style Italic

abcdefghijklmnopqrstuvwxyz

ABCDEFGHIJKLMNOPQRSTUVWXYZ

1234567890(&.,:;'""--·*$¢%/£)

Goudy Catalogue

abcdefghijklmnopqrstuvwxyz

ABCDEFGHIJKLMNOPQRSTUVWXYZ

1234567890 (&.,:;!?'""--·*$¢%/£)

Goudy Bold

abcdefghijklmnopqrstuvwxyz

ABCDEFGHIJKLMNOPQRSTUVWXYZ

1234567890 (&.,:;!?""''--·*$¢%/£)

Goudy Bold Italic

abcdefghijklmnopqrstuvwxyz

ABCDEFGHIJKLMNOPQRSTUVWXYZ

1234567890 (&.,:;!?""''--·*$¢%/£)

Goudy Extra Bold

abcdefghijklmnopqrstuvwxyz

ABCDEFGHIJKLMNOPQRSTUVWXYZ

1234567890 [&.,:;!?""''--·*$¢%/£]

Frederic W. Goudy's early twentieth-century designs were modeled after the Renaissance letterform. Convex serifs are a definite Goudy style. The italics are almost vertical; in fact *m* and *n* are upright. Several bold versions of Goudy were designed by Morris F. Benton. Goudy Catalogue and Goudy Handtooled (not shown) are both display faces with no italics or bold.

Grotesque No. 9

abcdefghijklmnopqrstuvwxyz

ABCDEFGHIJKLMNOPQRSTUVWXYZ

1234567890 (&.,:;!?'""-[]*$¢%/£)

Grotesque No. 9 Italic
abcdefghijklmnopqrstuvwxyz
ABCDEFGHIJKLMNOPQRSTUVWXYZ
1234567890 (&.,:;!?'""-*$¢%/)

Grotesque No. 18
abcdefghijklmnopqrstuvwxyz
ABCDEFGHIJKLMNOPQRSTUVWXYZ
1234567890 (&.,:;!?'""-*$¢%/)

This face is based on one of the early sans serifs, designed by William Thorowgood in 1832 and called Grotesque.

Helvetica Light
abcdefghijklmnopqrstuvwxyz
ABCDEFGHIJKLMNOPQRSTUVWXYZ
1234567890 (&.,:;!?"""-—·*$¢%/£)

Helvetica Light Italic
abcdefghijklmnopqrstuvwxyz
ABCDEFGHIJKLMNOPQRSTUVWXYZ
1234567890   (&.,:;!?'""-—·()*$¢%/£)

Helvetica
abcdefghijklmnopqrstuvwxyz
ABCDEFGHIJKLMNOPQRSTUVWXYZ
1234567890 (&.,:;!?'""-*$¢%/£)

Helvetica Italic
abcdefghijklmnopqrstuvwxyz
ABCDEFGHIJKLMNOPQRSTUVWXYZ
1234567890 (&.,:;!?'""·$¢%/£)*

Helvetica Medium
abcdefghijklmnopqrstuvwxyz
ABCDEFGHIJKLMNOPQRSTUVWXYZ
1234567890 (&.,:;!?'""-—·*$¢%/£)

Helvetica Medium Italic
abcdefghijklmnopqrstuvwxyz
ABCDEFGHIJKLMNOPQRSTUVWXYZ
1234567890(&.,:;!?''"" "-—·*$¢%/£)

Helvetica Bold
abcdefghijklmnopqrstuvwxyz
ABCDEFGHIJKLMNOPQRSTUVWXYZ
1234567890 (&.,:;!?''""-*$¢%/£)

Helvetica Bold Italic
abcdefghijklmnopqrstuvwxyz
ABCDEFGHIJKLMNOPQRSTUVWXYZ
1234567890(&.,:;!?''''""""-—·*$¢%/£)

Helvetica Regular Condensed
abcdefghijklmnopqrstuvwxyz
ABCDEFGHIJKLMNOPQRSTUVWXYZ
1234567890(&.,:;!?''"--·*$¢%/£)

Helvetica Bold Condensed
abcdefghijklmnopqrstuvwxyz
ABCDEFGHIJKLMNOPQRSTUVWXYZ
1234567890 (&.,:;!?'""-*$¢%£/)

Designed by Max Miedinger in 1957, Helvetica is a traditional grotesque type following the nineteenth-century style. It has become a very popular typeface, known for its well-proportioned letters and easy readability.

Hobo
abcdefghijklmnopqrstuvwxyz
ABCDEFGHIJKLMNOPQRSTUVWXYZ
1234567890 (&.,:;!?'""-*$¢%/£)

Hobo was designed by Morris F. Benton in 1910. The vertical strokes and bars are curved inward, stressing the central part of the character. The descenders have been cut off.

Janson
abcdefghijklmnopqrstuvwxyz
ABCDEFGHIJKLMNOPQRSTUVWXYZ
1234567890(&.,:;!?'""-*$¢%/£)

Janson Italic
abcdefghijklmnopqrstuvwxyz
ABCDEFGHIJKLMNOPQRSTUVWXYZ
1234567890(&.,:;!?'""-*$¢%/£)

The original face dates from about 1690 and was cut by Nicholas Kis, a Hungarian in Amsterdam.

Kabel Medium
abcdefghijklmnopqrstuvwxyz
ABCDEFGHIJKLMNOPQRSTUVWXYZ
1234567890(&.,:;!?'""--·*$¢%/£)

Kabel Bold
abcdefghijklmnopqrstuvwxyz
ABCDEFGHIJKLMNOPQRSTUVWXYZ
1234567890 (&.,:;!?'""-«»$¢%£/)

Kabel Heavy
abcdefghijklmnopqrstuvwxyz
ABCDEFGHIJKLMNOPQRSTUVWXYZ
1234567890(&.,:;!?'""'""--·[]*$¢%/£)

Designed by Rudolf Koch in 1927, Kabel is geometric sans serif. Unlike Futura, the feet on the light, medium, and bold weights are angled. The original Klingspoor versions of Kabel are no longer available, and the face has been redesigned for photocomposition. It remains popular with graphic designers.

Kaufmann Bold

abcdefghijklmnopqrstuvwxyz

ABCDEFGHIJKLMNOPQRSTUVWXYZ

1234567890 &.,:;!?'"''"-,$¢%

Designed by M. R. Kaufmann in 1936, this monoweight script has close-fitting letters and soft turns. The style appears to be drawn with a broad nib pen.

Lightline Gothic

abcdefghijklmnopqrstuvwxyz

ABCDEFGHIJKLMNOPQRSTUVWXYZ

1234567890 (&.,:;!?'"""-*$¢%£/)

Lightline Gothic was designed by Morris F. Benton in 1908. For contrast, News Gothic, News Gothic Bold, and Trade Gothic Bold are suggested.

Lilith

abcdefghijklmnopqrstuvwxyz

ABCDEFGHIJKLMNOPQRSTUVWX

YZ1234567890 (&.,:;!?""''--.*$¢%/£)

Lilith, designed by Lucien Bernhard in 1930, is a decorative fat face, which is slightly oblique. Notice the nodules added to the capitals for decoration.

Mandate

abcdefghijklmnopqrstuvwxyz

ABCDEFGHIJKLMNOPQRSTUVWXYZ

1234567890 (&.,:;!?'"""-[]*$¢/)

Designed by R. H. Middleton in 1934, Mandate is a medium-weight informal script, with connecting lowercase letters.

Melior

abcdefghijklmnopqrstuvwxyz

ABCDEFGHIJKLMNOPQRSTUVWXYZ

1234567890 (&.,:;!?''""-*$¢%£/)

Melior is a square roman face with short ascenders and descenders. Designed by Hermann Zapf in the early 1950s, it has some lowercase letters that relate to nineteenth-century designs, especially the squared-off c and g. The italics are slight.

Meridien Light

abcdefghijklmnopqrstuvwxyz

ABCDEFGHIJKLMNOPQRSTUVWXYZ

1234567890 (&.,:;'""'!?-—·*$$¢¢%/£)

Meridien Medium

abcdefghijklmnopqrstuvwxyz

ABCDEFGHIJKLMNOPQRSTUVWXYZ

1234567890 (&.,:;!?""''-—·*$¢%/£)

Meridien Bold

abcdefghijklmnopqrstuvwxyz

ABCDEFGHIJKLMNOPQRSTUVWXYZ

1234567890 (&.,:;!?''""'-—·*$¢%/£)

Designed by A. Frutiger and created by the Deberny & Peignot Foundry in Paris in 1957, Meridien is a classical roman type style with angular serifs.

Metropolis Bold
abcdefghijklmnopqrstuvwxyz
ABCDEFGHIJKLMNPQRSTUVWXYZ
1234567890 (&.,:;!?'""''-*$¢%£/)

Metropolis Bold is a fat face with definite 1930 period influences. (It was manufactured by Stempel after the design by W. Schwerdtner in 1932.) The vertical strokes are all wedge-shaped, thicker on top. A similar face is Lucien Bold.

MICHELANGELO
ABCDEFGHIJKKLMNOPQQRR
SSTUVWXYZ (&.,:;!?'""''-—·[]*$¢%/£)
1234567890

Designed by Hermann Zapf in 1950, Michelangelo is based on stone-cut Roman inscriptions. There are no lowercase letters. Sistina, by the same designer, is a companion type.

MICROGRAMMA NORMAL
ABCDEFGHIJKLMNOPQRSTUVWXYZ
(&.,:;!?'""''-*$¢%£/) 11234567890

MICROGRAMMA BOLD
ABCDEFGHIJKLMNOPQRSTUVWXYZ
(&.,:;!?'""''-✻*$¢%£/) 11234567890

MICROGRAMMA CONDENSED
ABCDEFGHIJKLMNOPQRSTUVWXYZ
11234567890 (&.,:;!?""''-—·*$¢%/£)

MICROGRAMMA EXT.
ABCDEFGHIJKLMNO
PQRSTUVWXYZ
1234567890 (&.,:;!?""''--·*$¢°lo/£)

MICROGRAMMA BOLD EXT.
ABCDEFGHIJKLMNOPQR
STUVWXYZ (&.,:;!?""''-*$¢°lo£/)
1234567890

Microgramma, designed by A. Butti and A. Novarese in 1952, is an angular sans serif, with no lowercase. The letters are basically square with rounded corners. Eurostile offers the compatible lowercase.

Mistral
abcdefghijklmnopqrstuvwxyz
ABCDEFGHIJKLMNOPQRSTUVWXYZ
1234567890 (&.,:;!?''""--·*$¢%/£)

Mistral is an informal brush script designed by Roger Excoffon in 1955. It is similar to Choc, but lighter in line.

NEON
ABCDEFGHIJKLMNOPQRSTUVWXYZ
1234567890 (&.,:;!?''""--·*$¢%/£)

Neon is a three-dimensional sans serif face designed by W. Schaefer in 1936.

NEULAND
ABCDEFGHIJKLMNOPQRSTUVWXYZ
1234567890 (&.,:;!?'`'""--•[]★$¢%/£)

NEULAND BLACK
ABCDEFGHIJKLMNOPQRSTUVWXYZ
1234567890 (&.,:;!?'""--•*$¢%/£)

NEULAND OUTLINE NO.2
ABCDEFGHIJKLMNOPQRSTUVWXYZ
1234567890 (&.,:;!?'""--◇[]*$¢%/£)

Designed by Rudolf Koch in 1923, Neuland is a soft, angular bold sans serif, with a woodcut quality. The monotype face Othello is an imitation of this design.

News Gothic
abcdefghijklmnopqrstuvwxyz

ABCDEFGHIJKLMNOPQRSTUVWXYZ

1234567890 (&.,:;!?'""-*$¢%£/)

News Gothic Bold
abcdefghijklmnopqrstuvwxyz

ABCDEFGHIJKLMNOPQRSTUVWXYZ

1234567890 (&.,:;!?'""-*$¢%£/)

News Gothic Condensed
abcdefghijklmnopqrstuvwxyz
ABCDEFGHIJKLMNOPQRSTUVWXYZ
1234567890 (&.,:;!?'""-*$¢%£/)

News Gothic Extra Condensed
abcdefghijklmnopqrstuvwxyz
ABCDEFGHIJKLMNOPQRSTUVWXYZ
1234567890 (&.,:;!?'""-*$¢%£/)

News Gothic was originally designed by Morris F. Benton for the American Type
Founders in 1908. The new, bold version—designed under the direction of H. R.
Freund—is slightly narrower than the original. Additional weights were added in
1958–60. In addition to the bold or italic versions of News Gothic, the Alternate Gothic
series offers a possible contrast.

Nobel Light
abcdefghijklmnopqrstuvwxyz
ABCDEFGHIJKLMNOPQRSTUVWXYZ
1234567890 (&.,:;!?""''--·*$¢%/£)

Nobel Light Italic
abcdefghijklmnopqrstuvwxyz
ABCDEFGHIJKLMNOPQRSTUVWXYZ
1234567890 (&.,:;!?""''--·*$¢%/£)

Nobel, or Nobel Grotesque, is a sans serif, designed after the Continental model.

Novel Gothic
abcdefghijklmnopqrstuvwxyz
ABCDEFGHIJKLMNOPQRST
UVWXYZ& 1234567890$.,-:;""""!?

Designed by H. Becker in 1929, Novel Gothic is a bold sans serif with wide characters. Notice that several of the vertical strokes are angled, and that the E and F have triangular arms touching the stem.

Nubian Black
abcdefghijklmnopqrstuv
wxyz ABCDEFGHIJKLM
NPQRSTUVWXYZ (&.,:;!?
'""",-,-.*$¢%/£) 1234567890

Nubian, designed by W. T. Shiffin in 1928, is a fat face with extra weight.

Optima
abcdefghijklmnopqrstuvwxyz
ABCDEFGHIJKLMNOPQRSTUVWXYZ
1234567890 (&.,:;!?'""-*$¢%£/)

Optima Italic
abcdefghijklmnopqrstuvwxyz
ABCDEFGHIJKLMNOPQRSTUVWXYZ
1234567890 (&.,:;!?'""-*$¢%£/)

Optima Semibold
abcdefghijklmnopqrstuvwxyz
ABCDEFGHIJKLMNOPQRSTUVWXYZ
1234567890 (&.,:;!?'""--·*$¢%/£)

Optima Semibold Italic
abcdefghijklmnopqrstuvwxyz
ABCDEFGHIJKLMNOPQRSTUVWXYZ
1234567890 (&.,:;!?'""--·*$¢%/£)

Designed by Hermann Zapf in 1958, Optima is a sans serif roman face. Some designers have classified this face as a calligraphic roman.

ORPLID
ABCDEFGHIJKLMNOPQRSTUVWXYZ
(&.,:;!?'""="*$%) 1234567890

This three-dimensional sans serif was designed by Hans Bohn in 1929.

Palatino
abcdefghijklmnopqrstuvwxyz
ABCDEFGHIJKLMNOPQRSTUVWXYZ
1234567890 (& .,:;!?'""-*$¢%£/)

Palatino Italic
abcdefghijklmnopqrstuvwxyz
ABCDEFGHIJKLMNOPQRSTUVWXYZ
1234567890 (&.,:;!?'``''-*$¢%/£)

Palatino Semibold
abcdefghijklmnopqrstuvwxyz
ABCDEFGHIJKLMNOPQRSTUVWXYZ
1234567890 (&.,:;!?''-*$¢)

Palatino Bold
abcdefghijklmnopqrstuvwxyz
ABCDEFGHIJKLMNOPQRSTUVWXYZ
1234567890(&.,:;!?'""--·[]*$¢%/£)

Palatino is a roman face with strong, inclined serifs. Designed by Hermann Zapf in 1950, it resembles a Venetian style and is named after the Italian sixteenth-century writing master. Notice that the M and W are especially wide.

Parisian
abcdefghijklmnopqrstuvwxyz
ABCDEFGHIJKLMNOPQRSTUVWXYZ
1234567890 (&.,:;!?'"'"--·*$¢%ƒ£)

This Art Deco type style was designed by Morris F. Benton in 1928 for the American Type Founders. The thins occupy much of the letter. Notice that the S has an angled axis.

Peignot Light
abcdefghijklmnopqrstuvwxyz
ABCDEFGHIJKLMNOPQRSTUVWXYZ
1234567890 1234567890 (&.,:;!?'""--·*$¢%/£)

Peignot Demi Bold
abcdefghijklmnopqrstuvwxyz
ABCDEFGHIJKLMNOPQRSTUVWXYZ
1234567890 1234567890 (&.,:;!?'"''––·*$¢%/£)

Peignot Bold
abcdefghijklmnopqrstuvwxyz
ABCDEFGHIJKLMNOPQRSTUVWXYZ
1234567890 1234567890 (&.,:;!?'"''––·*$¢%/£)

Designed by A. M. Cassandre in 1937, Peignot has a contemporary French look. Some biform characters are available.

Perpetua Roman
abcdefghijklmnopqrstuvwxyz
ABCDEFGHIJKLMNOPQRSTUVWXYZ
1234567890 (&.,:;!?'"''"'––·*$¢%/£)

Perpetua Italic
abcdefghijklmnopqrstuvwxyz
ABCDEFGHIJKLMNOPQRSTUVWXYZ
1234567890 (&.,:;!?'"''"''––·*$¢%/£)

Perpetua Bold
abcdefghijklmnopqrstuvwxyz
ABCDEFGHIJKLMNOPQRSTUVWXYZ
1234567890 (&.,:;!?'" "-*$¢%/)

Perpetua Bold Italic
abcdefghijklmnopqrstuvwxyz
ABCDEFGHIJKLMNOPQRSTUVWXYZ
1234567890 (&.,:;!?""''--.*$¢%/£)

Designed by Eric Gill around 1925–30, this face was originally used in a privately printed translation of *The Passion of Perpetua and Felicity*. The roman style was named Perpetua and the italic, cut later, was called Felicity. The serifs are sharply cut and horizontal. Notice that the figures are old face, and that the italic *g* has a calligraphic tail.

Plantin
abcdefghijklmnopqrstuvwxyz
ABCDEFGHIJKLMNOPQRSTUVWXYZ
1234567890 (&.,:;!?'-–·[]*$¢%/£)

Plantin Italic
abcdefghijklmnopqrstuvwxyz
ABCDEFGHIJKLMNOPQRSTUVWXYZ
1234567890 (&.,:;!?'""--·*$¢%/£)

Plantin Bold
abcdefghijklmnopqrstuvwxyz
ABCDEFGHIJKLMNOPQRSTUVWXYZ
1234567890(&.,:;!?'‘""”-[]*$¢%/£)

Plantin Bold Italic
abcdefghijklmnopqrstuvwxyz
ABCDEFGHIJKLMNOPQRSTUVWXYZ
1234567890(&.,:;!?'‘""”- – ·[]$¢%/£)*

Designed by F. H. Pierpont for the Monotype Corporation, this old style roman typeface is named after the famous Antwerp printer, Christophe Plantin. It was modeled on a sixteenth-century type that was never used by Plantin.

PRISMA
ABCDEFGHIJKLMNOPQRSTUVWXYZ
(&.,:;!?"-*$‹%/)
1234567890

Prisma is an inline version of Rudolf Koch's Kabel. The inlines are parallel white lines. Only capitals and figures are available. The suggested contrast is Kabel Bold.

PROFILE
ABCDEFGIJKLNPQRSTUVX
YZ (&.,:;!?'""”-*$G%/£)
1234567890

Designed by Eugen and Max Lenz in the 1940s, Profile offers three-dimensional capitals and figures. Notice the drop-shadow effect at the lower right side.

Radiant Bold

abcdefghijklmnopqrstuvwxyz

ABCDEFGHIJKLMNOPQRSTUVWXYZ

1234567890 [&.,:;!?'""-*$¢%/]

Radiant, designed by R. H. Middleton, is a sans serif that is slightly thick and thin and modestly condensed.

Raffia Initials

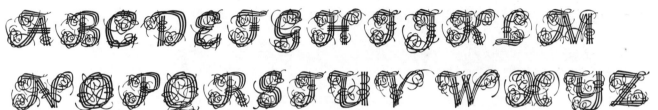

Raffia Initials, a pen-drawn set of initials with flourishes, were designed by Henk Krijger in 1952.

Reiner Black

abcdefghijklmnopqrssttthuvwxyz fffifl

ABCDEFGHIJKLMNOPQRSTUVWXYZ

1234567890 [&.,:;!?'""-—.*$¢%/£]

This bold brush script was designed by Imre Reiner in 1955.

Salto

abcdefghijklmnopqrstuvwxyz

ABCDEFGHIJKLMNOPQRSTUV WXYZ 1234567890 (&.,:;!!'""-*$¢)

Salto is a strong brush script, which is slightly oblique. The capitals are higher and stronger in intensity than the lowercase letters.

SANS SERIFS SHADED
ABCDEFGHIJKLMNOPQRSTUVWXYZ
(&.,„:;!?""""-[]'°$¢%/£) 1234567890

This sans serif was called Sans Surryphs when it was first shown by William Thorowgood in 1839. The letters are monoweight with a drop shadow.

Signal Medium
abcdefghijklmnopqrstuvwxyz
ABCDEFGHIJKLMNOPQRSTUVWXYZ
1234567890 (&.,:;!?'""''-*$¢%/)

Signal, designed by W. Wege in 1931, is an informal script, which resembles many German scripts. The alignment is deliberately irregular but contained by the monoweight letterform.

SISTINA TITLING
ABCDEFGHIJKLMNOPQQRSTUVWXYZ
1234567890 (&.,:;!?''""''--·*$¢%/£)

Designed by Hermann Zapf in 1951, Sistina apppears to have the same character structure as Zapf's typeface Michelangelo. Sistina, however, is twice as heavy and can therefore be considered a bold version of Michelangelo.

SOLEMNIS
ABCDEFGHIJKLMNOPQRST
UVWXYZ (@.,:;!?"'""''-*$¢%/)
1234567890

Solemnis, designed by G. G. Lange in the 1950s, is a biform or common-case calligraphic type. It is similar to American Uncial and Libra.

Standard Medium
abcdefghijklmnopqrstuvwxyz
ABCDEFGHIJKLMNOPQRSTUVWXYZ
1234567890 (&.,:;!?'""”-*$¢%/£)

Standard, a Continental-style sans serif in four weights, was very popular in the 1950s. It is also called Akzidenz Grotesk.

STENCIL
ABCDEFGHIJKLMNOPQRSTUVWXYZ
(&.,:;!?'""”-*$¢%/) 1234567890

This boldface, serif stencil letter was designed in the late 1930s.

Stradivarius
abcdefghijklmnopqrstuvwxyz
ABCDEFGHIJKLMNOP
QRSTUVWXYZ (&.,:;!?"-*$¢/£)
1234567890

Stradivarius, designed by Imre Reiner in 1945, is a decorative script with end turns that look like musical notes. In Germany the type is called Symphonie.

Studio Bold
abcdefghijklmnopqrstuvwxyz
ABCDEFGHIJKLMNOPQRSTUVWXYZ
1234567890(&.,:;!?‘’""”---[]*$¢%/£)

Designed by A. Overbeek in 1946, Studio is a freely drawn face based on the printed script style. The bold is also called Flambard.

Stymie Medium
abcdefghijklmnopqrstuvwxyz
ABCDEFGHIJKLMNOPQRSTUVWXYZ
1234567890 (&.,:;!?'´"""-*$¢%/£)

Stymie was originally designed by Morris F. Benton; it was later redesigned by Sol Hess and Garry Powell. There are four weights and a compressed version. Stymie Antique Shaded, however, does not relate to this group.

TEA CHEST
ABCDEFGHIJKLMNOPQRSTUVWXYZ
1234567890 (&.,:;!?'""--·*$¢%/£)

Tea Chest is a condensed, stencil roman face. Notice that the serifs protrude on only one side of the stem.

Thorowgood Roman
abcdefghijklmnopqrstuvwxyz
ABCDEFGHIJKLMNOPQRSTU
VWXYZ (&.,:;!?'""--·*$¢%/£)
1234567890

Thorowgood Italic
abcdefghijklmnopqrstuvwxyz
AABCDEFGHIJKLMMNNOPQ
RSTUVVWWXYYZ (&.,:;!?'""-*$
¢%/£) 1234567890

Thorowgood, cut by the English type founder Robert Thorne in the early nineteenth century, was revived in 1953. Overall, it is a distinctive fat face with very black strokes, contrasting hairline serifs, and turns for the italics.

Times Roman
abcdefghijklmnopqrstuvwxyz
ABCDEFGHIJKLMNOPQRSTUVWXYZ
1234567890 (&.,:;!?'""-*$¢%/£)

Times Italic
abcdefghijklmnopqrstuvwxyz
ABCDEFGHIJKLMNOPQRSTUVWXYZ
1234567890 (&.,:;!?""--·$¢%/£)

Times Roman Bold
abcdefghijklmnopqrstuvwxyz
ABCDEFGHIJKLMNOPQRSTUVWXYZ
1234567890 (&.,:;!?'""-*$¢%/£)

Times Bold Italic
abcdefghijklmnopqrstuvwxyz
ABCDEFGHIJKLMNOPQRSTUVWXYZ
1234567890 (&.,:;!?'""-*$¢%/£)

Designed by Stanley Morrison for the *London Times* in 1932, Times New Roman does not need a strong increase in tonal value for emphasis.

Torino Roman
abcdefghijklmnopqrstuvwxyz
ABCDEFGHIJKLMNOPQRSTUVWXYZ
1234567890 (&.,:;!?'""""-[]*$¢%/£)

Torino Italic
abcdefghijklmnopqrstuvwxyz
ABCDEFGHIJKLMNOPQRSTUVWXYZ
1234567890 (&.,:;!?" "-*$¢%/£)

Torino is a modern roman face, slightly condensed and with a strong contrast in color. Hairline serifs balance the letterforms.

TRUMP GRAVUR
ABCDEFGHIJKLMNOPQRSTUVWXYZ
&.,:;!?'' '' ''-$•/•£
1234567890

Trump Gravur is a relief version of Trump Mediaeval (see below). It has an open three-dimensional design, with the shadows on the right side of the letter.

Trump Mediaeval
abcdefghijklmnopqrstuvwxyz
ABCDEFGHIJKLMNOPQRSTUVWXYZ
1234567890 (&.,:;!?'"-*$¢%/£)

Trump Mediaeval Italic
abcdefghijklmnopqrstuvwxyz
ABCDEFGHIJKLMNOPQRSTUVWXYZ
1234567890 (&.,:;!?''" "-*$¢%/£)

Trump Mediaeval was designed by Georg Trump in 1954. The Germans use the term *Mediaeval* in place of *Venetian*, but in this case the type can be classified as old face.

Univers 45
abcdefghijklmnopqrstuvwxyz
ABCDEFGHIJKLMNOPQRSTUVWXYZ
1234567890 (&.,:;!?"-*$¢%/£)

Univers 55
abcdefghijklmnopqrstuvwxyz
ABCDEFGHIJKLMNOPQRSTUVWXYZ
1234567890 (&.,:;!?""""-*$¢%/£)

Univers 56
abcdefghijklmnopqrstuvwxyz
ABCDEFGHIJKLMNOPQRSTUVWXYZ
1234567890 (&.,:;!?"-$¢%/£)*

Univers 57
abcdefghijklmnopqrstuvwxyz
ABCDEFGHIJKLMNOPQRSTUVWXYZ
1234567890 (&.,:;!?'"-*$¢%/£)

Univers 58
abcdefghijklmnopqrstuvwxyz
ABCDEFGHIJKLMNOPQRSTUVWXYZ
1234567890 (&.,:;!?'"-$¢%/£)*

Univers 65
abcdefghijklmnopqrstuvwxyz
ABCDEFGHIJKLMNOPQRSTUVWXYZ
1234567890[&.,:;!?'''""-*$¢%/£]

Univers 75
abcdefghijklmnopqrstuvwxyz
ABCDEFGHIJKLMNOPQRSTUVWXYZ
1234567890[&.,:;!?'''""-*$¢%/£]

Univers is a popular grotesque face combining characteristics of both English and Continental sans serif types. The styles are compatible according to a numerical formula (see page 29).

Vendome
abcdefghijklmnopqrstuvwxyz
ABCDEFGHIJKLMNOPQRSTUVWXYZ
1234567890(&.,:;!?'""--·*$¢%/£)

Vendome Italic
abcdefghijklmnopqrstuvwxyz
ABCDEFGHIJKLMNOPQRSTUVWXYZ
1234567890(&.,:;!?'""--·$¢%/£)*

Vendome was designed in 1952 by François Ganeau, who was influenced by seventeenth-century French types. Notice that the serifs are sharp and that the letters appear to be angled slightly, although not as much as the italics. The condensed version should not be used as a contrasting type as it is too severe for the open letter.

Walbaum
abcdefghijklmnopqrstuvwxyz
ABCDEFGHIJKLMNOPQRSTUVWXYZ
1234567890 (&.,:;!?'´"“”-[]*$¢%/£)

Walbaum Italic
abcdefghijklmnopqrstuvwxyz
ABCDEFGHIJKLMNOPQRSTUVWXYZ
1234567890(&.,:;!?'"“”--·$¢%/£)*

J. E. Walbaum, the founder at Goslar and Weimar, cut this modern face in the early nineteenth century. Walbaum followed Didot rather than Bodoni in his design.

Weiss Roman
abcdefghijklmnopqrstuvwxyz
ABCDEFGHIJKLMNOPQRSTUVWXYZ
1234567890 (&.,:;!?'""-[]*$¢%/£)

Weiss Italic with Regular and Swash Caps
abcdefghijklmnopqrstt_uvwxyz
AABBCCDDEEFFGGHHIIJJJKKLLMMNNO
PPQRRSTTUUVVWWWXXYYZZ Qu Th
1234567890(&.,:;!?'"“”"--·[]$¢%/£)*

Weiss Roman Bold

abcdefghijklmnopqrstuvwxyz

ABCDEFGHIJKLMNOPQRSTUVWXYZ

1234567890 (&.,:;!?'""-[]*$¢%/£)

Weiss Roman Extra Bold

abcdefghijklmnopqrstuvwxyz

ABCDEFGHIJKLMNOPQRSTUVWXYZ

1234567890 (&.,:;!?'""-[]*$¢%/£)

WEISS Initials No. 1

ABCDEFGHIJKLMNOPQRSTUVWXYZ

1234567890 (&.,:;!?'""""--·*$¢%/£)

WEISS Initials No. 2

AABCDEEFGGHIJKLMNOPQRSTUVWXYZ

1234567890 (&.,:;!?'""-$¢%/)

WEISS Initials No. 3

ABCDEFGHIJKLMNOPQRSTUVWXYZ

1234567890 (&.,:;!?'""-*$/)

Designed by Emil Rudolf Weiss, this classic twentieth-century type offers a variety of swash capitals and terminal letters.

Edited by Susan Davis and Sue Heinemann
Graphic production by Ellen Greene
Text set in 11-point Century Expanded